MADE IN TAIWAN is an expansive volume that embraces the breathtaking diversity of Taiwanese cookery. For the first time ever, here is a cookbook that celebrates the island nation's unique culinary identity—despite a refusal by the Chinese government to recognize its sovereignty. Written by Taipei-based journalist Clarissa Wei, it contains deeply researched essays and more than one hundred recipes inspired by the people who live in Taiwan today.

For generations, Taiwanese cuisine has been miscategorized under the broad umbrella term of Chinese food. Backed by historical evidence and interviews, Wei makes a case for why Taiwanese food should get its own spotlight. *Made in Taiwan* includes classics like Peddler Noodles, Braised Minced Pork Belly, and Three-Cup Chicken, and features never-before-seen recipes and techniques such as how to make Stinky Tofu from scratch and broth tips from an award-winning beef noodle soup master.

Made in Taiwan is an earnest reflection of what food is like in Taiwan today. Photographed, researched, and written entirely on the island by an all-Taiwanese team, this book is a visually stunning compendium that tells the story of a proud nation—a self-sufficient collective of people who continue to forge on despite unprecedented ambiguity.

台灣製造
MADE IN TAIWAN

Recipes and Stories
from the Island Nation

台 灣 製 造

MADE
IN
TAIWAN

CLARISSA WEI 魏貝珊
with **IVY CHEN** 陳淑娥

Simon Element
New York London Toronto Sydney New Delhi

[Neither] race, language, nor culture form a nation, but rather a deeply felt sense of community and shared destiny.

—TAIWANESE DEMOCRACY ACTIVIST PENG MING-MIN 彭明敏
   IN HIS MEMOIR *A TASTE OF FREEDOM*

Contents

Introduction

Here in Taiwan, we mind our own business. We wake up each day to a cloak of humidity, a scattering of birdsong, hot steamers' bellies full of fresh soy milk or congee. Wet-market vendors set out their goods in the early morning, unloading cartloads of lime-green guavas and bundles of sharp bamboo shoots freshly picked from the mountains, as aunties with striped nylon bags do their grocery shopping for the week. During the lunch-hour rush, cafeteria-style canteens are packed with patrons wolfing down quick meals of pork chops over rice with pickled greens. Some of us might end the day with a home-cooked meal—pork ribs and chunks of daikon bobbing in soup, pan-fried fish rubbed with white pepper, a quick stir-fry of seasonal vegetables. Others pop into the closest neighborhood joint and slurp on a bowl of noodles while watching the in-house television spew out news about the rising prices of popcorn or about a monkey that broke into a local university and was photographed sitting in a cubicle. All things considered, our country does well for itself; we have low rates of crime, impeccable public transportation, a world-class health care system, peaceful elections, and, as this book will delineate, fantastic food and markets.

Yet when I turn on the international news, I always feel incredibly disoriented. Every other month, it seems, Taiwan appears on news tickers accompanied by the words *China*, *threat*, and *conflict*; our island is constantly framed as a flash point to potential world war. The Chinese government has made us a target—a so-called renegade province they say is theirs to take—despite the fact that we're a self-ruled democracy of 23.5 million people who have never in our history been ruled by the People's Republic of China. Over the years, I've come to realize that the very act of being Taiwanese is a constant fight against unrelenting Chinese state attempts to obliterate our identity. Unlike Taiwan, China does not mind its own business, and rarely do we get the opportunity to freely tell our own stories without having to deal with their very influential, very public displays of outrage.

And so, with food as the focus, this is my take on the Taiwanese story. This book, the recipes, and the stories herein revolve around the central premise that Taiwanese cuisine stands on its own. While one could argue that Taiwanese cuisine is just another provincial expression of Chinese food at large, our food isn't a subset of Chinese food because Taiwan isn't a part of China. While many of our dishes have Chinese roots or were brought over by immigrants from China, physical and diplomatic isolation, entirely separate governments, and, most important, a nascent yet powerful Taiwanese identity movement in the face of increasing cross-strait political tensions have given shape to a redefined food culture that's completely and unquestionably unique. And as the world sees an alarming rise in autocracy and affronts to democracy, it's more important than ever to remember what makes us different.

I'll be the first to admit that I didn't always feel this way. I was born in Los Angeles to apolitical Taiwanese immigrants and raised in a heavily East Asian suburb, where I went to school with kids from China, Taiwan, and Hong Kong. In the 1990s, we all just collectively referred to ourselves as Chinese—mostly because it was easier to explain ourselves to outsiders that way. But also, no one told me it was important to make the distinction. My parents were born in the '60s, before the democratic transition of Taiwan, when the island was a dictatorship put under martial law by the Nationalist Chinese government in exile. In my parents' youth, Taiwanese schoolchildren were told they were Chinese and taught more about the history of China than the history of their own people. Anyone who spoke up and said anything contrary risked being thrown in jail, exiled, or executed. The government at that time also portrayed Taiwan as a mecca of regional Chinese cuisine. While this was true to some extent because of the surge of Chinese refugees in Taiwan from the war, it was the food of the ruling elite and confined mostly to Taipei. Meanwhile, the cuisine of the majority who had been here for centuries—rooted in humble ingredients like shellfish, pork, sweet potatoes, and rice—was staunchly ignored and seen as second-class.

By now, more than 70 years have passed since the last wave of Chinese immigrants, and even our regional Chinese food in Taiwan today is irrefutably different from that of our neighbors across the strait. While Chinese culture and cuisine is no doubt a beautiful and important part of the Taiwanese identity at large, it doesn't define us, because we don't want it to.

It's extremely important to point out our differences because cultural homogenization is a frequently used tool in the Chinese state's pursuit of conquest and unity. China molds hearts and minds with coercive storytelling, by forcing Uyghurs to memorize Chinese history in internment camps, and by plastering the Chinese leader's photograph in the classrooms of many Buddhist colleges in Tibet, where almost a quarter of the curriculum is dedicated to learning about the Chinese Communist Party. The Chinese government has a tendency to weaponize Chinese culture and cuisine to its advantage, oftentimes using them as excuses to claim even the diaspora as their own. But it's my strong opinion that the food of a place can tell a story far more vividly than any textbook—and the food of Taiwan tells a tale of a country that has been subjected to multiple colonial influences but remains vibrant in its self-expression.

The story of an entire cuisine cannot be told from one perspective alone, which is why this book includes recipes and stories from home cooks from all walks of life and lauded chefs from around the country. Though it's written in my voice, it's a collaborative effort with Ivy Chen, a Taiwanese cooking instructor here on the island whose guidance forms the backbone of this book. Ivy—who has been teaching the ins and outs of the cuisine for more than two decades—worked tirelessly to develop the recipes in this cookbook. Coincidentally, both our families are from Tainan in southern Taiwan and have been on the island for more than 200 years. But unlike me, who was raised in the States and whose early memories of Taiwan are centered around the cities, Ivy spent her formative years in the country-side and watched her grandmother cater all sorts of now-antiquated religious festivities, weaving together thin strands of wheat noodles into the shapes of goats and chiseling blocks of white sugar into delicate miniature pagodas. Ivy's childhood playground was her grandfather's rice vermicelli factory, where long hairs of translucent rice noodles were churned out and sun-dried on large mesh bamboo trays.

Because of her unique background, Ivy has a deep relationship with Taiwanese flavors that most younger city folks like myself lack. When cooks around the country gave us their recipes for this book—many of them verbally thrown at us or haphazardly scribbled down—Ivy handled them with immense care, making sure we preserved the taste, texture, and intent of the original dishes. There were numerous times when, faced with a particularly difficult set of instructions, I impatiently wanted to delete an ingredient or a couple of steps, but Ivy resisted, believing that if we diluted the progression of a dish, we would lose out on its story. And the whole point of this book is to tell the story of Taiwan as best as we can before it's too late.

Unfortunately, the odds are not in our favor. Taiwan isn't formally recognized as a country by most of the world, China has been actively stripping us of our few remaining diplomatic allies, and we are in the midst of an existential threat. In his speeches, Chinese president Xi Jinping has repeatedly called for unification with Taiwan and hasn't ruled out using brute force to do so. Since 2020, a record number of Chinese warplanes have encroached on our island's air defense zone in a blatant act of intimidation, and in 2022, China conducted a series of unprecedented live-fire drills in the Taiwan Strait.

In light of these grim facts, all I can do is celebrate our humanity through the lens of food. I hope the world can see Taiwan as more than just a geopolitical chess piece or a controversial island near China with great night markets. Despite the occasional bouts of amnesia due to colonial influences, for generations and centuries we have considered ourselves our own people. Many of our dishes and rituals cannot be found anywhere else in the world, and even our core pantry items—like soy sauce, vinegar, rice wine, salt, and sugar—have always been and continue to be made in Taiwan. Our cuisine is a hodgepodge of cultures, colored by our indigenous tribes, influenced by Japanese colonists, inspired by American military aid, and shaped by all the various waves of Chinese immigrants and refugees who have arrived and made this island their home. We are not a tiny territory off the coast of China. We are not Chinese. We are Taiwanese, and we are a proud island nation—a self-sufficient collective of people who, despite unprecedented ambiguity, continue to forge on. This is our story.

A Note on Language and Romanization

Taiwan is a multilingual country, which makes translating the names of people, places, and dishes into English really difficult. Some dishes have only Taiwanese names, while others have only Mandarin names. Though Mandarin is technically the lingua franca in Taiwan, it arrived on our island in full force only during the mid-20th century with the Chinese refugees. The descendants of the initial waves of Chinese settlers from the 17th to the 19th centuries primarily spoke Taiwanese (which I sometimes refer to as Taiwanese Hokkien throughout the book), a dialect originally from the Fujian province of China that is still spoken by roughly 70 percent of the Taiwanese population. We also have significant pockets of Hakka speakers, but there are variations in their language depending on where they live. And, of course, Taiwan has a motley of Austronesian languages—the original indigenous languages of our island that have existed for millennia. There are currently more than a dozen unique Austronesian languages still in use today, and they aren't all mutually intelligible.

For posterity's sake, I've added Chinese characters after the names of people and shops that don't have English equivalents. Without these notations, it would be virtually impossible for many of the people I interviewed to find themselves in this book. It's important to me that not only people's stories but their identities remain intact. I've also included diacritics over most of the Mandarin, Taiwanese, and Hakka romanizations to help with pronunciation. Lastly, all the Chinese characters are written in traditional Chinese because, well, that's just how it's done in Taiwan.

■ FOR MANDARIN (IN BLUE): In Taiwan, proper nouns are anglicized using the Wades-Giles system. For everything else, I've resorted to Hanyu pinyin because I find that it's a much easier format to pick up and pronounce; it's also what most beginner Mandarin students around the world are taught. However, because Hanyu was a romanization system originally developed in China, it has long been a controversial flash point on the island. Many argue that Tongyong pinyin, which was created in Taiwan, more accurately reflects Taiwan-accented Mandarin and is therefore the more patriotic choice. There is no single correct method, and the choice of romanization in Taiwan remains frustratingly inconsistent. In Taipei, Hanyu pinyin is used for many of the highways, street names, and train stops. But if you drive south to Kaohsiung, Tongyong pinyin is the norm. It's confusing, but an apt metaphor for how Taiwanese identity isn't easily defined.

■ FOR TAIWANESE (IN GREEN): Also sometimes referred to as Taiwanese Hokkien or Tâi-Gí, Taiwanese is the language of my ancestors and arrived with the early Chinese settlers more than 200 years ago. While mutually intelligible with other Hokkien dialects around the world like in southeast China and parts of Southeast Asia, our language—like our food—has evolved to become distinct and includes vocabulary and sentence structures unique to our island. I'm using the Tâi-lô romanization system, which is used by Taiwan's Ministry of Education. The pronunciation of certain words also differs a bit depending on where in Taiwan people are from, so keeping true to my roots, we're using southern-style Taiwanese.

■ OTHERS (IN RED): Because of all the endless variations out there, the indigenous and Hakka romanizations were directly cross-referenced with the people I interviewed. The indigenous romanization comes from the Taromak tribe in southeastern Taiwan, a subset of the Rukai people. The Hakka dialect is from Meinong, a hilly, rural Hakka village on the outskirts of Kaohsiung.

Culinary History of Taiwan

A verdant green island at the far edge of the Pacific Ocean, Taiwan is shaped like a sweet potato—curvy and fat in the middle, gently tapered off at the ends. Sticky and hot with constant summer rains, our jungles are lush, like houseplants on steroids. Humidity clings to every living thing—that is, until you trek high up our alpine mountain range, which forms the magnificent spine of the island. Up there, a cascade of snowy mountain peaks reigns over all things, comfortably perched on thrones above the clouds.

For millennia, the stewards of our island have been a robust group of Austronesian nations whose cuisines perfectly mirror the diversity of our geography, flora, and fauna. Mountainous tribes, like the Bunun and Rukai, are agile hunters who can track down heavy boars and shoot leaping flying squirrels at night; the men can easily scale to soaring heights where the air is uncomfortably thin. It's in the alpine regions, after all, where many of their gods reside. Ocean-faring tribes like the Amis can read the tides and hold their breath underwater for incredible spans of time; some women are still fluent in all the different varieties of edible seaweed.

In the spring, gleaming schools of silvery flying fish leap across the east coast of Taiwan, and the Tao people of Orchid Island will row their canoes out and catch nets of them for sustenance. And deep in the central mountains is an important fig vine that snakes around the trunks of tall, ethereal trees. A couple of times a year, an indigenous wasp burrows itself into the belly of a fig and lays her eggs inside. The fig is pollinated by the dead maternal wasp and bulges until it's fat and

juicy. When this happens, the men of the Tsou tribe know to scale the massive trees to harvest the fruit. They bring it back home, dig out the seeds, dry them, and mix them with water to form aiyu—a delicious, citrine-hued jelly native to Taiwan.

Our indigenous custodians cultivated brooms of yellow millet and pearly handfuls of javanica rice. They drew from the vast ocean around us and spread their culture across the world. The Austronesian languages, spoken from the Philippines to New Zealand to Hawaii, are widely said to have originated in Taiwan. The food of Taiwan's indigenous people—stunning and grounded—is a testament to the beauty and bounty of our island. But while all the aforementioned ingredients and traditions still exist in pockets of Taiwan today, we've strayed incredibly far from our original, indigenous food culture because we're a nation of people who have colonized and been colonized. And with every new regime change has come a tidal wave of completely new dishes.

Today, with a population of 23.5 million squeezed into a land mass roughly about the size of Maryland,

Taiwan is misunderstood by the world as a Mandarin-speaking collective of people who may or may not be Chinese. We are, by cliché, the land of glitzy night markets and hearty beef noodle bowls. And while these descriptors may be true on some level, they only skim the surface.

And so, what is Taiwanese food?

It's impossible to write a book about Taiwanese cuisine without oversimplifying it in some way, because what's traditional to one family differs vastly from the traditions of the next. Ninety-five percent of the people in Taiwan are ethnically Han Chinese, though that's an extremely broad generalization and doesn't indicate much, because Han Chinese is but a vague umbrella term for people who have ancestry in China. The first wave of Chinese immigrants who arrived in the 17th century were primarily Hokkien-speaking folks from the southern Chinese province of Fujian who brought over their love of seafood, rice, and pork. Then came the Chinese refugees who landed with the Nationalist government in the mid-20th century, whose influence further broadened our culinary palate. Throw in intermarriage, colonial influences from the Japanese, and a lot of time, and out tumbles a rather eclectic menu particular to Taiwan. Given the shared ancestry, our cooking techniques and flavors are undeniably similar to those of our Chinese cousins across the strait. Food is fried or braised in large woks, or softened in hot and steamy bamboo baskets stacked up on top of one another. Because the first Chinese settlers in Taiwan came primarily from Fujian, we possess a common love for lightly seasoned food, occasionally heightened with a minimalistic trinity of ginger, garlic, and scallions. While its roots in China have shaped our taste preferences, Taiwanese cuisine ultimately revolves around the ingredients that thrive here. For carbs, sweet potatoes and rice dominate. A cheap and easy-to-grow root vegetable, sweet potatoes spring up like weeds, and rice does particularly well with the ample subtropical rains. Because two-thirds of our small island is covered by mountains, we lack large tracts of grazing land, and so the pig—which doesn't need a lot of space—is our de facto protein. Of course, by virtue of our being an island nation, seafood has remained a constant. I must point out that Taiwanese coastal waters have been considered overfished since the 1950s; however, there is a robust aquaculture industry, and fish and shellfish are consistently churned out by the boatload. Although not endemic, tropical fruits like mangoes, papayas, guavas, and pineapples have thrived here for centuries and usually punctuate the end of a great meal. And as for the Taiwanese pantry, it's stuffed with simple but effective condiments like soy sauce, sesame oil, rice vinegar, and rice wine. All things considered, this is a rather plain collection of staples—but our food has never needed much bling to shine.

For the last three centuries, and at the expense of the indigenous people here, Taiwan has been a land of immigrants with influences from around the world. The Chinese and Japanese have had the most significant impact on our cuisine; the European influence is imperceptible mostly because their colonial outposts didn't last very long (though it's said that the Dutch inspired our culture of deep-frying). Western food started to make an appearance only during the Cold War in the 1950s, when the United States flooded Taiwan with billions of dollars in economic aid and filled our coffers with large shipments of wheat and soybeans. There are a lot of threads to unpack. So, in order to properly synthesize our incredible cuisine, I've broken it down into six major historical time periods.

The Dutch and a Chinese Pirate (16th Century—1683)

Taiwan has had visitors from China for more than 600 years, and by the 16th century there were already a handful of Chinese settlements on the southwestern half of the island, albeit seasonal and sparsely populated. But then the Dutch arrived and established a small colony in the south of Taiwan in 1624. In order to milk the island for taxes, the Dutch recruited droves of farmers and fishermen from China to work the land and sea, which jump-started one of the first waves of Chinese immigration to the island. They started sugarcane and rice farms and, with the help of Chinese fishermen, set up some of the first primitive aquaculture systems on the island. They also purchased venison and deer hide in bulk from the indigenous Taiwanese and sold them to China and Japan, respectively.

In 1661, the Dutch were ousted by a Japanese-born Chinese pirate named Koxinga (sometimes known as Zheng Chenggong), who brought more people over from China during his military expeditions. Koxinga is often credited with the invention of the Taiwanese oyster omelet. Legend has it that when the Dutch opposition hid his supply of rice, he made due by feeding his soldiers oysters dipped in sweet potato starch. While likely just a tall tale, the story gives insight into the humble ingredients that were accessible at that time. Oysters could easily be farmed in brackish waters near the shore, an industry that's still very much alive today. And sweet potatoes were the carb of choice because most of the rice that was grown was reserved for export. Pickles and preserves were also incredibly important at this time. Leafy greens, bamboo shoots, and fruits like mangoes were salted and preserved, as were catches from the sea like fish and shrimp. All of these added much-needed pops of flavor to otherwise rather bland plates of food.

DISHES:

Fried Mackerel Thick Soup (page 97)
Pan-Fried Milkfish Belly (page 164)
Sweet Potato Leaves Stir-Fry (page 169)
Oyster Omelet (page 99)
Preserved Radish (page 351)

Qing Dynasty (1683–1895)

Koxinga's kingdom, known as the Kingdom of Tungning, was annexed by the Qing Dynasty in China in 1683 and some of Taiwan became a part of Fujian province. At first immigration was limited mostly to men, but by the late 18th and early 19th centuries, more than two million immigrants, primarily from Fujian and Guangdong, settled in Taiwan. Impoverished yet hopeful for new opportunities, my ancestors came over here for a chance at a new life. For the first time in Taiwan's history, the Chinese population outnumbered the indigenous, though there was significant intermarriage between the two groups at the cost of the indigenous women and their offspring, whose cultures and surnames were quickly erased.

The Chinese arrivals brought over with them their culinary traditions from across the strait, like making soy sauce with black soybeans and braising leftover bits of pork. They also set up large, permanent agrarian communities throughout the island. The

Hokkien-speaking folks from Fujian, who were used to living by the sea, settled on the western coastal plains; many were already expert fishermen and sea salt producers and continued their trades in Taiwan. The Hakka, who were used to living in the mountains, occupied the hills and made the most of their uneven terrain by carving out intricate terraces of tea and rice fields. They were also some of the first people to raise domesticated pigs, and the pig slowly became a central part of the Taiwanese household and a source of pride, food, and offering.

As the Chinese immigrants shifted from a pioneer society to a settler society, temples and ancestral altars were set up across the island, which created the need for tribute foods. Rice, which was time-consuming to grow, became a pivotal ingredient for offerings and was shaped into intricate dumplings and puddings called kueh. In 1858, the Qing Dynasty opened Taiwan's ports to the world, and Taiwanese tea, then marketed as Formosa Oolong, became an international export and brand. And as Taiwan became an increasingly profitable colony, it transformed from a prefecture of Fujian to a province in 1887, and stayed that way for seven years.

It's important to note, though, that while parts of Taiwan were under Qing control for these 200 years, only isolated pockets of the island were actually claimed by the Chinese. The rest of Taiwan was still run by indigenous stewards, who were not subjugated until the Japanese came.

DISHES:

Oyster and Pork Intestine Vermicelli Stew (page 136)
Red Tortoise Kueh (page 269)
Daikon Kueh (page 274)
Braised Minced Pork Belly (page 90)
Savory Rice Pudding (page 101)
Shiitake and Pork Congee (page 46)
Rice Noodle Soup (page 43)

The Japanese (1895–1945)

In 1895, in the aftermath of the first Sino-Japanese War and without any input from the people of Taiwan, the Qing government in China handed Taiwan over to Japan. They were met with hefty opposition, and even a declaration of independence that lasted for about five months. It was a brutal handover, and violent battles among the Japanese arrivals, the Chinese settlers, and the indigenous people raged on for years. Japan used the legal concept of *terra nullius*—meaning nobody's land—to claim ownership over what was previously considered indigenous territory. Many tribes were kicked out of their ancestral lands and forced to assimilate.

Japan set off on a mission to modernize Taiwan, and one way of doing that was through sugar, which was considered an ingredient of luxury and refinement. The empire of Japan was reliant on imported sugar, and Taiwan's subtropical climate meant that it was the perfect place to establish a proper sugarcane industry to supply domestic demand. Though Taiwan already had a history of sugarcane cultivation dating back to the Dutch days, the Japanese raised it to another level. Dozens of modern plantations and factories were set up, and by the early 20th century, sugarcane growers made up one-third of all rural households in Taiwan.

Within elite circles, the Japanese invented a brand-new cuisine known as Taiwanese ryori (táiwān liàolǐ 台灣料理), inspired by their limited understanding of Chinese cuisine. These were elaborate 13-dish banquets with bird's nests, pigeon eggs, shark fins, crab, white fungus, soft-shelled turtles, sea cucumbers, and other rare ingredients. But just as Indian curry is a figment of the British colonial imagination, so was this new genre of haute cuisine a figment of the Japanese imagination. Chefs from southern China were brought over to execute these meals, which were described to diners as exotic Taiwanese flavors with a tropical flair. Served in elaborate buildings with free-flowing alcohol and pretty girls, Taiwanese ryori was exclusively geared toward the wealthy, including the Japanese royal family.

The Japanese rule of Taiwan lasted only 50 years, but it had a long-lasting impact on our cuisine because it industrialized and monopolized so many of our core ingredients. Most of our core pantry items, including soy sauce, rice vinegar, and rice wine, are still made in the Japanese fashion today.

DISHES:

Taiwanese Tempura (page 255)
Haishan Sauce (page 370)
Railway Bento Box (page 144)

Nationalist China (1945–1980)

At the end of World War II, Taiwan was taken over by the Republic of China, which, at that point, was in control of most of China. But in 1949, it was defeated by Communist forces and the government was forced to flee the Chinese mainland for Taiwan. With them came about one million soldiers and refugees, and the food of Taiwan radically changed once again. Whereas the first waves of Chinese immigrants mostly came from southeastern China, this new batch of people hailed from all over. They brought with them a diverse spread of regional Chinese cuisine never seen before in the history of Taiwan. Northerners introduced fried crullers, scallion pancakes, and flatbread. Folks from Shanghai brought over soup dumplings and rice rolls. Sichuan immigrants were partial to spicy broad-bean paste, which formed the foundation of beef noodle soup.

While these immigrants made up only 10 to 15 percent of the population, they were very much the ruling elite, both literally and culturally. The people of Taiwan were told that they were being returned to the fatherland and that Taiwan was the last bastion of traditional Chinese food and culture. Celebrated celebrity chef Fu Pei-Mei 傅培梅, Taiwan's first TV chef and considered by many to be the Julia Child of Chinese cookery,

was sent by the government to countries around the world as an ambassador for Chinese cuisine. Her programs were broadcast internationally and promised the Chinese diaspora a taste of home. It's here where the perception of Taiwanese food is often stuck in time. While this era was indeed rich in regional Chinese feasts, it eventually faded, and many of the dishes have evolved to become virtually unrecognizable from their mainland progenitors in both flavor and ingredients. I currently live in a neighborhood in Taipei with a lot of restaurants and veterans from this era, and the food tastes very different from what I've experienced during my extensive travels in China. Generally speaking, Chinese food in Taiwan is significantly sweeter than its modern Chinese counterparts.

Meanwhile, as the world was being told that Taiwan was a hub for Chinese cuisine, the majority of people—like my parents and Ivy—only knew of these Chinese dishes from television or during rare visits to Taipei. Most folks were eating the plebeian meals of Taiwan's middle class, which were still very much rooted in sweet potatoes, rice, cheap seafood, and lots of pickles.

DISHES:

Fried Crullers (page 54)

Sesame Flatbread (page 58)

Beef Noodle Soup (page 128)

Soup Dumplings (page 125)

Sticky Rice Roll (page 52)

Pickled Mustard and Pork Noodle Soup (page 146)

The Americans (1945–1990s)

While the United States never colonized Taiwan, its policies made a durable impact on our food culture. After World War II, it was the Americans who forced the Japanese to surrender Taiwan to the Republic of China; and as an enemy of the Communist Chinese forces in mainland China, Taiwan naturally became an American ally. From the late 1940s to the 1960s, the States pumped billions of dollars in military aid and agricultural exports into Taiwan. Products like soybeans and wheat were shipped in en masse. The soybeans were used for animal feed, soy sauce, oil, and tofu products. Taiwanese chefs were sent to America to learn how to make bread with the wheat, and the recently arrived refugees from northern China happily molded the mountains of wheat into dumplings, flatbreads, and noodles. Even American turkey eggs were shipped in, which created a niche industry of turkey-over-rice restaurants. All these raw ingredients are still very much in vogue today and continue to be shipped in, mostly from the United States.

In part because of American aid, Taiwan's economy soared, and it became an East Asian superpower. American hegemony and soft power eventually inspired a new genre of dishes. In the 1970s and '80s, the Taiwanese became particularly enamored of American culture. Hamburger breakfast chains were set up as aspirational interpretations of concession-stand food.

Cheap steak houses were erected at night markets across the country, where stringy cuts of meat were smothered with sweet black-pepper sauces. The first coffee shops in Taiwan arrived during this time, and sipping slow cups of coffee in air-conditioned spaces became a symbol of status. It was also during this era when many Taiwanese interpretations of American classics were born. Fried chicken was turned into popcorn chicken. Chicken pot-pie morphed into a chicken liver chowder in deep-fried bread, a dish called coffin bread. Despite the prosperity, this also marked an era of significant Taiwanese emigration. Highly educated but faced with very limited job opportunities, many college graduates left Taiwan during this period to obtain advanced degrees. My parents were part of this wave, and in the late 1980s they left Taiwan for California—where I was born.

DISHES:

Turkey Rice (page 134)

Pork Floss Milk Bread (page 65)

Coffin Bread (page 112)

Fried Chicken Cutlet (page 236)

Black Pepper Steak and Spaghetti (page 242)

A New Taiwanese Identity (1980–Today)

Taiwan transitioned into a democracy in the 1980s, and by then, enough generations had passed that the rampant discrimination and disparate identities of the past had begun to fade. Most people of today's Taiwan no longer see themselves as Chinese, and a completely new identity distinct from those of our former colonial occupants has formed. In the 1980s, a new class of outdoor beer restaurants known as rè chǎo 熱炒 popped up, serving cheap lagers with quick plates of food that combined regional Chinese influences, Japanese condiments, and local seafood into one large fusion genre unique to the island.

When the Democratic Progressive Party assumed power for the first time after the elections of 2000, then president Chen Shui-Bian hosted a banquet featuring street food from southern Taiwan, like savory rice pudding and milkfish soup—a momentous gesture that celebrated what most people on the island actually ate. In contrast, previous presidents had insisted on ethereal Chinese banquet dishes like shark fin soup, abalone, and lobster—purposefully eschewing local cuisine because it was considered inappropriate and low-class.

Today, there is a small yet influential cohort of fine-dining chefs channeling native ingredients and products that have been cultivated here for centuries. In a way, we're coming back full circle to an awareness of our indigenous roots, while also acknowledging our messy colonial past. In the grand context of all this history, the notion that Taiwanese cuisine is its own distinct genre is extremely new. But it's an increasingly common perspective that's being adopted by many who live on the island today, especially in light of cross-strait tensions and as we look for ways to set ourselves apart from our aggressors. And it's through this perspective that this book was born.

DISHES:

Poached Squid with Five-Flavor Sauce (page 214)
Pineapple Prawns (page 225)
Stir-Fried Fiddleheads (page 207)

Status Quo

The idea that Taiwanese cuisine is its own unique genre isn't controversial here in Taiwan at all. The majority of people in Taiwan identify as solely Taiwanese, not Chinese. Yet outside Taiwan, our food often gets conflated with Chinese food because of a general lack of understanding of modern Taiwanese identity politics (in 2022, only 2.4 percent of people in Taiwan identified as exclusively Chinese, compared to 25.5 percent in 1992, according to an ongoing survey by National Chengchi University). But also, despite being a self-ruled island with peaceful elections, Taiwan isn't recognized as a country by most of the world—which has a significant impact on how our cuisine is perceived internationally.

A nation's identity is shaped by its history. So in order to properly understand why the idea of a distinct Taiwanese identity is contentious to outsiders, it's imperative to understand the progression of events that led us to where we are. In just three generations—from my grandparents to my parents to myself—Taiwan has shifted from a Japanese colony to a Chinese dictatorship and finally to a functioning democracy. These transitions have been incredibly violent but instrumental to defining who we are.

The formal name of Taiwan is the Republic of China, and it's in this nomenclature where a lot of the confusion lies. A government that, indeed, originated in China, the Republic of China ruled the Chinese mainland when it overthrew the centuries-long reign of the Qing Dynasty in 1912. But it wasn't able to hold on to control for long, and in 1927 China was thrown into a chaotic state of civil war as the Republic of China (also commonly referred to as the Nationalists) wrestled for power and control with what would later be known as the People's Republic of China (the Communists). To add fuel to all the pandemonium, the Japanese decided to invade Northeast China in 1937, and World War II broke out.

My paternal grandmother, who was born when Taiwan was under Japanese rule, told me stories from this era. Born in Madou, a district in the southern Taiwanese city of Tainan, her earliest memories of life were punctuated by the sound of exploding steel against concrete and loud, menacing American planes zipping across gray skies. For 50 years, Taiwan was a Japanese colony, and my grandmother spoke more Japanese than she did Mandarin. She was a small schoolgirl; she had classmates who were killed. She didn't have any shoes, and food was prohibitively expensive. I kept trying to get her to tell me about the bombings by American warplanes, but she kept circling back to the shoes. "We were so poor we couldn't afford shoes. We had to borrow shoes," she said. "Most schoolchildren didn't have shoes."

On August 6, 1945, the United States of America dropped a nuclear bomb on Hiroshima and then another three days later on Nagasaki, effectively ending the war. Nine days after that, Japan surrendered, and two months later, at the behest of the Americans, they handed Taiwan over to the Nationalist army of the Republic of China as part of reparations for the war.

When the Japanese surrendered to the Allied forces, they were told by the Americans to give Taiwan to the Chinese Nationalist government and not to the Communists—even though the Chinese Civil War was far from settled. And so the Republic of China became the new custodian of our verdant island, set up an office in Taipei, and declared Taiwan a province of their China. At that time, with the exception of the indigenous population, most of the people in Taiwan were descendants of ethnically Chinese immigrants and felt cautiously optimistic about the new colonial power because of their shared cultural heritage. They were told that they were being returned to "the fatherland." All of a sudden, my grandmother, whose native tongue was Taiwanese Hokkien and who was born a Japanese subject, was told that she was Chinese.

Unfortunately, the honeymoon phase was over before it could start. Corruption and bribery were rampant. The newly arrived soldiers from China terrorized the people and took away private property as they pleased. The economy tanked. Rice in Taiwan sold for twice the price it did in Shanghai. The Nationalist government ruled Taiwan with an iron fist, forcing people to learn, speak, and write Mandarin. And if they didn't, they were belittled and discriminated against. The Taiwanese, who were used to a strict but fair rule of law as enforced by the Japanese, began to resent their new colonizers and pine for the past.

The Taiwanese people, fed up with their oppressors, took over the radio stations and called for an uprising. They were quickly rebuffed, and more than 18,000 people were killed by military forces. Protest organizers were thrown in jail and executed by the thousands. The incident, now known as the 228 Massacre, was so brutal and violent that the leadership of the Nationalist party—still in China fighting the civil war—dismissed and replaced their governor in Taipei.

Two years later, in 1949, the Communists gained full control of the Chinese mainland and Mao Zedong formally established the People's Republic of China, still the ruling government of China today. Generalissimo Chiang Kai-Shek, the head of the Nationalist government, was forced to flee to Taiwan. Taipei was officially declared the temporary capital of the Republic of China, and more than 1.2 million Chinese refugees began to trickle into the island.

A motley group made up of veterans, military families, exiled students, Chinese prisoners of war, and government bureaucrats, these newcomers made up only 10 to 15 percent of the population, but their politics, food, and culture dictated the lives of the majority. Taiwan was put under martial law for 38 years. It's a period that's now referred to as the White Terror, the second-longest continuous period of martial law in recorded history, after Syria's. Under these conditions, resentment between the Taiwanese and the new Chinese arrivals continued to flare up. The former proudly called themselves sweet potatoes—the tuber's shape resembles that of the island of Taiwan—and new arrivals were called taros. The children of sweet potatoes and taros were also discriminated against and disparagingly known as mutts.

My parents—both sweet potatoes—were born in the 1960s, during the period of martial law, and from birth they were indoctrinated with anti-Communist but pro-Chinese-culture propaganda. They read about how the Communists destroyed Chinese culture in the Cultural Revolution, burned books, pulverized ancient temples and gods, and stripped the Chinese language of its soul by creating simplified Chinese. They were told that Taiwan—in language, religion, and spirit—was the last vestige of traditional Chinese culture, and that one day the Nationalists would reclaim their old territories and fulfill their manifest destiny as the sole rulers of all of China.

Of course, that never happened.

In 1979, the United States established official relations with the People's Republic of China, cutting diplomatic ties with Chiang Kai-Shek's Republic of China and sending Taiwan into international purgatory. Now, Taiwan isn't a victim by any means, and much of this was actually self-inflicted. Taiwan likely could have achieved international recognition and gotten away with it, but the stubbornness of the ruling class took priority over the desires of the people. During the 1976 Olympic Games in Montreal, the Taiwanese leadership was given an opportunity by the International Olympic Committee to compete under the formal banner of Taiwan. But the Nationalist government—hell-bent on being recognized as the Republic of China and offended that the title of China was given to the Communists—decided to boycott the Games in retaliation. Four years later, when Taiwan rejoined the Olympics, China insisted Taiwan compete under the banner of Chinese Taipei, which is the title we're forced to use in the Games today. A similar script had played out in the United Nations a couple of years prior, where the Republic of China was kicked out in favor of the People's Republic of China. Today, Taiwan remains excluded from most international organizations. Our status as a nation stuck in international purgatory is in part a result of the greed of our political forefathers, whose ambitions to blindly conquer were not unlike those of Chinese leader Xi Jinping today.

But while Taiwan is still the Republic of China on paper, attempts to reclaim the Chinese mainland were eventually abandoned as Taiwan slowly transitioned from an autocratic dictatorship to a democracy. In 1986, an opposition party known as the Democratic Progressive Party was born, offering an alternative to the one-party system. Martial law was lifted a year later, and in the 2000s, the Democratic Progressive Party won their first presidential election by supporting the idea of a distinct Taiwanese identity.

Democracy, though, did not come easy. There were multiple presidential assassination attempts, physically charged brawls in parliament, and rampant streaks of corruption. As a kid, I watched television broadcasts of Taiwanese legislators hurling punches, food, and water bottles at one another, a tradition that continues to this day (albeit sparingly). Back then, I was convinced that this was just how politics was conducted around the world. While messy and rough around the edges, this democracy somehow produced a new Taiwanese identity, separate from China and notable in its sense of self-determination.

While the Chinese Civil War was never formally settled, over the decades, the people of Taiwan have made it increasingly clear that they do not want any Communist Chinese involvement on their shores. In 2014, the Nationalist party hastily passed a trade treaty that would make Chinese investment in Taiwan legally easier. They did so without the required public discussion and transparency, and many citizens took that as an assault on democracy. Hundreds of students and protesters angrily burst into the legislative and executive chambers and occupied the buildings for weeks in a protest known as the Sunflower Movement. They argued that the trade pact would make Taiwan vulnerable to political pressure from Beijing.

The movement gave birth to a new cohort of politicians who were more vocal than ever against China, and in time, many prominent Sunflower activists were eventually elected to office. In 2016, Tsai Ing-Wen, a former law professor and Democratic Progressive Party politician who ran on a platform of not bowing to pressure from Beijing, was voted in as president. Four years later, in 2020, as cross-strait tensions continued to ramp up and Beijing began to escalate its crackdown on Hong Kong, Tsai was reelected with more than eight million votes—the highest number of votes any presidential candidate has ever received in Taiwan's short democratic history.

Today, tensions between China and Taiwan continue to climb to unprecedented heights as the Chinese side becomes increasingly hostile and the Taiwanese side becomes increasingly outspoken. Over the years, Xi Jinping has continuously reiterated his desire to fold Taiwan into the People's Republic of China. In 2021, he vowed to "smash" any attempts at Taiwanese independence, and since then, record numbers of Chinese military planes have been sent into Taiwan's air defense identification zone in a blatant act of intimidation. Chinese ships have illegally dredged sand on Taiwanese territorial seas, and tidal waves of targeted disinformation campaigns are continuously lobbed at us.

Domestically, flare-ups between the two major political parties in Taiwan are almost always sparked by fundamentally different views on China. The Nationalist party (also known as the Kuomintang), which decades ago dropped its ambitions to retake China, wants friendly relations and free trade with China. Their official line is that Taiwan's issue of sovereignty is something for future generations to take care of. The Democratic Progressive Party's current stance is that Taiwan does not need to declare independence because it's already an independent, self-ruled country. Despite all their differences, neither group wants unification or a direct declaration of independence. Both want to keep the status quo, which means "no unification, no independence, and no use of force"—a delicate stance that the Chinese state is actively trying to topple to their advantage.

The status quo can be uncomfortable and might one day prove to be untenable, but it's what the majority of Taiwanese people—roughly 87.1 percent, according to polls—want to uphold. Unification with China would mean the destruction of our way of life. But an outright formal declaration of independence would also mean imminent war. This gray space, awkward as it may be, is perhaps the safest place to be. Many people of the older generations—like my grandmother, standing in a swirl of dust left behind by bombs, or the war refugees from China, forever estranged from their families in the Chinese mainland—still viscerally remember the heartbreak of war.

It may not seem like it, but the people of Taiwan are well aware of the realities and risk of armed conflict. Yet life goes on as normal because it must, and as China becomes more aggressive, we find ourselves becoming increasingly more Taiwanese.

Taiwan	China
Republic of China	People's Republic of China
Used to be referred to as Nationalist China	Used to be referred to as Communist China
Major political parties: Kuomintang (sometimes called the Nationalists) and the Democratic Progressive Party	Major political party: Chinese Communist Party
Democracy	Autocracy

The Taiwanese Pantry

Even at the pantry level, Taiwanese cuisine stands on its own. All our condiments and seasonings are produced on the island, and have been for centuries. We are very much a self-sufficient country.

LARD (zhū yóu 豬油): Pork is integral in our cuisine, and lard—a hearty by-product of it—is the core ingredient many swear on for flavor's sake. Every single home cook over the age of 50 has stressed to me that it is absolutely mandatory. Traditional families will have a decorative ceramic lard jar in their refrigerator that they replenish constantly; I just use a simple glass Mason jar. For instructions on how to make lard at home, see page 358.

VEGETABLE OIL (zhí wù yóu 植物油): The vegetable oil of choice in Taiwan has shifted with the times. From the 17th to 19th century, the early Chinese immigrants had manually powered wood mills that churned out peanut and sesame oil. But because it was done on an extremely small scale back then, lard was still very much the de facto fat of choice. It wasn't until the early 20th century, when the Japanese invested in hydraulic oil presses, that peanut oil became a regular fixture of the Taiwanese pantry. In the late 20th century, Taiwan entered a string of trade deals with the United States and soybeans were imported into Taiwan en masse, which gave way to the rise of soybean oil. Of course, these days, we also have grape seed oil, canola oil, and all sorts of other exotic variants, but these are largely imported from abroad.

SESAME OIL (zhī má yóu 芝麻油): There are two major types: toasted sesame oil (zhī má xiāng yóu 芝麻香油), which is made from white sesame seeds, and black sesame oil (hēi má yóu 黑麻油), made from black sesame seeds. They are derived from two completely different varieties of sesame. White and black sesame oil cannot be used interchangeably. Toasted white sesame oil is lighter and more versatile, and is mostly used as a marinade or to add a subtle pop of flavor in sauces and at the end of stir-fries. It's also great as a final drizzling touch on a dish. Black sesame oil has a darker and smokier taste. It's regarded as more medicinal, and because it has a lower smoking point, it must be cooked carefully at low heat or added at the end of the cooking process.

SUGAR (táng 糖): Coarse raw sugar is the preferred and traditional sugar of choice in Taiwan. It's an unrefined light golden brown sugar known domestically as Cane Sugar #2 (èr shā táng 二砂糖); the closest equivalent is demerara. Unlike white sugar, coarse raw sugar has subtle notes of toffee and molasses, flavors that are especially accentuated in long braises. Considered to be much more aromatic, coarse raw sugar keeps better in the Taiwanese tropics because it has larger, coarser grains that don't clump with the humidity. For most dishes, it can be used interchangeably with white sugar, but I've listed it specifically as an ingredient in the recipes where I find it absolutely essential. As a former cash crop, sugar is incredibly important to Taiwanese cuisine and was considered a status symbol, especially during the Japanese colonial era. We also have dark brown sugar (hēi táng 黑糖) and rock sugar (bīng táng 冰糖) on the island, but these are typically reserved for desserts.

SALT (yán 鹽): As in many ocean-faring countries around the world, sea salt is king. In the 17th century, residents started to divert seawater into shallow ponds to harness the power of evaporation to make piles of salt. But because of water pollution and how time-consuming this process was, these salt pans have largely been retired, though some of the more historical ones are now functional tourist attractions that can still produce salt on a small scale. Today, most of Taiwan's salt is produced by Taiyen Biotech, which

sells both fine sea salt (produced by electrodialysis) and iodized table salt. Coarse salt is quite rare in Taiwanese cooking.

SOY SAUCE (jiàng yóu 醬油): This foundational condiment was brought over in the 17th century by Chinese immigrants, and in the early days was exclusively made with black soybeans, which have a deeper, almost earthier flavor than the more common yellow soybean that dominates the soy sauce market internationally. Originally, black soybean soy sauce production in Taiwan was concentrated in Lukang township in the west of the island. But it declined dramatically when the Japanese took over Taiwan and brought their soy sauce processing techniques, which used yellow soybeans and toasted wheat. Yellow soybean soy sauce became the standard in northern Taiwan and in all the big cities. All the recipes in this book were developed using yellow soybean soy sauce from Kimlan, which is the largest soy sauce brand in the country. Stylistically,

Kimlan soy sauce is most similar to Japanese all-purpose soy sauce (koikuchi shoyu), so if you can't find Kimlan, Kikkoman is the best brand alternative.

While black bean soy sauce (which is gluten-free) still exists in pockets of Taiwan, it's a smaller, more artisanal market based mostly in Xiluo, an urban township in Yunlin County. I'm partial to Yu Ding Xing, a family-owned business that wood-fires all their soy sauces and ages them in terra-cotta vats. They also scribble little love notes on the sides of the vats for good luck, which is a lovely and adorable bonus.

Unlike China, Taiwan doesn't have light or dark soy sauce. There's a dark soy sauce–like variant here in Taiwan called bottom-vat soy sauce (which is a much more concentrated formula designed specifically for braises and stews), but unlike Chinese dark soy sauce, it doesn't contain molasses and will not color your food as prominently. If you're using bottom-vat soy sauce for any of the recipes in this book, start with half the amount listed and taste your way up from there.

TAIWANESE SOY PASTE (jiàng yóu gāo 醬油膏): This is a condiment unique to Taiwan, made with soy sauce and sugar thickened with glutinous rice flour. With a viscosity and color similar to those of oyster sauce, soy paste is used to add complexity to braises or is mixed with water and sugar to make a dipping sauce. There are many variants of this item, depending on the region and brand. Northern versions will add a hint of licorice powder, and in the south, the paste is extremely saccharine and has a light caramel color instead of a dark, coffee-like hue. The recipes in this book were developed using Kimlan soy paste. For instructions on how to make this condiment yourself, see page 366.

WHITE PEPPER (bái hú jiāo 白胡椒): Ground white pepper—which is derived from the seeds of a whole black peppercorn—is the default pepper of choice in Taiwan. It's used in most dishes as an accent, as a marinade for meats, or as a finishing touch to anything soupy. Unlike black pepper, which can be quite sharp around the edges, white pepper has a gentleness to it that most Taiwanese people prefer.

FIVE-SPICE POWDER (wǔ xiāng fěn 五香粉): I get my five-spice powder from my local Chinese medicine store, which is where most people in Taiwan procure their spices. Different stores will have their own proprietary blends, but fundamentally, the powder is made with ground Sichuan red peppercorns, cinnamon, star anise, cloves, and fennel seed. Five-spice is what gives a lot of Taiwanese deep-fried snacks their signature pop. It can be quite overpowering, so be gentle with it.

MONOSODIUM GLUTAMATE (MSG) (wèi jīng 味精): Most chefs and street vendors are pretty heavy-handed with MSG; it's what gives food in this part of the world an extra layer of depth and umami. But, like lard, it's something that appears in every grandma's house but is frowned upon by the younger generation for health reasons. Of course, a flavor agent is sometimes needed, and many Taiwanese households today will instead stock boxes of hondashi—a "healthier" instant granular form of Japanese dashi which, ironically, also contains MSG (but don't tell my mom—she has no idea). I didn't include MSG or hondashi in any of the recipes in this book, but feel free to add a pinch to any of the savory recipes if you'd like.

DRIED FLOUNDER (biǎn yú 扁魚): The Japanese have bonito, and Koreans use anchovies. Here in Taiwan, we're partial to a palm-size dehydrated whole flatfish known as the olive flounder. The fish, which is about as big as a business card, is usually cut into squares, fried, and then scattered in soups. Or it can be crushed into a powder and folded into braises for flavor. Unfortunately, because many home chefs now prefer granulated instant flavoring like hondashi or bouillon cubes, dried flounder is getting increasingly harder to find, even in Taiwan.

In the West, it's also sometimes labeled as dried stockfish, brill fish, dà dì yú 大地魚, or ròu yú 肉魚. Korean dried pollack is an acceptable alternative as well. To store, cut the whole dried fish into small, one-inch chunks and keep it in the freezer. Don't be intimated by the head and the eyes of the fish; use and cook them like you would the rest of the fish. Chinese medicine stores might also have this in stock, sometimes in powdered form. If you can only get your hands on the powder, substitute it 1:1 by weight.

BLACK VINEGAR (hēi cù 黑醋): In China, Japan, and Korea, black vinegar is made by steaming rice and then aging it in clay pots for at least six months. But here in Taiwan, our black vinegar—inspired by Japanese-style Worcestershire sauce—is more of an infusion than it is an aged vinegar. First, a basic rice vinegar is made with sticky rice. Then it's steeped with fruits and vegetables for months, and then sometimes flavored with a sprinkle of licorice and caramel. The result: a fruity, full-bodied hit of acid that's usually drizzled to taste over a thick soup. The most common Taiwanese black vinegar brand is Kong Yen. If you can't find that, Chinkiang vinegar from China, although not made the same way, is a decent-enough substitute.

RICE VINEGAR (mǐ cù 米醋): A transparent vinegar with yellowish undertones, this is a really simple condiment that's mostly used for quick pickling vegetables like cucumbers, daikons, or carrots. The most common brand is Kong Yen, which makes a Japanese-style vinegar out of glutinous rice, salt, and a little bit of fructose. Slightly less acidic than Western styles of vinegar, rice vinegar is made using a process similar to that for making sake. If you can't find a Taiwanese brand, the best substitute is a seasoned Japanese rice vinegar.

TAIWANESE RICE WINE (michiu or mǐ jiǔ 米酒): In the old days, rice wine was created by incorporating long-grain rice with white koji and fermenting it. However, because koji can be unpredictable, this method gave funky and inconsistent results. When the Japanese took over Taiwan, they learned about a new rice wine–brewing technology from Vietnam, which isolated the bacteria from the koji. This created a more even and consistent brew and is how most of our rice wine is produced today. In Taiwan, rice wine comes in all sorts of different alcohol percentages. The most common one is the Red Label, which is 19.5 proof. If you can't find Taiwanese rice wine, cooking sake is the best alternative.

SHACHA SAUCE (shā chá jiàng 沙茶醬): Made with a special blend of dried flounder, garlic, shallots, and dried shrimp and brought over by Teochew immigrants from China, this sauce used to be a heavily guarded secret just a few generations ago. Families would make it behind closed doors and serve it with hot pot or in lamb or beef stir-fries. Shacha is easy to find in Asian grocery stores; the most common brand is Bullhead Barbecue Sauce, but for instructions on how to make it from scratch, see page 371.

SWEET POTATO STARCH (dì guā fěn 地瓜粉 or fān shǔ fěn 蕃薯粉): Taiwanese starches are one of the most mislabeled items in both the English- and Chinese-speaking world, which is extremely frustrating because for select dishes like crystal meatballs, the type of starch that's used makes a really big difference. Sweet potato starch is the original starch of the island and, when molded into dough, is quite firm and hardens when it cools. Sometimes you can buy sweet potato starch in thick granular form, which is ideal for dishes that are deep-fried.

TAPIOCA STARCH (mù shǔ fěn 木薯粉 or shù shǔ fěn 樹薯粉): Made from dehydrated cassava, tapioca starch yields a much softer dough than sweet potato starch, which is why the two starches are often used in conjunction with each other to achieve the right texture. Because sweet potato and tapioca starches are often mislabeled for each other in English, double-check the ingredient list on the back of the packaging and cross-check the Chinese characters if you can. For some dishes, it's important to distinguish between the two because of the textural differences. Tapioca starch is also a popular thickener because it produces a glassy and translucent finish, which is a typical feature of many southern Taiwanese soups.

POTATO STARCH (tài bái fěn 太白粉): This is a common, generic starch in Taiwan used for thickening and marinades. It's described in English as potato starch, but in fact it's just a hodgepodge of cheap, miscellaneous starches that's mostly potato starch. I don't usually buy this; I'll use tapioca starch as my default thickener because it has the same effect.

CHILI SAUCE (là jiāo jiàng 辣椒醬): Taiwanese cuisine tends to be mild and sweet, and therefore we don't really have a robust hot-sauce scene. And in keeping with this theme, our chili sauce tends to be—well—mild and sweet. Even then, it's rarely used by itself and is usually mixed with sugar and ketchup to make a sweet chili sauce. The best replacement for Taiwanese-style chili sauce is Lee Kum Kee chili garlic sauce or Huy Fong sambal oelek.

FERMENTED BROAD BEAN PASTE (dòu bàn jiàng 豆瓣醬): Fermented broad bean paste originated in Sichuan, but when it made its way to Taiwan via Chinese immigrants in the 1950s, it was tweaked so much over the generations that it's now virtually unrecognizable from its original form. Taiwanese broad bean paste is more bean-heavy than it is spicy. It's used only in select dishes, like beef noodle soup and braised beef shank.

DRIED FERMENTED BLACK BEANS (dòu chǐ 豆豉): These are soybeans that have been inoculated with a mold, salted, and then left to wrinkle and cure. They're like salty capers, but with the funkiness of a deeply aged cheese. Time breaks down the protein in the bean, which combines with the sodium in the salt to form a natural MSG. These pair especially well with stir-fried fiddleheads or steamed fish.

DRIED SHIITAKE MUSHROOMS (xiāng gū 香菇): Taiwan has a robust shiitake mushroom cultivation industry, and the mushrooms come in all different sizes. The rule of thumb is to soak them in room-temperature water to coax out most of the flavor. You could technically reconstitute the mushrooms in boiling water, but they lose a lot of their fragrance that way. The soaking water can also be reserved and used in lieu of water in any of the recipes. If you can, look for organically grown shiitakes; fungi are quite sensitive to their surroundings and can pick up heavy metals if they're grown in subpar conditions. Rehydrate these in a French press if you have one; the plunger will keep the mushrooms submerged in the water.

DRIED SHRIMP (xiā mi 蝦米): An absolutely essential pantry item, these sun-dried shrimp are about the size of a fingernail and infuse salty complexity in any stir-fry or braise. Look for shrimp that are a vibrant orange. They should be even in color and shouldn't be too ragged around the edges. A tip I learned from the auntie I buy my dried shrimp from: store them in your freezer. They'll last a lot longer that way.

FRIED SHALLOTS (yóu cōng sū 油蔥酥): Fried shallots are used as a garnish or thrown directly into braises or soups for an infusion of flavor. You can make these at home (see page 368), but most people in Taiwan don't bother. Pre-fried shallots are available in nearly every corner store in Taiwan. Asian grocery stores in the West also stock them. I keep a big bag of these in my pantry at all times.

WHEAT FLOUR (miàn fěn 麵粉): Most flour in Taiwan is milled domestically and made with wheat berries imported from the United States. The protein levels are the same, but the way the berries are milled and the additives that are incorporated are slightly different. For more on the nuances and history of wheat flour, see page 56.

RICE VERMICELLI (mǐ fěn 米粉): These are dried strands of thin rice noodles that are reconstituted with water, and can be thrown into a stir-fry or soup. Ivy's tip is to blanch the noodles in boiling water instead of just soaking them in water for a couple of hours like most people do. Blanching softens the noodles so that they're perfectly al dente; soaking them overnight will make them far too mushy. When buying rice vermicelli, look for the package with a red and yellow tiger on it. These noodles are made in northern Taiwan and can be procured at most major Asian supermarkets.

BAMBOO LEAVES (má zhú yè 麻竹葉): These long green leaves are derived from the sweet bamboo (*Dendrocalamus latiflorus*) plant and are sold in dehydrated packets at Asian specialty stores. They're the default wrappers for southern Taiwanese–style zongzi. They must be boiled and washed thoroughly before use.

MALTOSE (mài yá táng 麥芽糖): Also known as malt sugar, maltose can be a bit of an intimidating ingredient because it straddles the medium between a solid and a liquid. It's thicker than honey but softer than caramel. With a brilliant amber-like shine, maltose is best pried out of the jar with a wet stainless steel spoon or with wet hands. It will dissolve easily in water, and if you're folding it into flour, just pull it apart with your hands in the flour until it's thin and stringy like a spiderweb. Eventually—like magic—it will disappear. Maltose is a really common ingredient in Taiwanese desserts and is the secret for keeping dishes like mochi soft and supple for hours. There's no substitute for it; the most common brand outside of Taiwan is Elephant King.

GINGER (jiāng 薑): There are two types of ginger: old ginger (lǎo jiāng 老薑) and young ginger (nèn jiāng 嫩薑). The former can be found in most grocery stores around the world, and in Taiwanese cuisine, it's usually sliced up—unpeeled—and put into soups or stir-fries. Young ginger is quite rare outside Taiwan, and even on the island, it shows up only around the spring. It's a delicate, tender, almost ivory-like root that's finely julienned and used in dipping sauces or soups. If you can't get your hands on young ginger, peel old ginger, slice it up thinly, and soak it in water for 30 minutes to tone down its piquancy.

GARLIC (suàn tóu 蒜頭): This is a pretty straightforward, universal aromatic. How we usually process it: smash it with the back of a cleaver, peel off the skin, and chop or mince accordingly.

SCALLIONS (cōng 蔥): My rule of thumb for scallions is to reserve the white parts for stir-frying and the green parts for folding into the end of the dish. If they're needed in soup, you can tie them into a knot and plop them right in; this makes them easier to pluck out afterward. My local vegetable vendor taught me a nifty little trick for preserving scallions: trim off the bottom, separate the whites and greens, and then freeze.

PORK FLOSS (ròu sōng 肉鬆): An old way to preserve excess pork, pork floss is made by boiling chunks of meat, shredding them, and then pan-frying until the meat is dry, fluffy, and stringy. Pork floss can be sprinkled over morning congee or bread. For instructions on how to make this from scratch, see page 364.

PLUM POWDER (méi zi fěn 梅子粉): Made from dehydrated brined plums, plum powder was, in the old days, given out for free at fruit stalls across the country. It has a distinct sweet and sour taste and is usually sprinkled over fresh slices of guava.

Cordia dichotoma (phuà pòo tsí 破布子): These are the pickled seeds of the bird lime tree, a tropical plant distributed across Asia. They taste like sweet capers and are usually steamed with fish or sautéed with tender fern shoots. They add a delicious layer of brininess to a dish.

MAQAW (mǎ gào 馬告): A seed derived from the *Litsea cubeba* tree, maqaw is an indigenous Taiwanese peppercorn with spicy and floral lemon notes. Used primarily by the Atayal tribe, it's one of the few indigenous ingredients that has crossed over into mainstream Taiwanese cooking. It's a popular spice in wild boar sausages; I've also had maqaw in both coffee and pineapple cake, which works surprisingly well.

Rice

I live next to a small family-owned bulk food shop in Taipei, where heaps of rice, grains, and miscellaneous legumes are piled up neatly in individual white bins, and then measured out using an antique scale with miniature brass weights. It's here where the residents of my neighborhood have been congregating for generations to buy dried pulses and grains, and for the uninitiated, it can be really intimidating.

"I'm looking to buy, uh, rice to make daikon cake with," the teenager ahead of me in line says nervously, clutching his phone.

"Long-grain or glutinous?" the auntie who manages the store asks.

"I don't know. The one that makes daikon cake?" he says, looking down at his phone screen, referencing a shopping list someone sent him out to fulfill.

As he does that, Auntie scoops up some rice and puts it in a bag. "Long-grain," she says as she hands it to him.

Then it's my turn.

"I'd like four kilograms of short-grain regular rice and one kilogram of short-grain glutinous rice," I say, pleased with myself for knowing the difference.

Auntie doesn't look impressed. "Okay, what district do you want the rice to be from? Chishang or Guanshan?" she asks dryly.

I make an educated guess, get my order, and leave incredibly humbled.

Rice in Taiwan is an incredibly nuanced topic that can take many lifetimes to grasp. And because of our colonial history, the type of rice that we eat on a daily basis changed depending on who controlled the island. The original variety of rice was javanica, which was cultivated on a small scale by indigenous residents and by the early Dutch settlers. Difficult to grow, it was eventually replaced by indica and japonica rice, brought over by colonists from China and Japan, respectively.

Today, there are four basic types that dominate the island: short-grain rice (japonica), long-grain rice (indica), short-grain glutinous rice (japonica glutinous), and long-grain glutinous rice (indica glutinous). Different varieties have varying levels of amylose and amylopectin, and like gluten in wheat flour, these variables greatly affect texture. Amylose is what gives slender, long-grain rice like basmati and jasmine their light, fluffy texture. When these varieties are cooked, they don't stick together at all. Amylopectin is the carbohydrate responsible for the stickiness of short-grain and glutinous rice. It's the reason sushi rice—a short-grain rice—can be packed into a sushi roll with ease. And it's why mochi, which is made with glutinous rice, is gooey when you bite into it.

Short-grain rice has high amounts of amylopectin but low amounts of amylose. Long-grain rice is the exact opposite. Glutinous rice has high levels of amylopectin and almost no amylose. And if all that wasn't confusing enough, the age of the rice matters, too. Dishes like savory rice puddings are made out of long-grain rice that has been aged for at least

a year; newly harvested rice would make the pudding far too sticky.

All these nuances might seem disorienting, but it's actually not that complicated. The vast majority of the rice Taiwanese people eat on a daily basis today is a short-grain japonica rice. Long-grain indica rice, introduced by Chinese settlers in the 17th century, used to be the dominant strain in Taiwan because of its ability to thrive in the hot and humid climate. Similarly, a lot of other tropical countries have a similar predilection for long-grain rice. India, for example, has basmati, and Thailand has jasmine.

But the Japanese colonists in the early 20th century grew up eating short-grain rice and weren't fans of the long-grain variety. So, they got to work, and after many failed attempts over many years, finally had a

Rice Kernels

A. Short-grain glutinous rice (japonica glutinous), also known as sweet rice Yuán Nuò Mǐ 圓糯米	Amylose content: 0–5%	Extremely sticky kernels usually used to make desserts with.	Taiwanese Mochi (page 327) Tang Yuan (page 302) Red Tortoise Kueh (page 269)
B. Long-grain glutinous rice (indica glutinous), also known as sticky rice Cháng Nuò Mǐ 長糯米	Amylose content: 0–5%	A long-grain sticky rice usually reserved for savory festive dishes.	Oil Rice (page 287) Zongzi (page 279)
C. Short-grain rice (japonica), like sushi rice Péng Lái Mǐ 蓬萊米	Amylose content: 15–20%	The rice that is most commonly served at home and at restaurants. Plump, sticky, great for absorbing sauces.	Shiitake and Pork Congee (page 46) Fried Rice (page 210) Quick Seafood Congee (page 158) Braised Minced Pork Belly (page 90)
D. Long-grain rice (indica), like extra long-grain rice, basmati, or jasmine Zài Lái Mǐ 在來米	Amylose content: Over 25%	Used a lot in steamed pastries, the rice is often aged for a couple of years which helps improve the texture.	Savory Rice Pudding (page 101) Crystal Meatball (page 108) Daikon Cake (page 285)

breakthrough with a short-grain cultivar bred in the mountains of Yangmingshan, a national park just north of Taipei. In 1926, they named that new cultivar péng lái 蓬萊 after Mount Penglai, a mythical mountain in Chinese and Japanese folklore that houses the elixir for eternal life. And the old long-grain rice of Taiwan—an indica variety—was named zài lái 在來, which means "has-been." This new nomenclature signaled that indica's reign as the dominant rice strain on the island was officially over, eternally replaced by the superior japonica.

Today, Taiwan is one of the few subtropical countries in the world where japonica is the de facto rice of choice—a grain more typical of temperate and mountainous climates. Indica still exists in Taiwan, though its role has largely shifted from a daily rice to an ingredient used in steamed pastries. Most of the long-grain rice in the market these days is sold in flour form, or meant to be taken home, soaked overnight, and blended with water to form rice milk, which is then steamed to make pastries.

There's also glutinous rice, which also comes in long-grain and short-grain varieties. Both variants are quite dense and distinguished by their pearly, opaque kernels. A special-occasion grain reserved for weddings, funerals, and religious holidays, glutinous rice tends to be pricier because there's less farmland dedicated to it. Short-grain glutinous rice, sometimes called sweet rice, is reserved for sweet rice desserts like mochi and tang yuan. And long-grain glutinous rice is used for festive savory dishes, like oil rice, which marks the birth of a baby boy, or for zongzi, which celebrates the Dragon Boat Festival.

And as the auntie at the bulk grain store so bluntly pointed out to me, terroir also plays a huge role in how a bowl of rice turns out. It's a lot to unpack, but the changing nature of rice in Taiwan reflects the shifting tides of Taiwanese identity. From javanica to indica to japonica, even our staple, core foundational grain hasn't stayed constant through the generations—a testament to how we're constantly redefining what it means to be Taiwanese.

Rice Flour

Rice flour, also known as Thai rice flour or common rice flour Zài Lái Mǐ Fěn 在來米粉 or Zhān Mǐ Fěn 粘米粉	Made with long-grain rice flour. Usually mixed with water to form rice milk and then steamed into a cake or savory pastry.	Savory Rice Pudding (page 101) Daikon Cake (page 285)
Glutinous rice flour, also known as sweet rice flour Nuò Mǐ Fěn 糯米粉	Most commonly made with a mix of long-grain and short.	Taiwanese Mochi (page 327) Tang Yuan (page 302) Red Tortoise Kueh (page 269)

NOTE:
When buying rice flour outside Taiwan, always go for water-milled rice flour. I highly recommend the Erawan brand. If you use dry-milled or stone-ground rice flour, the flour-to-water ratio might need to be adjusted.

Equipment

Depending on your perspective, the average Taiwanese kitchen is either really janky or quite charming. When I first moved into my 40-year-old sixth-floor walk-up in Taipei, I was convinced of the former. We don't have hot water in the kitchen or a dishwasher, and when I run out of gas—oftentimes when I'm in the middle of cooking—I have to call a number and patiently wait for a courier to carry a new tank of gas up six flights of stairs. There's simply no way around it. If anything, living in an old apartment in Taipei has given me a deeper appreciation for Taiwanese cuisine and its inherent simplicity. You don't need a large, grandiose setup to create a wonderful, home-cooked meal.

These are the bare essentials:

GAS STOVE (wǎ sī lú 瓦斯爐): Gas stoves in Taiwan are like infernos, and even the lowest heat can bring a small pot of water to a rolling boil if you're not careful. Our stoves here are quite difficult to control, but the benefit is that the high heat is great for wok-frying and imparts a lovely smoky finish to the food. An electric or induction stove, of course, is fine; just make sure your wok is sufficiently heated before you add your oil and aromatics.

WOK (chǎo cài guō 炒菜鍋): For Western kitchens, I recommend a 14-inch (35-cm) flat-bottomed carbon steel wok. Carbon steel is lightweight, distributes heat evenly, and develops a gorgeous patina over time if it's properly seasoned. Carbon steel is traditional in Taiwan and is the de facto wok material in restaurants across the country, though more home cooks are now becoming partial to nonstick because it makes for easier cleanup. It's a real shame, because unlike nonstick woks, a properly cared-for carbon steel wok can truly last forever, and might eventually become a family heirloom.

How to season a wok: Using a dish brush, scrub the inside and outside of the wok with mild dish soap.

Rinse off the soap. Heat the wok over high heat until the water evaporates. Tilt and rotate the wok so all the sides and edges are heated. It will start to change color and become dark brown with a blue tinge. Turn off the heat and let it cool down again. Rinse under running water and scrub with a dish brush. Heat the wok over high heat until all the water has evaporated again. Turn off the heat. Swirl in 2 tablespoons of oil and, with a folded paper towel held in a pair of tongs, spread the oil all over the inside of the wok. It can be used immediately.

How to clean a wok: Rinse your wok in the sink with hot water and scrub it with a plain sponge. If things are especially sticky, use a dish brush (you can splurge on a fancy wok brush, but a nylon dish brush with a scraper edge will do the trick). To finish, heat the wok on the stove over high heat until all the water beads have evaporated. Washing your wok with a tiny bit of baking soda or mild dish soap is okay when it's absolutely needed, but don't overdo it.

WOK LID (guō gài 鍋蓋): Wok lids in Taiwan are traditionally made out of cheap aluminum or stainless steel. I have a gorgeous Japanese cedar lid that nestles perfectly on top of my wok, and I love it because it makes my kitchen smell like a sauna. The wood prevents condensation from building up and dripping onto the food.

METAL WOK SPATULA (chǎo cài chǎn 炒菜鏟): Don't worry about scratching up your wok with this; carbon steel woks are quite resistant, and the scratches will even out with time. A hefty metal spatula is necessary for stir-fries and for scraping up any junk that accumulates on the bottom of the wok.

CLEAVER (cài dāo 菜刀): Everyday tools for slicing, dicing, and smashing, most cleavers in Taiwan are made with either stainless or carbon steel and have rectangular blades. Look for a lightweight cleaver that's comfortable on the wrists. While I've met people who use heavier meat cleavers that can cut through bone to do all of the above as well, it takes quite a bit of skill and experience to maneuver that on a daily basis. A lightweight cleaver is easier to manage for beginners and great for everyday use—especially if you aren't butchering on a regular basis.

CUTTING BOARD (zhēn bǎn 砧板): Old-school households in the countryside use a smooth cross-section of a tree trunk as their cutting board. That setup isn't as practical for many home cooks today, though a heavy, round piece of wood at least 1.5 inches (4 cm) thick and about a foot (30 cm) in diameter is ideal. Traditional wooden cutting boards are made from an indigenous magnolia known as black heart stone (wū xīn shí 烏心石) or a native elm called Zelkova (jǔ mù 櫸木). I use my wooden cutting board exclusively for meats and a regular plastic board for vegetables. The oil from the meat will keep the board naturally lubricated, but if you have a wooden board dedicated to vegetables, make sure to rub it with vegetable oil often or else it might crack over time. To clean, rinse the board with hot water and vinegar after use and dry completely.

ROLLING PIN (gǎn miàn gùn 擀麵棍): Taiwanese rolling pins are usually made out of wood and are much thinner and shorter than their Western counterparts, which makes them easier to maneuver with one hand. Be sure to oil your rolling pin regularly so that it doesn't crack.

METAL LADLE (tāng sháo 湯杓): A necessary tool for ladling soup. These ladles aren't as steeply angled as Western ladles, and some restaurant wok chefs will sometimes even use the back side for stir-frying.

SPIDER STRAINER (lòu sháo 漏杓): Also sometimes known as a skimmer spoon, this is one of my favorite tools. It's especially great for lifting deep-fried food from a bubbling vat of hot oil or noodles from a pot of boiling water. Think of it as a lightweight colander on a stick. Old-school Taiwanese spider strainers are large metal spoons dotted with perfectly round holes; newer models are made with woven metal.

BAMBOO STEAMER (zhú zhēng lóng 竹蒸籠): There are many different types of steamers out there, but I highly recommend one made out of bamboo. If you're using a 14-inch (35-cm) wok, buy a 12-inch (30-cm) steamer with at least two or three tiers. Bamboo is preferred because, unlike stainless steel, it won't allow condensation to build up on top of the lid and drip back down onto the food. This doesn't make a difference if you're steaming meat or vegetables, but if you're cooking a delicate rice pastry like a kueh, condensation could mean the difference between a gloopy, wet pastry and a firm, intact one. If you only have a stainless steel steamer, wrap a large cloth around the lid to prevent condensation from falling onto the food.

How to use a steamer: Pour 1 to 1½ inches (2.5 to 4 cm) of water into a wok. Bring it to a rolling boil, then nestle the covered bamboo steamer with the food inside over the water. The bottom rim of the steamer should be submerged in water at all times, or else it might char. Make sure the floor of the steamer doesn't touch the water, though, or the food will get drenched. Depending on how long your steam time is, you might have to replenish the water occasionally. I always keep a kettle of boiling water on the side for a quick top-off.

How to clean a bamboo steamer: Wash the steamer with mild soap and warm water and then air dry. If there are chunks of food stuck to the steamer, scrub them off with a nylon brush. If you live in a particularly dry area, you can occasionally brush a bit of vegetable oil on the outside and inside of the steamer to keep it from cracking and falling apart.

An important note: Using a carbon steel wok for steaming can wear down the patina of the wok. If you have the means to do so, dedicate an old wok to steaming and smoking. For instructions on how to smoke food with a wok, see page 188.

ROUND STEAMER RACK (zhēng jià 蒸架): If you're just steaming a small plate of food, you can perch it on top of a wire rack instead of using a bamboo steamer. Fill the wok with water, put the rack in the middle, bring the water to a rolling boil, put the food on top of the rack, cover, and steam.

TATUNG STEAMER (dà tóng diàn guō 大同電鍋): An electric steamer made in Taiwan with a single on-off switch, the Tatung steamer can reheat food, cook rice, and push out long, earthy braises. Like a Russian matryoshka doll, it consists of a small pot nestled within a fixed bigger pot. Just pour a couple of cups of water into the outer pot, add your food to the smaller pot inside, and flick the switch. For more on the Tatung, see page 70.

GRATER (páo sī bǎn 刨絲板): Typically used for grating large chunks of daikon or taro, Taiwanese graters are made out of wood or plastic and are traditionally just flat, skinny planes that can be propped up in a bowl or against a table. You're totally welcome to use a box grater as well.

MUSLIN CLOTH (dòu jiāng bù 豆漿布): This cloth can be used for making soy milk and rice-based snacks made from raw rice kernels. It's important to find a tightly woven muslin cloth to make rice-based dishes, because if you use a cheesecloth with a loose weave, the rice flour will literally fall through the cracks.

早

餐

Breakfast

The Morning After

It's Sunday, August 29, 1971, at two a.m., and my dad's hometown baseball team—the Tainan Giants—is up to bat against the US North team at the Little League World Series in Williamsport, Pennsylvania. He and his brothers are sprawled out in front of the television in the living room, knuckles white with anticipation. My dad is eight years old, and staying up late at night and into the early morning with his two older brothers huddled around the television watching baseball is one of his favorite pleasures. Lanky, tan, and still mostly children, the Taiwanese players aren't that much older than him. The kids are wearing blue caps and have the words Far East printed on the front of their pin-striped jerseys in bold red capital sans serif letters.

It's a thrilling experience for my dad and his brothers to watch these young baseball players represent their city and nation on the international stage. And they aren't the only ones who feel that way; that morning, ten million Taiwanese people—approximately two-thirds of the island's population—are also wide-awake and glued to the game. It's a tense moment that means a lot more to the Taiwanese people than just a baseball score. It comes at a time when diplomatic relations between Taiwan (which was known internationally as Nationalist China at the time) and the rest of the world are souring. Taiwan had just lost its United Nations seat in favor of Communist China the year before, and a year later, President Nixon would visit China to normalize relations, setting the stage for the United States to switch diplomatic recognition from Taipei to Beijing. The writing is on the wall already, and the baseball players—young as they are—know that they're playing for much more than just a trophy. Taiwan's hopes for international honor are resting on their small, preteen shoulders.

They don't disappoint. The Taiwanese boys wipe out the Americans by a stunning 12 to 3. And when they officially clinch the Little League World Series title in the late afternoon, it's five a.m. in Taiwan. The island erupts in cheers. Firecrackers fizzle and explode on the streets. Teary-eyed viewers flood outside in raucous celebration, with many eventually filing into nearby northern Chinese–style breakfast shops for sustenance. They fill up on long, crunchy sticks of deep-fried dough dipped in hot, creamy soy milk and scarf down sesame-dotted flatbreads stuffed with egg.

Now, prior to these baseball games, these breakfast eateries—which were opened by northern Chinese immigrants to Taiwan—were largely eschewed by the local Taiwanese population, who saw the relatively new Chinese presence as an infringement on their way of life. Breakfast in Taiwan traditionally consisted of a large pot of plain congee served with a collection of accoutrements like pickled bamboo shoots, plain peanuts, and pork floss. But because being a die-hard baseball aficionado required staying up all night and into the next day to watch the games, northern Chinese breakfast vendors were eventually wholeheartedly embraced by the mainstream because they were some of the few places that were open early.

For folks like my dad, a hearty northern Chinese–style spread is forever linked with rich and vivid memories of baseball. Sometimes after a particularly late night, he and his brothers would fall asleep on the couch when the game ended, exhausted from excitement. Their grandmother would wake up in the morning to a tired pile of young boys and venture out to buy them breakfast. And they'd wake up to the smell of steaming soy milk and deep-fried dough sticks—the best way to start the morning after watching a big game.

This warm noodle soup is many people's preferred way to start the day. Rice is freshly milled each morning, made into a dough, pushed through a sieve directly into boiling water, and then served in a hearty broth with a kiss of braised minced pork on top. The noodles can also be wok-fried into a hearty stir-fry, or even served as dessert, drenched in icy sugar water with tapioca pearls and shaved ice. Ivy says that when she was a child, fresh rice noodles were a common snack her parents would serve to visitors—a mark of the utmost hospitality. The recipe below uses rice flour, but for directions on how to make it with raw rice, see page 45.

SERVES 2

Rice Noodle Soup

米苔目
Mǐ Tái Mù

米篩目
Bí Thai Bàk

FOR THE RICE NOODLES:

- 2 cups (260 g) Thai rice flour, such as Erawan
- ¼ teaspoon fine sea salt
- Canola or soybean oil

FOR THE SOUP:

- 4 cups (1 L) Bone Broth (page 357) or low-sodium chicken stock
- 6 fresh garlic chives, cut into 1-inch (2.5-cm) chunks
- 1 teaspoon fine sea salt
- ½ teaspoon ground white pepper
- ½ cup (140 g) Braised Minced Pork Belly (page 90)
- ½ cup (80 g) minced celery (for garnish)
- 2 tablespoons fried shallots (store-bought or homemade; page 368) (for garnish)

MAKE THE RICE NOODLES: In a large bowl, mix the rice flour, salt, and 1½ cups (355 ml) water. Whisk to combine, and let the mixture rest at least 1 hour at room temperature or up to overnight in the refrigerator so the rice flour can properly hydrate.

Give the rice mixture another stir, and pour it into a medium saucepan. Set the pan over low heat, and cook the rice mixture, stirring constantly with a wooden spatula, until a dough begins to form and solidifies into a sticky, white mass with some translucent bits, 3 to 4 minutes. Turn off the heat, and transfer the dough to a clean work surface.

When the dough is cool enough to handle, grease your hands with oil, and knead the dough thoroughly until it's smooth and evenly white, about 2 minutes. Divide the dough in half, and roll it into 2 balls.

With a pastry brush, brush the blade of a sharp knife with oil. Prepare an ice bath and set aside.

Bring a medium pot of water to a rapid simmer over medium-high heat. Place 1 dough ball into a potato ricer with solid sides, and squeeze it over the

SPECIAL EQUIPMENT:
stainless steel potato ricer with solid sides

(RECIPE CONTINUES)

bubbling water (it'll be quite tough, so put some muscle into it). Use the knife to slice off the hanging noodles from the bottom of the potato ricer. Gently give the noodles a nudge with chopsticks (do not stir vigorously). Cook until the noodles all float, 2 to 3 minutes. During this process, the noodles might break into shorter segments; that is normal and typical of this dish. Reduce the heat to low. If the noodles are still floating, they're done. Don't overcook them or they will get mushy and disintegrate.

Drain the noodles through a fine-mesh sieve, immediately transfer them to the ice water bath, and let the noodles cool down completely, about 20 seconds. Scoop the noodles out with a spider strainer, transfer them to a sheet pan, and drizzle them with oil so that they are lightly coated. Toss and mix the noodles so they don't stick together. Prepare another ice bath and repeat the cooking process for the remaining dough ball. Divide the noodles into serving bowls.

MAKE THE SOUP: In a medium pot over high heat, bring the bone broth to a rolling boil. Add the chives, salt, and white pepper. Turn off the heat and ladle the hot soup over the noodles. Divide the pork belly among the bowls. Garnish with the celery and shallots.

SERVES 2

How to Make the Rice Noodles with Raw Rice Kernels

¾	cup (150 g) basmati rice	3	tablespoons tapioca starch
½	cup (100 g) jasmine rice	¼	teaspoon fine sea salt

SPECIAL EQUIPMENT:
high-speed blender or food processor; stainless steel potato ricer with solid sides

Briefly rinse the basmati and jasmine rice under running water. Transfer the rice to a large bowl and add enough water to cover. Soak the rice for at least 4 hours at room temperature or overnight in the refrigerator.

Drain the rice through a sieve and transfer it to a blender. Add the tapioca starch, salt, and 1 cup (240 ml) water. Blend on high speed until it's completely smooth and milky, about 1 minute.

Pour the rice milk into a medium saucepan. Set the heat to low and cook, stirring constantly with a wooden spoon, until a dough begins to form and solidifies into a sticky, white mass with some translucent bits, 3 to 4 minutes. Turn off the heat and transfer the dough to a clean work surface.

When the dough is cool enough to handle, grease your hands with oil, and knead the dough thoroughly until smooth and evenly white, about 2 minutes. Divide the dough in half and shape it into two balls. Cook according to directions on page 43.

Shiitake and Pork Congee

香菇肉鹹粥
Xiāng Gū Ròu Xián Zhōu

香菇肉糜
Hiunn Koo Bah Muâi

For most of Taiwan's modern history, breakfast revolved around rice. Morning provisions consisted of plain congee and a collection of simple sides, like pickled bamboo shoots, pork floss, peanuts, and perhaps a boiled sweet potato or two when rice was scarce. This recipe is a rather luxurious take on congee, dotted with shiitake mushrooms, thin slivers of pork tenderloin, and dried shrimp. While there are a couple of breakfast specialists across the island who sell this in the early mornings, it's actually much more commonly made at home. A thick grain porridge, after all, is a universally cheap and quick way to feed a family. Cook it low and slow over the stove, or, if you have an electric steamer or rice cooker, just pop all the ingredients in, press a button, and let time work its magic.

5	medium dried shiitake mushrooms
1	tablespoon small dried shrimp
1	cup (200 g) short-grain rice, also known as sushi rice
8	cups (2 L) Bone Broth (page 357) or low-sodium chicken stock
¾	pound (340 g) pork tenderloin, cut into matchsticks
2	tablespoons soy sauce
1	tablespoon toasted sesame oil, plus more to taste
2	teaspoons Taiwanese rice wine (michiu) or cooking sake
3	tablespoons canola or soybean oil
2	teaspoons fine sea salt
½	teaspoon ground white pepper
½	cup (80 g) minced celery (for garnish)
½	cup (40 g) fried shallots (store-bought or homemade; page 368) (for garnish)

In a medium bowl, add the dried shiitake mushrooms, cover with water, and soak until soft, about 1 hour. If you are in a rush, soak them in boiling water for 30 minutes (though they won't be nearly as flavorful). In a small bowl, submerge the dried shrimp in water for 10 minutes. Drain the dried shrimp in a fine-mesh sieve. Remove the shiitake mushrooms from the bowl and squeeze out any excess water. Trim the stems and discard. Thinly slice the caps and set aside.

Put the rice in a fine-mesh sieve, and rinse it under running water for a couple of seconds. Don't over-wash it; we want to keep as much of its starch as possible. This will help thicken the congee.

In a large stockpot over high heat, combine the washed rice and the bone broth, cover, and bring to a boil. Reduce the heat to low, and simmer with the lid slightly ajar. Cook, stirring often so the grains don't stick to the bottom of the pot, until the congee is thick and creamy and the rice grains

NOTE:
As the congee cools down, it will continue to thicken. To thin it out again, just add more bone broth to taste, and bring to a boil before serving.

PHOTOGRAPHY NOTE:
Yen Wei, the food stylist for this book, inherited this table from her grandmother.

swell, 25 to 40 minutes. If you'd like it a little bit thicker, simmer for an additional 20 minutes.

In a small bowl, combine the pork tenderloin, soy sauce, sesame oil, and rice wine, and marinate for 15 minutes.

In a wok, heat the canola or soybean oil over medium-high. When the oil is hot and shimmering, toss in the sliced shiitakes and shrimp, and cook, stirring, until it smells lovely, about 40 seconds. Add in the marinated pork tenderloin, and cook, stirring, until no longer pink, about 1 minute. Turn off the heat and set the wok aside.

When the congee is sufficiently thick, transfer the cooked shiitakes, shrimp, and pork tenderloin into the congee pot, and give it one big stir. Set the pot over low heat, and simmer everything together for an additional 5 minutes.

Turn off the heat, and mix in the salt and white pepper, adding more if you'd like. To serve, ladle some congee in a bowl. Garnish with a pinch of the minced celery and fried shallots, then finish off with a light drizzle of sesame oil.

At nearly a century old, Tung Yu-Chu 董玉珠 dresses impeccably every time he leaves the house with a neatly ironed shirt and shiny, polished shoes, a habit from his military days. Born in 1934 in Zhangjiakou, Hebei, China, he came to Taiwan at the age of 16 as an air force soldier and was stationed on Kinmen, a Taiwanese-owned island just four miles off the coast of the Chinese mainland, at the height of the Chinese Civil War. He remembers the bombs that were lobbed over by the Communists every other day and says surviving was just a matter of luck.

Like many other men who came over with the armed forces, Yu-Chu moved to Taiwan with the hopes of eventually returning home. But history had other plans. Yu-Chu ended up falling in love and marrying a local Taiwanese woman, and he never got an opportunity to see his hometown ever again, even when cross-strait family visits finally opened up in 1987. Yet after all these years, he still vividly remembers the food of his northern Chinese hometown, a cold, dry region resplendent with thick, scallion pancakes; hearty dumplings; and dreamy, cloud-like baos. A prolific home cook in his younger days, he re-created the flavors of his heritage entirely from memory, and this is his recipe for scallion pancakes. He can no longer cook at his advanced age, but he spelled out the instructions for this dish in meticulous, handwritten calligraphy for his family as a keepsake.

I made a couple of adjustments to the original recipe. Because American all-purpose flour is milled differently than Taiwanese all-purpose flour, the proportion of water to dough is different. Yu-Chu's original recipe also contains monosodium glutamate (MSG), which I've omitted because while a sprinkle of MSG can go a long way, it's completely optional and admittedly not for everyone. The use of lard is mandatory, though, because according to Yu-Chu, "it really wouldn't be a scallion pancake otherwise."

Scallion Pancakes

蔥油餅
Cōng Yóu Bǐng

SPECIAL EQUIPMENT:
stand mixer (optional)

NOTE:
To make the scallion pancakes for the Beef Roll (page 78), use half the amount of scallions as directed above, and roll the pancakes into six 9-inch (23-cm) pies.

PHOTOGRAPHY NOTE:
The scene in this photograph reflects what breakfast might have looked like in an old military house—the residences that veterans like Yu-Chu were put in when they first arrived on the island. Built out of wood with very low windows, these homes were meant to be temporary accommodations and were quite small and cramped in order to save money on materials. Most of them have been torn down by now. Ryan, the photographer for this cookbook, also grew up in a military village and drew on his memories to style this photo.

2	scallions, minced
2	cups (250 g) all-purpose flour, plus more for dusting
1	teaspoon fine sea salt, divided
¼	cup (60 ml) boiling water
¼	cup and 2 tablespoons (90 ml) room-temperature water
1	tablespoon plus 2 teaspoons lard or unsalted butter, divided, softened
4	teaspoons canola or soybean oil, divided, plus more for frying

Spread the scallions out evenly on top of a paper towel–lined plate. Air dry them for at least 30 minutes. This gets rid of excess moisture and prevents the scallions from weighing down the pancakes later.

In a large bowl or the bowl of a stand mixer, combine the all-purpose flour and ½ teaspoon of the salt. Gradually pour in the boiling water, stirring as

(RECIPE CONTINUES)

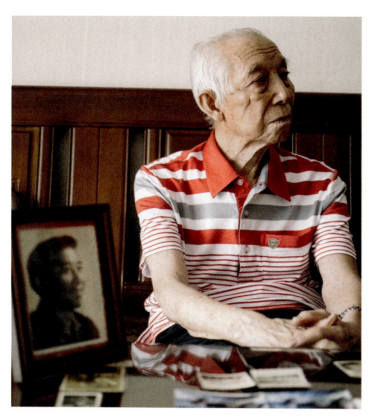

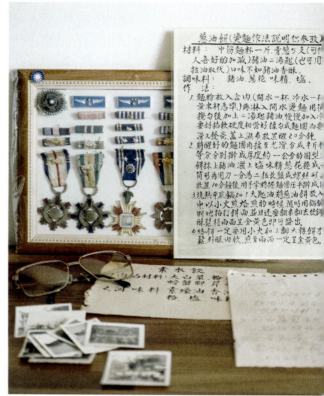

you add it. Pour in the room-temperature water and mix everything together until it forms a shaggy dough. Add 1 tablespoon of the lard, then knead the dough with your hands until it forms a solid mass and is completely smooth, about 3 minutes. (Alternatively, churn the dough in a stand mixer with the dough hook attachment on low speed for about 2 minutes.) The dough should be soft and slightly gummy. Cover the dough with plastic wrap, and let it rest at room temperature for 30 minutes.

Divide the dough into 4 equal pieces; the pieces should weigh about 103 g each. Flatten each piece with your palm and with a rolling pin, shape the dough into 4 round discs, each measuring 9 inches (23 cm).

In a small bowl, mix together the remaining 2 teaspoons of the lard and the remaining ½ teaspoon salt. With a pastry brush, brush the seasoned lard mixture on the dough discs. Evenly divide the scallions among each of the discs.

Tightly roll up each disc into a thin log and pinch the seams and sides so that everything is sealed. Gently stretch one log so that it elongates into a 10-inch- (25-cm-) long rope. Place your palms face down on the rope, with one palm on each side. Swipe the right palm up and the left palm down at the same time so that the rope begins to twist onto itself. Take one end of the rope and begin to coil it up against itself like a snail shell. Pinch it closed and cover it with plastic wrap. Repeat with the remaining pieces. Let the dough rest at room temperature for 15 minutes.

On a lightly floured surface, flatten a snail shell dough piece with the palm of your hand, then with a rolling pin, gently shape it into a round pancake, about 6 inches (15 cm) in diameter. Gently dust flour on the pancake as you roll so it doesn't rip or get too oily. Repeat with the remaining pieces.

Heat a well-seasoned skillet over medium heat, and then swirl in ½ teaspoon of the oil. When the oil is hot and begins to shimmer, put a scallion pancake in the pan, and cook until dark golden brown spots appear on the bottom, 1 to 2 minutes. Lift up the pancake with tongs, add ½ teaspoon more oil to the pan, flip the pancake, and cook for another 1 to 2 minutes. Repeat with the remaining scallion pancakes, adding more oil in between batches. Remove from the heat and enjoy immediately. Uncooked pancakes can be stored in the freezer for up to 2 months. To reheat, cook the pancakes in a well-oiled pan on medium heat until warm, about 5 minutes.

Sticky Rice Roll

飯糰
Fàn Tuán

Brought over by immigrants from eastern China, rice rolls are a breakfast staple doled out with immense speed by street vendors at the height of the morning traffic rush. A mat of sticky rice is stuffed with a sprinkle of pickled mustard greens, preserved radish, and a bit of pork floss before it's compacted into a large pill shape and slung into a plastic bag. Originally an on-the-go breakfast item geared toward blue-collar workers, this recipe is inspired by the rice rolls at Tzu-Yin Grandma's Rice Roll 慈音古早味阿婆飯糰 in Taipei. Born in Taichung, the stall's namesake Wang Tzu-Yin 王慈音 started selling rice rolls in the early 1990s at the age of 50 as a way to make money. She was a relative latecomer to the scene, but set herself apart by selling her rice rolls exclusively at night. Today, the stall is run by her daughter and granddaughter, who are still following her recipe exactly. Tzu-Yin's version uses fish floss instead of pork floss "because it's less likely to clump up that way," they tell me. But because fish floss is rather rare outside Taiwan, I've kept pork as the protein of choice.

2   cups (400g) long-grain glutinous rice, also known as sticky rice

3   ounces (85 g) preserved radish, also known as salted daikon (store-bought or homemade; page 351)

3   ounces (85 g) pickled mustard greens (store-bought or homemade; page 347)

2   Fried Crullers, about 6 inches (15 cm) long (page 54)

1   teaspoon canola or soybean oil, divided

1½ teaspoons white sugar

½   cup (35 g) pork floss (store-bought or homemade; page 364) or fish floss

Cook the long-grain glutinous rice according to instructions on page 360. Cover to keep warm.

Preheat the oven to 350°F (175°C).

Rinse the preserved radish and pickled mustard greens under running water. Put the preserved radish and pickled mustard greens into separate small bowls, cover with water, and soak for 10 minutes. Drain, squeeze out the excess water, and pat dry with paper towels. Mince the radish and mustard greens finely, keeping them separated still, and set aside for later.

Cut the crullers in half and toast them in the oven until they are a dark golden brown, 5 to 8 minutes. They should be very crispy, but not burnt.

In a wok over low heat, swirl in ½ teaspoon of the oil. When the oil is hot, add the preserved radish, and cook, stirring constantly, until it's dried out and

fragrant, about 5 minutes. Transfer the radish to a plate and set aside for later. Add the remaining ½ teaspoon oil to the wok. Add the pickled mustard greens and the sugar, and cook, stirring constantly, until the sugar has dissolved and the greens are withered and dried out, 5 to 7 minutes. Transfer the greens mixture to a plate and set aside for later.

Now assemble the rice roll. Take a clean hand towel and fold it in half so that it forms a rectangle, roughly 7 × 6 inches (18 × 15 cm). Keep the towel in the landscape orientation and lay a sheet of plastic wrap on top of the towel so that it's covered completely.

Dip a spoon in water and use it to scoop out ¼ of the cooked sticky rice. Spread it on the plastic wrap to form a thin 6 × 5-inch (15 × 13-cm) horizontally oriented rectangular mat on top of the towel. The long side of the rectangle should be facing you. Sprinkle a line of pork floss vertically down the middle of the rice rectangle, add the preserved radish and pickled mustard greens on top, and then finally add a chunk of the fried cruller lined up vertically on top of everything. Gently lift up the towel and with your hands, then gently squeeze and shape everything together so that the sticky rice is formed into an oblong-shaped rice roll. Repeat with the remaining ingredients. Enjoy immediately.

Fried Crullers

油條
Yóu Tiáo

For commercial bakers, the secret to these deep-fried dough sticks is ammonium bicarbonate, an old-school leavening agent used before the advent of baking powder and baking soda. It's what makes the cruller balloon to twice its size, with paper-thin walls and a porous, crunchy cavity. The only downside is that the cruller will smell like urine if it isn't cooked well. Thankfully for the home cook, the same effect can be achieved with baking powder and baking soda without any of the noxious side effects. Restaurant-size crullers are about a foot long and difficult to manage even with a large wok, so I've scaled down this recipe significantly to make reasonable 6-inch (15-cm) bread sticks.

1 cup (125 g) bread flour, plus more for dusting	¼ cup plus 1 tablespoon (75 ml) water
½ teaspoon baking powder	1 tablespoon canola or soybean oil, plus an additional 4 cups (1 L) for deep-frying
¼ teaspoon fine sea salt	
¼ teaspoon baking soda	

In a large bowl or the bowl of a stand mixer, combine the bread flour, baking powder, salt, and baking soda. Drizzle in the water and mix the ingredients together with chopsticks until the dough is lumpy. Add in 1 tablespoon of the oil and knead the dough with your hands until it comes together and is completely smooth and shiny, about 5 minutes. (Alternatively, mix the dough in a stand mixer with the dough hook attachment on low speed until it forms a smooth ball, about 2 minutes.) Cover the dough with plastic wrap and refrigerate it for at least 8 hours or overnight.

Transfer the dough to a lightly floured work surface and with a rolling pin, roll it out into a 3 × 10-inch (8 × 25-cm) rectangle. Cover it with plastic wrap and bring it to room temperature, 1 to 2 hours.

In a large wok, heat the remaining 4 cups (1 L) oil over medium-high heat until it registers 400°F (205°C) on an instant-read thermometer.

Unwrap the dough, and cut it crosswise into 10 even strips, about 1 inch (2.5 cm) wide. Make a set by carefully placing one strip on top of another. Lay a chopstick lengthwise in the middle of the set. Press firmly so that the top layer angles up in a V-shape and the 2 strips stick together. Take the set of dough, and pull the edges with your fingers so that it stretches out like a rope to about double its length, around 6 inches (15 cm) long.

Gently lower the rope into the hot oil, letting the middle part dip in first before quickly letting go of the edges. Once immersed in the oil, the dough

SPECIAL EQUIPMENT:
stand mixer (optional)

will immediately start to puff up and the oil will shine and fizzle around the edges. Cook until golden brown, flipping it over with tongs often so that it cooks evenly, 30 seconds to 1 minute. Remove the cruller with tongs, and then transfer to a paper towel–lined plate or wire rack set in a rimmed baking sheet to drain.

Repeat with the remaining dough strips, maintaining the oil temperature at 400°F (205°C). You should have 5 crullers in total; it's important to assemble and fry them one at a time. Serve while hot.

All-American Wheat

In 1954, the Eisenhower administration started a food aid program in the midst of the Cold War that gave American aid to developing countries in the form of wheat. Later renamed the Food for Peace Program under President John F. Kennedy, the initiative was "a far better weapon than a bomber in our competition with the Communists for influence in the developing world," George McGovern, who served as a director of the program, said. And as part of this initiative, Taiwan—a natural enemy of Communist China—and other countries around the world received large shipments of the grain, relieving the United States of its food surpluses in exchange for diplomatic leverage and influence. For the Taiwanese, the wheat was a signal of solidarity from the United States at a time when tensions between Taiwan and the Chinese mainland were high, and, naturally, folks were thrilled with the show of support.

Problem was, the people of Taiwan didn't have much experience working with the grain. Wheat doesn't grow well in Taiwan, and the main carbs in the Taiwanese diet at that point came from the crops that do grow well there, like rice and sweet potatoes. The very few wheat dishes that existed in the Taiwanese culinary repertoire were mostly noodle-based; they were consumed in very small portions and considered luxurious treats.

To make good use of the gift from the Americans, a massive marketing campaign to promote wheat was launched: cooking demos were held, and students were sent to the American Institute of Baking to learn how to bake bread and cakes. Absurd marketing slogans linking wheat consumption to whiter skin and a taller frame began to emerge, with many of them falsely claiming that wheat dishes were inherently more nutritious than rice dishes. Yet despite all the hype, it still took a while for wheat to gain traction.

The first people in Taiwan to take advantage of the influx of wheat were the people who actually knew how to use it. Refugees from China's arid northern regions who came in with the Nationalist army in the mid-20th century began opening up eateries centered around the wheat products they ate back home. Many grew up with baos, noodles, and dumplings as their staples, and for them, comfort food meant a large, steaming bowl of soy milk with deep-fried bread and glorious discs of lard-infused scallion pancakes.

Eventually, wheat milling companies in Taiwan started pastry schools and industry-sponsored baking competitions, fostering a cohort of talented bakers in an attempt to sell their products. It worked like a charm. Bakeries began to pop up en masse in the 1960s in neighborhoods across the country, churning out platters of soft milk breads graced with distinctly local toppings like pork floss and scallions. In time, a new and distinctly Taiwanese culture around wheat flour emerged, and today bakeries with tantalizing displays of freshly baked bread are as much a mainstay on the streets of Taipei as they are on the streets of Berlin.

An Important Note:

While the vast majority of the wheat berries imported into Taiwan come from the United States—averaging more than one million tons per year—Taiwan mills most of its own wheat. This means that Taiwanese wheat flour and American wheat flour are inherently different and, depending on the recipe, cannot always be substituted 1:1.

The real difference lies in the flour stabilizers and preservatives that are used and how the wheat is milled. Generally speaking, American wheat is more finely milled than Taiwanese wheat, so the water-to-flour ratio will differ. Not to worry—all the recipes in this book have been adapted so that they work with American flour.

Sesame Flatbread

燒餅

Shāo Bǐng

These hearty flatbreads are exclusive to breakfast, traditionally baked in a steel drum tandoor and served either stuffed with a fried egg and scallions or a large fried cruller (page 54). A northern Chinese import, they can also be eaten plain or paired with a hot cup of soy milk. Whipping up a batch of these at home is always an extremely satisfying experience. I love hovering in front of the oven and watching as they expand and puff up. Moisture in the bread evaporates into steam, which then pushes the layers of the dough up against themselves. When the flatbreads come out of the oven, they're delightfully swollen and plump, like balloons—but cut into them and you'll find thin layers of soft bread nestled inside the crisp crust of the toasted flatbread.

2 cups (250 g) all-purpose flour, plus 2 tablespoons more for sprinkling	3 tablespoons (45 ml) lard or canola or soybean oil
½ teaspoon fine sea salt	¼ cup plus 1 tablespoon (50 g) cake flour
3 tablespoons plus 1 teaspoon (50 ml) boiling water	2 tablespoons raw white sesame seeds
¼ cup plus 3 tablespoons (100 ml) room-temperature water	

In a large bowl or the bowl of a stand mixer, combine 2 cups (250 g) of the all-purpose flour and the salt. Gradually pour in the boiling water, quickly stirring with chopsticks as you add it. Add the room-temperature water and mix everything together until it forms a shaggy dough. Bring the dough together with your hands and knead until it forms a solid mass and is completely smooth, about 5 minutes. (Alternatively, mix the dough in a stand mixer with the dough hook attachment on low speed until it forms a smooth ball, about 3 minutes.) The dough should be soft and slightly gummy. Cover it with plastic wrap, and let it rest at room temperature for 30 minutes.

Meanwhile, make a roux. In a small saucepan, combine the lard and cake flour, and cook over medium heat, stirring often with a silicone spatula, until it begins to shimmer and bubble. Stir until the mixture is the color of peanut butter and is similar to the texture of a thick condensed milk, 4 to 5 minutes. Remove from the heat, and cool to room temperature. It will get thicker as it cools down.

On a lightly floured surface, flatten the dough with a rolling pin into a long rectangular sheet, about 16 × 8 inches (40 × 20 cm). With a pastry brush or the back of a spoon, spread the roux all over the dough, leaving about a finger-width of empty space on the edges. Then sprinkle with the remaining 2 tablespoons all-purpose flour.

SPECIAL EQUIPMENT:
stand mixer (optional)

(RECIPE CONTINUES)

From the long end of the rectangle, roll the dough into a long cylinder, and pinch the edges so that they are completely sealed. Hold up the cylinder with one hand, and with the other hand, pinch off 6 even pieces.

Pinch the edges of each piece closed so the roux does not leak out. With a rolling pin, shape each piece into a long-rounded rectangle, about 3 × 6 inches (7.5 × 15 cm). Fold the top third of the rectangle down, and then fold the bottom third of the oval up, forming a small book. Rotate the dough 90 degrees and repeat. With a rolling pin, flatten the dough into a long-rounded rectangle, and then fold into thirds again, like you're folding a letter. Set aside and cover with plastic wrap. Repeat with the remaining pieces of dough.

With a pastry brush, brush the flat smooth side of each dough with water. Put the sesame seeds on a small plate, and then press the wet side of each dough piece into the sesame seeds so that they stick. Repeat until all the pieces are covered with sesame seeds. Cover with plastic wrap, and let it rest for 10 minutes.

Preheat the oven to 400°F (205°C).

With the sesame seed side of the dough facing down on the table, flatten each piece with a rolling pin into another long-rounded rectangle, but this time about 7 inches (18 cm) long and 3½ inches (9 cm) wide. You'll have 6 flatbreads in total. Flip the flatbreads so that the sesame side is facing up and arrange them on a large baking sheet.

Bake the flatbreads on the middle rack of the oven for 10 to 12 minutes, until they are golden brown and puffed up like balloons. Flip them over in the oven with tongs, and bake for an additional 4 minutes, until the other side is also golden brown.

Eat while they are hot. You can cut a pocket into them so that they're like a pouch and stuff them with fillings of your choice, like fried eggs with scallions, scrambled eggs, or a Fried Cruller (page 54). Cooked sesame flatbreads can be stored in the freezer for 2 months. To reheat, defrost the flatbreads and then bake them in a 300°F (150°C) oven for 5 to 6 minutes.

Taiwanese Egg Crepe

蛋餅

Dàn Bǐng

In the early years of Ivy's marriage, her husband approached her with a very specific request. There was a breakfast egg crepe he used to buy from a vendor in his university days, and he desperately craved it. Could she make it for him? There was just a slight problem: The vendor's stall was no longer there, and he had no idea what the dish was actually made of. But he could still vividly describe the texture of the batter: like a runny yogurt with finely chopped scallions embedded inside. The vendor would slosh a bit of it on a flat griddle, and when it became slightly opaque, an egg was thrown on top, then the whole thing was folded and sliced into bite-size pieces. Rarely deterred from a culinary challenge and determined to re-create one of her beloved's favorite dishes, Ivy tried her hand at the batter over and over again, and eventually nailed it after many iterations.

A suggestion: On its own, the crepe is quite plain. Nowadays, all sorts of crazy fillings like canned corn or bacon are thrown in, so feel free to get creative and put the fillings on top of the egg right before you roll it up. The crepe is just a foundation; build on it. My husband likes to order his with a thin layer of cheddar cheese. I like mine stuffed with kimchi.

1 cup (125 g) bread flour

1½ tablespoons tapioca starch

½ teaspoon fine sea salt, plus a pinch more for the egg

1¼ cups (300 ml) water

1 scallion, green part only, finely minced

1 tablespoon canola or soybean oil, divided

3 large eggs

Ground white pepper

Everyday Garlic Soy Dressing (page 367)

In a large bowl, mix together the bread flour, tapioca starch, and ½ teaspoon salt. Add the water and whisk thoroughly until there are no lumps. It should be the texture of a runny yogurt. Add the scallions and stir well. Cover and let rest for 15 minutes.

With a pastry brush or a paper towel, brush a nonstick pan or well-seasoned skillet that's at least 8 inches (20 cm) in diameter with ½ teaspoon of the oil. Set the heat to low, and when the pan is warm, pour in a third of the batter. For precision's sake: that's about ½ cup (150 ml). Immediately pick up the pan and tilt it so the batter is evenly distributed and fills out the entire 8 inches (20 cm). Increase the heat to medium-high, cover, and cook until the crepe is completely opaque, 2 to 3 minutes. Lift up the edge of the crepe with a chopstick, and carefully use a spatula to flip it. Cook the other side until it has set and has light golden spots on the bottom, another 1 to 2 minutes. Peel the crepe off the pan and transfer it to a clean plate. Turn off

the heat. Repeat with the remaining batter, but make sure to clean the pan in between batches if there are pieces of flour that have stuck.

Crack the eggs into a small bowl, add a pinch of the white pepper and salt, and whisk until smooth.

In the same pan set over low heat, heat ½ teaspoon of the oil and pour in a third of the egg mixture. Swirl the egg around the pan, then quickly layer 1 crepe on top of the egg while the egg is still very runny. Cook until the eggs set, 5 to 10 seconds. Turn off the heat, and carefully flip the crepe upside down onto a clean plate, with the egg side facing up. Roll the crepe into a burrito—egg layer facing in—and cut into 4 or 5 even pieces. Repeat with the remaining oil, crepes, and the rest of the egg mixture. Serve hot with the Everyday Garlic Soy Dressing.

Hamburgers for Breakfast

If you walk around Taipei in the mornings, you might notice a chain of breakfast shops with red-and-yellow-striped countertops whipping out hamburgers for breakfast. It's a curious sight, especially given that hamburgers are very much a Western import. But ask a young Taiwanese person about it, and they'll tell you that hamburgers are early morning comfort food and that these shops have been here since long before they were born.

In the early 1980s, a man named Lin Kun-Yen 林坤炎 was obsessed with watching American baseball, and was inspired by the colorful striped hot dog concession stands he saw on television. "What if I did this in Taiwan, but sold hamburgers instead?" he likely asked himself. So he took out a loan and opened up a hamburger stand in Taipei called Mei Er Mei 美而美. It was wildly successful, and pretty soon copycat concepts began to spring up across the country. This was before Taiwan had any copyright laws, and now there are literally thousands of these rip-off Mei Er Mei shops around the nation, serving hamburgers with thin crispy pork patties; crustless triangle sandwiches stuffed with iceberg lettuce, cucumbers, and ham; and cold cups of milk tea. To be honest, the burgers aren't anything special; they tend to be quite sweet. But it's become a necessary favorite for many, including my husband, who likes to order his with a slice of processed American cheese.

At the coffee shop where I meet her, Taiwanese pastry chef and teacher Yvonne Chen 陳郁芬 orders a plain piece of buttered toast with strawberry jam and rips it apart the moment it arrives at the table. It's an accordion of light, feathery wisps of dough. She inspects the bread closely, takes a deep whiff, and nods in mild approval as she dips chunks of it into the glistening jam.

Baking blogs around the world often credit Yvonne with inventing tāngzhōng 湯種, the creamy gelatinized substance in Asian breads made by whisking together scalding water and flour at a 1:5 ratio and heating it up to 150°F (65°C) to form a thick slurry. When combined with the rest of the ingredients, the slurry basically gelatinizes part of the dough, which helps the final bread retain moisture. It's what gives Asian breads their signature cloudlike texture, though Yvonne stresses that the credit is misdirected and she didn't actually invent tangzhong at all. A similar technique has been used all over East Asia for generations, and it was the Japanese who first coined and codified this particular procedure for bread. Yvonne picked it up during culinary school in Taiwan, and her name became synonymous with it only when she wrote a popular cookbook in 2007 called *65 Degrees C*, a nod to the temperature at which tangzhong is made. "It's normally used just for toast, but I apply it to everything," she tells me.

Pork Floss Milk Bread

肉鬆麵包
Ròu Sōng Miàn Bāo

肉酥麭
Bah Soo Pháng

FOR THE TANGZHONG:

1½ tablespoons (12 g) bread flour

¼ cup (60 ml) whole milk

FOR THE BREAD:

½ cup plus 2 tablespoons (90 ml) whole milk

1 teaspoon active dry yeast

2 cups (250 g) bread flour

1 large egg (50 ml)

2 tablespoons white sugar

¼ teaspoon fine sea salt

1½ tablespoons (20 g) unsalted butter, softened and cut into ½-inch (1-cm) pieces

Canola or soybean oil

FOR THE EGG WASH:

1 large egg

1 tablespoon whole milk

FOR THE TOPPINGS:

½ cup (115 g) Kewpie mayonnaise (see Note)

1¼ cup (80 g) pork floss (store-bought or homemade; page 364)

SPECIAL EQUIPMENT:
stand mixer with dough hook attachment (optional)

NOTE:
If you don't have access to Kewpie mayonnaise, mix ½ cup regular mayonnaise with 1½ tablespoons white sugar for a quick version.

Yvonne's original recipe uses milk powder and water, but I've substituted whole milk here instead.

(RECIPE CONTINUES)

MAKE THE TANGZHONG: In a small saucepan, combine the bread flour and milk, and stir until the flour is completely dissolved. Bring to a simmer over low heat and cook, stirring constantly, until the mixture is glue-like, about 3 minutes. Immediately remove from the heat, transfer to a container, and let it cool to room temperature. Refrigerate for a minimum of 2 hours or overnight ("It must be cold," advises Yvonne).

MAKE THE BREAD: In a small saucepan set over low heat, heat the milk until tiny bubbles begin to break on the surface and it starts to steam. Turn off the heat and wait until the milk is cool but still lukewarm and comfortable to the touch, about 105°F (40°C). Sprinkle the active dry yeast over the milk, stir to dissolve, and let it sit until frothy, about 5 minutes.

In a large bowl or the bowl of a stand mixer, combine the bread flour, egg, sugar, salt, the refrigerated tangzhong, and the yeast-milk mixture. Mix until it forms a shaggy dough. Add the butter one piece at a time and knead the dough with your hands until it forms a solid dough, about 5 minutes. (Alternatively, churn in a stand mixer with the dough hook attachment on low speed until it forms a smooth ball, about 3 minutes.) The dough should be soft and quite sticky.

Lightly grease the inside of a bowl with oil. Lift the dough out of the mixing bowl, shape it into a ball and place it in the oiled bowl. Cover it with plastic wrap and let it rest until it has doubled in size, 1 to 2 hours at room temperature or overnight in the refrigerator.

Punch the air out of the dough and scoop it out onto a lightly oiled surface. Using a bench scraper, divide the dough into 6 even pieces, about 78 g each. Gently knead each piece until it forms a very smooth ball. Cover the balls with plastic wrap and let rest at room temperature for 10 minutes.

With a rolling pin, flatten a dough ball into an oval, about 6 inches (15 cm) long. Starting from the top tip of the oval, tightly roll up the dough toward you into a log. Pinch the sides and seams together and fluff it up gently ("It should look like an olive," says Yvonne). Repeat with the rest of the dough balls. Place the logs on a baking sheet seam side down, leaving a couple of fingers' worth of space between each of them. Don't worry if the tops aren't completely smooth; they'll smooth themselves out when baked. Cover and let rest at room temperature until they have puffed up and are soft to the touch, 30 to 40 minutes. If you poke them gently, they should spring back up again slowly.

Preheat the oven to 350°F (175°C).

APPLY THE EGG WASH: In a small bowl, whisk together the egg and milk. Brush the egg wash on the tops and sides of the buns with a pastry brush.

Bake the buns until the tops are golden brown, about 15 minutes. Take the buns out of the pan and place them on a wire rack to cool down completely to room temperature.

FOR THE TOPPINGS: With a sharp knife, make a vertical incision into the buns (like it's a hot dog bun), but don't cut all the way through and don't cut to the edge. Spread some Kewpie mayonnaise inside, then cover up the incision by spreading more mayonnaise on top. Layer an even mat of pork floss on top of the mayonnaise. Repeat with the remaining buns. To store, put the buns in an airtight container and store at room temperature. The bread should be eaten within 2 days.

小菜

Side Dishes

The Steamer That Could

Every now and then, there comes an appliance that really takes off. And not in a fleeting and seasonal way, but in a way—like with the toaster or the microwave—that really revolutionizes how people cook and makes them forget what life was like before it. Introduced to Taiwanese housewives via enthusiastic salespeople stationed at wet markets in the 1960s, the Tatung steamer hit all these marks and changed the way we cook in Taiwan forever.

Fundamentally, it's just a plug-in electric steamer made up of a smaller pot nestled inside a larger outer pot. Put water into the latter, food into the former, cover it all with a lid, and then flick a switch to turn it on. It can steam fish, make rice, reheat leftovers, incubate yogurt, pop popcorn, and conjure up deep and earthy braises. Though Tatung didn't invent this technology (it was plagiarized from Japan's Toshiba), they managed to turn it from a novel gadget to such a cult classic that the company's name is now synonymous with the appliance. It was so embraced that it inspired volumes of cooking shows and cookbooks—some sponsored by the company, others emerging from a fervent, genuine fan base. With the steamer's introduction, home cooks no longer had to monitor an open flame for hours; all they had to do was pop in their ingredients and wait for the water in the outer pot to evaporate. And because gas stoves in Taiwan are like rocket engines—harsh and violent infernos really great for wok frying but terrible for maintaining a lazy simmer or a controlled sear—the Tatung began to replace the stove for dishes that required a gentle, low heat.

In Taiwan, many of our side dishes, like thin slivers of beef shanks and rings of pork intestines bathed in soy sauce, are made by braising the ingredients for hours in a Tatung. A style of cooking known as lǔ wèi 滷味, braising was a technique used in bygone days to cook up the leftover, tougher parts of an animal like pig's ears, pigskin, large intestines, duck heads, or chicken gizzards. These parts would be lazily simmered in a simple cocktail of soy sauce, sugar, and water, and the act of braising transformed the rubbery, otherwise inedible bits of meat into softer and more manageable bites.

All the braised dishes in this chapter and book can be made in a Tatung. For accessibility reasons, I've written them so that they all work on the stovetop, but feel free to sub in a Tatung anytime a recipe calls for a slow simmer over low heat. I usually bloom my aromatics in a wok until they smell divine, transfer all of that into my Tatung, toss in whatever I want to braise, and then top it all off with soy sauce, water, and some spices. Add water in the outer pot, push the button, and you're done. But there's a caveat: because the machine is relatively low-tech, two cups of water in the outer pot will keep the steamer chugging along for only 40 to 50 minutes. Once that evaporates, you have to refill it with a few more rounds of water.

By now, the Tatung's appeal goes beyond practicalities; for many Taiwanese people, it's a conduit of memories. For me, the smell of soy sauce and sugar wafting out of my olive-green steamer immediately triggers recollections of my childhood. I think of my paternal grandmother gently lowering a plate of steamed fish into it, or of her pulling out freshly wrapped bundles

of zongzi from the deep belly of the machine. Other days, my mom would open it up to reveal lunch—a pork belly braise blanketed with a thin, iridescent film of fat. Over the years, many of our appliances like toasters, blenders, and coffee machines were eventually put into storage, upgraded, or phased out, but the Tatung—in its monochromatic beauty—was always situated permanently in the center of our family kitchen.

Braised Egg, Bean Curd, and Seaweed

滷蛋, 豆乾, 海帶
Lǔ Dàn, Dòu Gān, Hǎi Dài

滷卵, 豆乾, 海帶
Lóo Nng, Tāu Kuann, Hái Tuà

There's a distinct elegance to eggs, bean curd, and kelp simmered in a sweet soy sauce–based liquid, cooled down, and then arranged neatly on a platter. An appetizer so ubiquitous that it can be found both in restaurants and at grandma's house, this recipe is inspired by instructions from my friend Xin-Yun's grandmother Chang Mei-Chih 張美枝, who has been making this regularly for more than six decades. Orphaned at a very young age, Mei-Chih moved to Taipei by herself at the age of 14 in 1957 to provide for her siblings, and quickly landed a job as a cook and cleaning lady at a medical clinic. She learned how to make this dish from the physician's wife, but notes that back then soy sauce was quite expensive and the braises were really watery. ("It was difficult to control the fire on the stove back then, so more water was added, and soy sauce was just a supplementary seasoning," she says.) The takeaway is that this recipe is rather forgiving. Use what you have. If you're feeding guests, feel free to make this a day ahead of time.

2	ounces (60 g) dried kombu kelp strips
½	pound (225 g) bean curd (dòu gān 豆乾) or extra-firm tofu
1	tablespoon canola or soybean oil
1	1-inch piece fresh ginger (10 g), unpeeled and sliced
3	garlic cloves, smashed
4	scallions, white and green parts separated
2	tablespoons coarse raw sugar, such as demerara
¾	cup (180 ml) soy sauce
2	tablespoons Taiwanese rice wine (michiu) or cooking sake
1	whole star anise pod
1	small cassia or cinnamon stick, about 2 inches (5 cm) long (optional)
1	dried tangerine or mandarin orange peel, about the size of a quarter (optional)
6	large soft-boiled eggs, peeled

Everyday Soy Dressing (page 367)

Toasted sesame oil (optional)

PHOTOGRAPHY NOTE:
This platter was lent to us by the Taiwan Bowl and Dish Museum. Made in Taiwan in the 1950s or '60s with local clay and fired in Yingge, it's embellished with a painting of a coconut tree and a sailboat on water—elements that portray Taiwan as a tropical oasis.

(RECIPE CONTINUES)

In a large bowl, cover the dried kombu kelp strips with water, and soak until they are pliable, about 30 minutes. Lift the kelp out of the bowl, and reserve 1 cup (240 ml) of the kelp water, saving the rest for another use (it's great for broth). If the rehydrated kelp strips are more than 1 foot (30 cm) long, cut them in half. Roll the kelp up tightly into individual cigars and secure them by spearing a toothpick through each roll. Set aside.

With a toothpick, poke multiple holes into each bean curd. The holes will help the bean curd absorb the braising liquid.

In a medium pot set over medium heat, add the oil. When the oil begins to shimmer, add the ginger, garlic, the white parts of the scallions, and sugar,

and stir until the sugar begins to dissolve, about 30 seconds. Immediately pour the soy sauce, rice wine, the reserved kelp water, and 2 cups of water (470 ml) into the pot. Plop in the star anise pod, cassia stick (if using), and dried tangerine peel (if using). The liquid will be a dark, amber brown and should taste as salty as the ocean. Cover the pot and increase the heat to high. When the liquid comes to a rolling boil, reduce the heat to low. Add in the kelp and bean curd, cover, and slowly simmer for about 30 minutes.

Remove the kelp from the pot with tongs and set it aside on a plate. Turn off the heat and add in the soft-boiled eggs. Keep the eggs and bean curd in the pot uncovered until the braising liquid cools down completely to room temperature, 1 to 2 hours.

Remove the eggs and bean curd from the pot. Strain the braising liquid through a fine-mesh colander into a large, clean bowl. Discard the solids but reserve the liquid. In a large glass storage container, combine the kelp, bean curd, and a couple of spoons of the braising liquid. The kelp and bean curd should only be lightly dressed with the braising liquid; they might disintegrate if they're soaked in it for too long.

In a separate medium glass storage container, combine the eggs and enough of the braising liquid to cover completely. Refrigerate the kelp, bean curd, and eggs until everything is fully chilled, about 2 hours or overnight. Save the leftover braising liquid for another use.

To serve, remove the toothpicks from the kelp, and cut the kelp into 1-inch (2.5-cm) strips. Slice the bean curd into ½-inch (1-cm) slices. Cut the eggs in half. Arrange all ingredients neatly on a serving platter.

Mince the scallion greens. Pour a couple of spoons of the reserved braising liquid over the ingredients and some Everyday Soy Dressing, to taste. Drizzle toasted sesame oil, if using, and garnish with the scallion greens. Enjoy immediately. This platter can be stored in the refrigerator for up to 2 days.

Ivy was raised in an extremely traditional household in the countryside of southern Taiwan during the 1960s, back when eating beef was still taboo across the island. At that time in agrarian Taiwan, cows were considered hard-working members of the family because they worked alongside people in the field. Ivy secretly ate beef for the very first time when she was 16, and one of the first dishes she learned how to make with the ingredient was this classic appetizer taught to her by a friend who had just graduated from culinary school. Delighted, she went back home and introduced it to her mother, who initially balked at the thought but became a convert once she took her first bite. This was the first and only beef dish her mom ever ate. This dish can be made ahead of time.

Braised Beef Shank

滷牛腱

Lǔ Niú Jiàn

- 2 teaspoons coarse salt
- 2 pounds (900 g) whole boneless beef shank
- 1 tablespoon canola or soybean oil
- 1 1-inch piece of fresh ginger (10 g), unpeeled and sliced
- 3 garlic cloves, smashed
- 4 scallions, white and green parts separated
- 2 tablespoons coarse raw sugar, such as demerara
- 2 teaspoons fermented broad bean paste (dòu bàn jiàng 豆瓣醬)
- ¼ cup (60 ml) soy sauce
- 2 tablespoons Taiwanese soy paste (store-bought or homemade; page 366)
- 2 tablespoons Taiwanese rice wine (michiu) or cooking sake
- 1 Spice Bag (page 131) or 1 teaspoon five-spice powder

Toasted sesame oil (optional)

Rub the salt evenly over the beef shank. Cover and refrigerate for at least 2 hours or overnight. This helps tenderize and draw out flavor from the meat.

In a large pot set over high heat, add the beef shank with enough water to cover. Bring the water to a boil, reduce the heat to medium, and simmer for about 5 minutes. Turn off the heat. Drain the liquid in a colander placed over the sink and rinse the beef under cool running water to get rid of any excess scum.

Place a medium pot over medium-high heat, and swirl in the oil. When the oil begins to shimmer, add the ginger, garlic, the white part of the scallions, sugar, and fermented broad bean paste, and cook, stirring, until the sugar begins to melt, about 20 seconds. Add the soy sauce, soy paste, rice wine, beef shank, spice bag, and 4 cups (1 L) water. At this point, the braising liquid should have the same color and opacity as a properly brewed cup of black tea.

(RECIPE CONTINUES)

Cover the pot and bring the liquid to a rapid boil. Reduce the heat to low, leave the lid slightly ajar, and gently simmer the shank until fork-tender, 1½ to 2 hours. If the beef isn't completely submerged, turn it occasionally so that it's exposed to the braising liquid on all sides. Check the meat; the shank is done when a knife can pierce through the meat with little to no resistance. Turn off the heat. Pluck out and discard the spice bag. Cover again, and let the meat cool down completely to room temperature in the pot for 1 to 2 hours. Remove the shank and set aside. Strain the braising liquid through a fine-mesh sieve and into a large clean bowl. Reserve the liquid and discard the solids.

In a large glass storage container, combine the shank with enough braising liquid so that it's completely submerged. If the shank is too big, cut it in half and divide between 2 storage containers. Chill in the refrigerator for a minimum of 1 hour or up to overnight before serving.

Mince the scallion greens. To serve, cut the beef shank against the grain into thin slices, about as thick as two nickels stacked on top of each other. Spoon a bit of the braising liquid over the beef, then drizzle with sesame oil to taste, if using. Garnish with the scallion greens. The braised beef shank can be stored for up to 2 days in the refrigerator.

How to Win
at the Wet Market

The secret to finessing your way through a wet market is to know exactly what you're buying before you step into it. The market is chock-full of opinionated aunties and uncles who will eat you alive if you hesitate. It's all about building a rapport and acting confident. I see it like a game; you must charm the vendors in order to get the best deals, the first choice of vegetables, and the finest cuts of meat. And even if you're a seasoned connoisseur or chef, the game resets itself the moment you step into a completely new wet market with unfamiliar vendors.

Strut in with confidence and sugarcoat your words. Call the aunties "big sister," refer to the uncles as "brother." Ideally speak in Taiwanese Hokkien. Compliment them on their perpetual youth, and never, under any circumstances, doubt their expertise on their products (even if they are truly in the wrong).

Wet markets are extremely social corners of Taiwan—community spaces that grew organically from the periphery of temples. In the old days, it was where farmers and fishermen would gather to sell their produce and catches. These days, most vendors are middlemen who buy everything in bulk at a wholesale fruit and vegetable distribution center and then sell the goods at their local market. Increasingly, indoor, air-conditioned supermarket chains are fierce competitors, with their much longer hours and exotic goods. But the wet market remains a bustling part of Taiwanese society because it's where many people still congregate to socialize, gossip, and, if you play the game right, get a couple of freebies and deals thrown in.

When Ivy and I were shopping for the ingredients for this cookbook, we did it at a completely unfamiliar market near our photographers' studio. At first it was a bit rough. Old men with attitudes. Aunties who wouldn't give us the time of day. By the time we hit the fifth day, Ivy—who speaks Taiwanese fluently—was starting to win the game.

"Can I get a red chili?" she asks a grumpy vegetable vendor we had been frequenting for the past week.

"How many?"

"Just one, but throw it in for free, please," Ivy says. "We've bought so much already."

The vendor obliges. And for the first time ever, I see her crack a smile.

Beef Roll

牛肉捲餅

Niú Ròu Juàn Bǐng

Beef rolls are one of the few side dishes more popular throughout the Taiwanese diaspora than they are in modern-day Taiwan. Mostly found on the menus at dumpling and beef noodle soup eateries in the country, it's a convenient way for chefs to use up any leftover braised beef or excess dough. Thin slices of beef are rolled up inside scallion pancakes, stuffed with cucumbers for crunch, and brushed with a thin layer of sweet wheat paste (also known as tián miàn jiàng 甜麵醬) for flavor. Because the quality of the sweet wheat paste out there varies wildly, I've found that brushing the pancake with hoisin sauce or a soy paste–based dressing is a better, more foolproof way to get a tasty roll. And hey—if you have some of the braising liquid from the beef left over, feel free to mix a couple of teaspoons of that into the sauce as well.

6   Scallion Pancakes (uncooked; page 49 and see instructions below)

2   tablespoons canola or soybean oil, divided, plus more if needed

Everyday Soy Dressing (page 367) or hoisin sauce

18   ounces (510 g) Braised Beef Shank, cut into ⅛-inch (3-mm) slices, about 24 pieces in total (page 75)

2   medium Japanese cucumbers or any small seedless cucumber, cut into matchsticks

3   scallions, thinly sliced at a diagonal

Make the scallion pancakes according to the instructions on page 49, but use half the amount of scallions indicated and roll the pancakes into six 9-inch (25-cm) pies instead of four 6-inch (15-cm) pies. They should be as thin as a tortilla; too many scallions will cause breakage. Heat a well-seasoned skillet over medium heat and add ½ teaspoon of the oil. Add the pancake and cook until it begins to slightly puff up, flipping occasionally, about 1 minute. Lift up the pancake and add another ½ teaspoon oil in the pan. Cook until there are dark golden spots, flipping often, another 1 to 2 minutes. Repeat with the remaining pancakes, adding more oil to the pan as needed.

Take a scallion pancake and with a pastry brush or the back of a spoon, paint an even layer of the Everyday Soy Dressing on top of the pancake. Line up 4 pieces of sliced beef shanks in a row toward the bottom half of the pancake, then add some cucumbers and scallions on top of the beef. Fold in the sides and roll away from you tightly into a burrito. With a knife, cut the roll in half at a steep diagonal. Repeat with the remaining pancakes and filling. Enjoy while hot.

Braised Intestines

滷大腸
Lǔ Dà Cháng

滷大腸
Lóo Tuā Tn̂g

NOTE:
The cooked intestines can be used in an Oyster and Pork Intestine Vermicelli Stew (page 136).

In America, store-bought intestines come already washed, but if they have a funky scent to them still or you're just not sure, scrub them again as a precaution.

I find the process of making this dish a lovely meditation on how my ancestors cooked; slow-cooking leftover parts of the pig to feed the family really embodies the scrappy origins of Taiwanese cuisine. This dish can be cooked in advance.

2	pounds (900 g) pork large intestines	3	scallions, tied into knots
2	cans soda, such as ginger ale	2	tablespoons (25 g) coarse raw sugar, such as demerara
¼	cup (45 g) coarse salt	¼	cup (60 ml) soy sauce
1	2-inch piece fresh ginger (20 g), unpeeled and sliced, divided	2	tablespoons Taiwanese rice wine (michiu) or cooking sake
1	tablespoon canola or soybean oil	1	whole star anise pod (optional)
3	garlic cloves, smashed		Everyday Garlic Soy Dressing (page 367) (for serving)

In a medium bowl, combine the intestines and soda. Wash the intestines thoroughly with the soda, like you're scrubbing your laundry, for 2 minutes. Drain in a colander. Cut the intestines into 6-inch (15-cm) segments and turn them inside out. Put them in a clean bowl, add the salt, and scrub the insides of the intestines thoroughly with the salt. Transfer the intestines to a colander again, and rinse under running water until the salt is completely washed off. Turn the intestines back outward.

In a medium pot set over high heat, combine the washed intestines, half the sliced ginger, and enough water to cover the intestines completely. Bring to a rolling boil, then reduce the heat to medium, and simmer for about 5 minutes. Turn off the heat. Drain the intestines and discard the ginger.

In a medium pot set over medium heat, add the oil. When the oil begins to shimmer, add the rest of the sliced ginger, the garlic, scallions, and sugar. Stir and cook until the sugar begins to dissolve, about 30 seconds. Immediately add the soy sauce, rice wine, intestines, star anise pod (if using), and 4 cups (1 L) water. Cover the pot and bring the liquid to a rolling boil. Reduce the heat to low and gently simmer, leaving the lid slightly ajar, for 1 to 1½ hours. The intestines are done when al dente and have a little bit of chew.

Turn off the heat, drain in a colander, and discard the aromatics. When the intestines are cool enough to handle, transfer them to a cutting board and cut at a steep angle into ½-inch (1.5-cm) segments. They can be eaten warm or chilled. Serve with the Everyday Garlic Soy Dressing as a dipping sauce.

Century egg isn't as intimidating as it sounds, and contrary to the name, it isn't actually 100 years old at all. It's merely a duck egg cured in a solution of soda ash, quicklime, salt, tea, and spices, then packed tightly with heavy mud. Transformed over a period of weeks, it slowly becomes gelatinous and Jell-O-like on the outside and creamy on the inside—somewhat like an over-ripe Brie. The finished egg is a stunning jet-black, and this dish showcases it over a raw plate of silken tofu. Century eggs can easily be purchased at most Asian grocery stores across the country. A simple soy paste–based sauce ties it all together, and the addition of bonito flakes as a garnish is a nod to our Japanese colonial heritage. This is a no-cook side dish. Just assemble, dress, garnish, and enjoy.

Tofu with Century Egg

皮蛋豆腐

Pí Dàn Dòu Fu

1   box (350 g) silken tofu

2   tablespoons Everyday Soy Dressing (page 367)

1   teaspoon toasted sesame oil

2   century eggs, peeled

1   scallion, minced (for garnish)

¼   cup (3 g) bonito flakes (for garnish; optional)

Gently unbox the tofu and place it on top of paper towel–lined plate. Let the tofu drain for about 5 minutes. Meanwhile, in a small bowl, mix the Everyday Soy Dressing and sesame oil to make the sauce.

Lift the tofu with a spatula and place it on a clean serving plate. Slice the tofu in half vertically, then cut it crosswise into 5 even pieces. Cut the century eggs into quarters, and carefully arrange them on top or around the tofu. Layer the scallion and bonito flakes (if using) on top and drizzle the sauce over everything. Enjoy immediately or chilled.

Petite, crunchy, and sweet, most of the cucumber varieties that exist in Taiwan today came via Japanese seed companies in the 1940s. But even though the cucumber is a warm-weather vegetable that grows well in the subtropics, rising average temperatures due to climate change have made growing them on the island increasingly difficult. To mitigate this, a few new local varieties in southern Taiwan have been bred over the last decade specifically for their heat resistance, which means that we now have cucumbers all year round. In order to reflect what a true cucumber salad is like in Taiwan, it's important to source a crisp, seedless varietal like a Japanese or a Persian cucumber. As for the marinade, rice vinegar is classic, but it can be swapped out based on what's in your pantry. White wine or apple cider vinegar are fantastic substitutes. Tip: Make this recipe a day or two before a big party.

Cucumber Salad

涼拌小黃瓜
Liáng Bàn Xiǎo Huáng Guā

- 4 medium Japanese cucumbers or any seedless cucumber, about 1 pound (450 g) in total weight
- 1 teaspoon fine sea salt
- ¼ cup (50 g) white sugar
- ¼ cup (60 ml) rice vinegar
- 2 garlic cloves, minced
- 1 fresh bird's eye chili, thinly sliced at a diagonal
- 1 tablespoon soy sauce
- 1 teaspoon toasted sesame oil

Cut the cucumbers in half and trim off the sides. With the flat side of a heavy cleaver or a large rolling pin, smash the cucumbers until they rupture. Cut them into bite-size 1-inch (2.5-cm) pieces.

Place the cucumbers in a bowl and mix the salt in with your hands so that the cucumbers are evenly coated. Cover and let rest at room temperature for 1 hour. Transfer the cucumbers to a colander under running water and rinse the salt off thoroughly. Drain and shake off the excess water.

In a large glass storage container with a lid, combine the sugar, rice vinegar, and ¼ cup (60 ml) water, and stir until the sugar is mostly dissolved. Add in the cucumbers. Cover, shake to combine, and chill in the refrigerator for at least 4 hours or up to overnight.

Drain the cucumbers in a colander and discard the marinade. In a clean serving bowl, combine the cucumbers, garlic, bird eye's chili, soy sauce, and sesame oil. Mix well and serve chilled. The cucumbers can be stored for up to 2 days in the refrigerator.

Wood Ear Mushroom Salad

涼拌黑木耳
Liáng Bàn Hēi Mù Ěr

A jelly-textured, dark mahogany fungus found all over the world, wood ear mushrooms grow wild in Taiwan. Bouquets of them can be found perched on decaying branches and logs in the jungle like wiggly, protruding ears, but the bulk of what's sold on the market is actually cultivated by mushroom farmers on the island. As a fresh product, the mushroom has a shelf life of only about two days before it starts deteriorating, so unless you stumble across a specialty grower, most wood ear mushrooms are sold dried and can be revived with a bit of water and time. The fungus itself doesn't have much of a taste; it's more of a conduit for flavor. This dish can be made a couple of days ahead of time.

½ cup (20 g) small dried black wood ear mushrooms

¼ cup (60 ml) rice vinegar

1 tablespoon white sugar

1 tablespoon soy sauce

1 teaspoon toasted sesame oil

1 1-inch piece of fresh young ginger (10 g), peeled and cut into matchsticks (see Note)

1 scallion, thinly sliced at a diagonal

In a medium heatproof bowl, cover the small dried black wood ear mushrooms with boiling water. Soak until they're soft, about 30 minutes. Drain in a colander, then wash them thoroughly under running water, making sure to get rid of any sand or grit stuck in the crevices. With a knife or scissors, trim off and discard any tough, craggy bits.

Fill a medium pot halfway with water and bring it to a vigorous boil over high heat. Prepare an ice bath to the side. Drop the wood ear mushrooms into the boiling water and cook for 3 minutes. Turn the heat off, drain the mushrooms in a colander, and immediately transfer them into the ice bath to cool down, about 20 seconds. This will keep them crunchy and crisp. Drain in a colander again.

In a glass storage container with a lid, combine the rice vinegar, sugar, soy sauce, and sesame oil, and stir until the sugar is mostly dissolved. Add in the wood ear mushrooms and ginger. Cover, shake to combine, and chill in the refrigerator for at least 2 hours or up to overnight. Mix in the scallions right before serving. The mushrooms can be stored for up to 4 days in the refrigerator.

NOTE:
Young ginger is less intense and slightly sweeter than regular, mature ginger. You can mimic its subtlety by soaking the peeled, sliced pieces of regular ginger in water for 30 minutes.

台南

TAINAN

City of Snacks

I'm working as a field producer for a documentary on cross-strait tensions and am just about to wrap up the multiweek shoot when my commissioning producer asks if I can find someone last-minute who can talk at length about Taiwanese identity and has enough of an interesting backstory that they can really pop on camera. There's something missing in the segment, he says. Too many talking heads and politicians. We need color and personality.

A couple of days later, I find myself in the southern Taiwanese city of Tainan interviewing Lin Tai-Yu 林泰佑, a rapper who goes by the moniker Gloj 阿雞. "Taiwan can't talk, its status is too low," he sings as we angle the cameras at him. "Only VIPs get attention. Taiwan has no status and no money. They'd sell out Taiwan for profit in an instant. The people of Taiwan have given their lives to safeguard Taiwan." He's the perfect on-camera interviewee. Gloj is charismatic, opinionated—and boy, the man can cook.

At night, Gloj spins out lyrics about identity almost exclusively in Taiwanese and has a whole track dedicated to the sounds of his hometown, the southern city of Tainan. But during the day, he's the chef and third-generation owner of Lin Family Braised Pork Over Rice 林家肉燥飯, a roadside food stall that specializes in braising chunks of succulent pork belly and fat for hours in soy sauce and sugar until it loses all resistance. Braised minced pork belly over rice is one of the most emblematic dishes of Tainan, the oldest city in Taiwan, the food capital of the nation, and where both sides of my family have resided for many centuries. While I was born and raised in the States, my parents made a point of lugging me and my brother back to Tainan during all our winter school breaks just so they could indulge in the food of their childhood.

Whereas Taipei is the high-powered economic and political capital of the island, dotted with metallic skyscrapers and a cavernous public transportation system, Tainan is its much more chilled-out southern cousin. A lot of food is still served by the road; people get around almost exclusively by scooters, and locals spend many afternoons either napping or sipping long, slow cups of coffee. Down south, the people are remarkably lax; there are many times when I've made plans to go to a coffee shop or restaurant only to realize that the owner decided at the last minute to take an impromptu personal day and shut down the business.

It's also the best place in the country to eat, and these are not controversial, fighting words. Many of Taiwan's most iconic dishes, like braised minced pork belly over rice or alkaline noodles topped with minced pork and a single plump shrimp, are unique to the city and doled out in small, palm-size bowls. You're supposed to snack your way around, hopping from vendor to vendor until it feels like the buttons of your pants are about to burst from the growing pressure of your belly. Or at least, that's what my parents taught me.

Tainan retains a wonderful artsy, gritty spirit that's getting harder to find in the globalized world today. In a city with nearly 400 years of history, the streets aren't arranged in neat narrow rows. There are countless meandering alleyways that still retain the chaos of preindustrial Taiwan, when towns were built exclusively for pedestrians. Many of the original markets and food stalls erupted in the vicinity of Taoist and

Buddhist temples and are still very much there today. Tainan has the highest concentration of temples in the country—more than 1,600 of them—and curvy vermilion roofs peek out from the cityscape everywhere you go. And in Taiwan, where there are temples, there definitely is food.

In preparation for his track on Tainan, Gloj wandered the streets recording everything he heard. He tells me he spent days trying to figure out what sounds encapsulated the soul and heart of Tainan. Was it the traffic? The markets? The temples? Or the sparse pockets of nature?

Eventually he got it. The answer was the sounds of his customers ordering lunch, because food is the backbone of the city, and the pursuit of good food is at the heart of what it means to be from Tainan.

Braised Minced Pork Belly

肉燥飯
Ròu Zào Fàn

肉燥飯
Bah Sò Pñg

NOTE:

To make a more luxurious version of this dish, use bone broth (page 357) or low-sodium chicken stock instead of water. This dish tastes better with time. Reserve the braise, refrigerate, and use it the next day. Scoop off and discard the white layer of fat that has accumulated on top and reheat it over medium-low heat until it begins to bubble. Add more water if needed.

When small pixels of pork fat and belly are braised for hours in soy sauce and sugar, they come out magical, bright, and quivering. The secret to this dish is procuring the fattiest, most succulent piece of skin-on pork belly you can find and using only the top half of it. If possible, employ the services of a local butcher, because the average prepackaged cut of pork belly in a regular grocery store is, unfortunately, far too lean. "I've been told that it's a three to seven meat to fat ratio, but to tell you the truth I just use all fat," says Gloj. While braising meat for hours in a soy sauce–based concoction is a technique used throughout Asia, this particular dish is special to Taiwan. There's no definitive story for how it came to be, but it's widely said that it was just a way for common folks to use up the cheapest part of a pig, especially the leftover skin, fat, and crumbs of meat. Gloj's recipe uses only pork, soy sauce, shallots, and sugar, but he achieves complexity by ladling in a portion of old braising liquid from the day before so that the final dish is infused with decades of flavor. My recipe adds soy paste, garlic, and rice wine to the ingredient list in order to mimic that intricacy, because the average home cook simply doesn't have access to three decades' buildup of braising liquid. This dish is also sometimes referred to as lǔ ròu fàn 滷肉飯, which is a term that's more widely used in Taipei and throughout northern Taiwan (and in most Taiwanese restaurants in the West). The difference is that lu rou fan includes a teaspoon of five-spice powder, perhaps a couple of chunks of star anise, and significantly less sugar. It also uses a leaner cut of pork and is therefore definitely not as tasty, but I know I think that only because of my preference for southern Taiwanese cuisine. This dish can be made a day ahead of time.

2	pounds (900 g) skin-on pork belly
1	tablespoon canola or soybean oil
3	garlic cloves, minced (optional)
2½	cups (600 ml) water, plus more if needed
½	cup (40 g) fried shallots (store-bought or homemade; page 368)
¼	cup plus 3 tablespoons (105 ml) soy sauce

2½	tablespoons coarse raw sugar, such as demerara
2	tablespoons Taiwanese soy paste (store-bought or homemade; page 366)
2	tablespoons Taiwanese rice wine (michiu) or cooking sake

Cooked short-grain rice (for serving)

Ground white pepper

Freeze the pork belly until partially frozen, about 1 hour. This will make it much easier to cut. Dice the pork belly into ¼-inch- (6-mm-) thick cubes.

In a large pot over medium-high heat, heat the oil. When it starts shimmering, add the diced pork belly. Cook, stirring often, until the pinkish color of the meat is gone and the fat begins to render a bit, about 4 minutes. Add the garlic, if using, and stir until fragrant, about 20 seconds. Add the water, shallots, soy sauce, sugar, soy paste, and rice wine. Cover, bring to a boil, and then slowly simmer over very low heat, leaving the lid slightly ajar. Cook, stirring occasionally with a wooden spoon, until pork is melt-in-your-mouth tender, 1½ to 2 hours. If you find that the braising liquid is reducing too fast and beginning to caramelize and stick to the bottom of the pot, add up to ¼ cup (60 ml) more water. The pork is done when it's soft and creamy.

To serve, drape a scoop of the finished braised pork belly over a bowl of cooked rice. Season with white pepper to taste.

Peddler Noodles

擔仔麵
Dān Zaǐ Miàn

擔仔麵
Tànn Á Mī

NOTES:

Fresh ramen noodles are another great alternative to homemade Oil Noodles. They can be found in the refrigerated section in many Asian specialty stores.

Technically, you could just put ground pork flavored with soy sauce on top, but you'll lose out on the heart and soul of the dish. The beauty of hand-mincing braised pork belly is that you retain the luscious fat that will seep into the broth and bind everything together.

PHOTOGRAPHY NOTE:

The bricks that you see in this picture are sourced from Anping and used to be held together by cement made from oyster shells. If you look closely enough, you can see the grayish remnants of the oyster cement.

In 1895, there was a man named Hung Yu-Tou 洪芊頭 whose job was to ferry passengers from the then islet of Anping to the city of Tainan. During the off-peak season in the summer evenings, he worked as a food vendor and would carry a shoulder pole balancing a bucket of broth and fresh noodles into the city. He'd often plop himself in the vicinity of a temple and illuminate his position with a red lantern inscribed with the words Du Xiao Yue 度小月, which means "overcoming the off-season." The dish was simple: an elegant broth infused with sweet shrimp, ladled over alkaline noodles and a bit of braised pork. Eventually, Hung lost his job and pivoted to being a full-time food peddler. It worked out in his favor, because Du Xiao Yue is now an icon in Taiwan, proudly serving the same dish that Hung did more than a century ago.

6 cups (1.5 L) Bone Broth (page 357) or low-sodium chicken stock

6 large shell-on shrimp

2 cups (150 g) bean sprouts

1½ pounds (680 g) Oil Noodles (uncooked; page 363) or 11 ounces (315 g) dried lo mein noodles

Canola or soybean oil

1½ teaspoons fine sea salt

¾ pound (340 g) Braised Minced Pork Belly (page 90)

3 fresh garlic chives, cut into 1-inch (2.5-cm) chunks

Garlic Puree (page 367)

Black vinegar

Ground white pepper

In a large pot over high heat, bring the bone broth to a boil. Add the shrimp, cover, and cook until pink, about 2 minutes. Remove the shrimp with a spider strainer. When the shrimp is cool enough to handle, peel and devein them, reserving the shrimp heads and shells but leaving the tails on. Set the cooked shrimp aside. Put the shrimp heads and shells back into the stock. Cover and simmer over low heat for about 30 minutes.

Bring a medium pot of water to boil over high heat. Place the bean sprouts in a spider strainer, and lower them into the boiling water for 40 seconds. Lift out the bean sprouts and set aside. Add the Oil Noodles to the boiling water and cook until al dente, 2 to 3 minutes. If using dried lo mein noodles, cook according to the package instructions. Drain in a colander, drizzle some oil over the noodles to coat, and toss to combine so they don't stick together.

When the shrimp stock is done simmering, season with the salt. Strain the stock through a fine-mesh sieve into a clean pot. Discard the shrimp shells.

Mince the pork belly finely so that it looks more like ground pork. To assemble, divide the noodles and blanched bean sprouts among 6 small

bowls. Pour hot broth over the ingredients and season with a couple of tablespoons of the pork belly, some chives, garlic puree, black vinegar, and white pepper to taste. Finally, arrange 1 cooked shrimp in the center of each bowl. Enjoy immediately.

Morning Beef Soup

牛肉湯

Niú Ròu Tāng

牛肉湯

Gû Bah Thng

NOTES:

If you have a hard time slicing your beef, freeze it for 15 minutes before slicing.

Young ginger is less intense and slightly sweeter than regular, mature ginger. You can mimic its subtlety by soaking peeled, sliced pieces of regular ginger in water for 30 minutes.

Three hours is the bare minimum for making a hearty stock. Of course, boiling the bones and meat for longer will yield a much more intense broth, which is what the vendors here in Taiwan do. If you have time to spare, push it to 6 to 8 hours, topping it off with more water as you go.

For tourists to Tainan, waking up the moment the sun rises and lining up for a bowl of beef soup for breakfast at five a.m. is a rite of passage. This dish is so beloved in modern-day Tainan that most people don't know that it became part of the culinary lexicon of Tainan only in the late 1990s and early 2000s, hyped up by the media and visitors to the city. Unlike Beef Noodle Soup (page 128), which is made mostly with imported meat from the West, beef soup from Tainan is made exclusively with local Taiwanese beef.

The secret to this dish is in the stock. In Taiwan, it's complex and rather gamey because vendors will throw in offal and any and all parts of the cow they can get their hands on. That intensity is difficult for the average cook to achieve, so to get that deep flavor at home, the best solution is to quickly wok-sear the bones and meat, which will create a nice, charred aroma. To serve, most vendors pour hot broth over raw meat. But depending on the temperature of the broth, that can sometimes create a cloudy, unappetizing bowl. The foolproof method below gives you a much clearer soup without compromising flavor.

12	cups (3 L) water
½	pound (225 g) Taiwanese flat cabbage or green cabbage, roughly chopped
1	yellow onion, peeled and halved
2	tablespoons Taiwanese rice wine (michiu) or cooking sake
2	tablespoons canola or soybean oil, divided
2	pounds (900 g) beef bones, marrow, or oxtail, cut into 2-inch (5-cm) pieces
2	pounds (900 g) bone-in beef short ribs, cut into 2-inch (5-cm) pieces
2	teaspoons fine sea salt
¼	teaspoon ground white pepper
¼	cup (70 ml) Everyday Soy Dressing (page 367)
1	3-inch piece of fresh young ginger (30 g), cut into thin matchsticks (see Notes)
1	pound (450 g) raw filet mignon or chuck steak, cut into ⅛-inch (4-mm) slices (see Notes)

Rice vinegar (optional)

In a large stockpot, combine the water, cabbage, onion, and rice wine. Bring to a rolling boil over high heat.

Meanwhile, in a wok set over medium-high heat, swirl in 1 tablespoon of the oil. When the oil is hot, add in the beef bones and cook, stirring constantly, until the bones are deeply golden brown on the edges and evenly seared, 5 to 6 minutes. Transfer the bones to the stockpot with the boiling water.

Drizzle in the remaining 1 tablespoon oil into the wok, increase the heat to high, and add the beef short ribs. Cook, stirring often, until the meat is

deeply golden brown and seared, 5 to 6 minutes. Turn off the heat and transfer the short ribs to the stockpot.

Reduce the stockpot heat to low, and slowly simmer the beef bones and short ribs, uncovered, until the liquid is reduced by half, 3 to 4 hours. Skim off any scum that floats up to the top. Strain out the stock through a fine-mesh sieve, discarding the bones, vegetables, and meat, and transfer the stock to a medium pot. Season the stock with the salt and white pepper.

To make a dipping sauce, in a small shallow bowl, pour the Everyday Soy Dressing, and arrange a pinch of sliced ginger on top. Set aside.

Set the pot with the filtered stock over high heat and bring it to a rolling boil. Arrange a small handful of the sliced filet mignon in a spider strainer, and quickly dunk it into the boiling stock until medium-rare, about 3 seconds. Transfer the beef to a small serving bowl and add a small pinch of sliced ginger. Ladle the hot broth over the filet. This is one serving. Repeat with the remaining beef slices and stock.

Enjoy immediately while hot. The dipping sauce is for the beef. If you'd like, add a couple of drops of rice vinegar into the soup to cut through the heartiness.

This thick, sweet, and savory soup accompanied by deep-fried nuggets of fish makes for a fortifying street snack all year round. When the Dutch ruled Taiwan in the 17th century, they wrote about immense catches of king mackerel off the coast of southern Taiwan. While it's not known exactly how this dish came about, some accounts claim that it was a technique taken from the Dutch, who had a history of deep-frying fish. Locals in Tainan saw it and thought it was interesting enough to adapt and make it their own.

FOR THE FISH MARINADE:

- 1   pound (450 g) King mackerel or Spanish mackerel, cleaned and deboned
- 1   tablespoon soy sauce
- 2   teaspoons Taiwanese rice wine (michiu) or cooking sake
- 2   teaspoons white sugar
- ⅛   teaspoon five-spice powder (optional)

FOR THE SOUP:

- 2   tablespoons canola or soybean oil
- 1   ounce (30 g) dried flounder, sometimes known as dried stockfish, cut into 1-inch (2.5-cm) squares (see Notes)
- ½   cup (10 g) bonito flakes
- ½   pound (225 g) Napa cabbage, cut into 1-inch- (2.5-cm-) thick segments

- 1   tablespoon white sugar
- 1½   teaspoons fine sea salt
- ½   teaspoon soy sauce
- ¼   teaspoon ground white pepper
- 2   tablespoons sweet potato starch or cornstarch

FOR DEEP-FRYING:

- 1   large egg
- 1   cup (160 g) thick sweet potato starch (see Notes)
- 4   cups (1 L) canola or soybean oil

TO SERVE:

- ¼   cup (30 g) Fried Garlic (for garnish; page 368), divided

Black vinegar

Fresh cilantro sprigs (for garnish)

MARINATE THE FISH: Cut the mackerel into 1 × 2-inch (2.5 × 5-cm) chunks, about ½ inch (1 cm) thick. You'll have around 20 to 25 pieces. Put the fish in a medium bowl and add the soy sauce, rice wine, white sugar, and the five-spice powder, if using. Massage the seasoning into the fish and let it rest in the refrigerator for 1 hour.

MAKE THE SOUP: In a wok set over low heat, add the oil. When the oil is hot and shimmering, add in the dried flounder. Fry the dried flounder pieces until they turn golden brown and begin to crisp up like bacon, about 4 minutes. Be very careful to make sure not to burn them; they will turn bitter. Turn off the heat and transfer the flounder pieces to a large tea bag or cheesecloth. Crush the bonito fish flakes with your hands, and stuff them into the same tea bag or cheesecloth. Tie to close.

Fried Mackerel Thick Soup

Tŭ Tuō Yú Gēng

Thôo Thoh Hî Kenn

SPECIAL EQUIPMENT:
large tea bag or cheesecloth

NOTES:
Thick sweet potato starch is coarse—similar to panko bread crumbs but a bit finer. Some brands will specify between thick and thin sweet potato starch. If you can only find thin, lightly spritz the starch with some water so that it clumps up and creates small beads.

Dried flounder (biǎn yú 扁魚) is also sometimes labeled brill fish, dà dì yú 大地魚, or ròu yú 肉魚. Chinese medicine stores might also have it in stock, sometimes in powdered form. If you can only get your hands on the powder, substitute it 1:1 by weight and add it directly into the cabbage mixture.

(RECIPE CONTINUES)

PHOTOGRAPHY NOTE:
This table was passed down from
food stylist Yen Wei's grandmother.

In a medium pot, add 4 cups (1 L) water, the tea bag, and the Napa cabbage. Cover and bring the soup to a boil over high heat. Turn off the heat and let the tea bag infuse for 10 minutes. Remove the tea bag, then increase the heat to medium, briskly simmering until the Napa cabbage has completely softened and wilted, about 5 minutes. Season the soup with the sugar, salt, soy sauce, and white pepper.

In a small bowl, make a slurry by mixing together the sweet potato starch with 2 tablespoons water. Trickle in a steady stream of the slurry into the soup and stir well until soup is thickened, about 30 seconds (this soup can be extremely thick in Tainan; if you'd like it thicker, just make and add more slurry). Cover and turn the heat off.

TO DEEP-FRY: In a small bowl, crack the egg and whisk until smooth.

Take the bowl of marinated fish out of the refrigerator, pour the scrambled egg over the fish, and mix with your hands until the fish is completely coated. Put the sweet potato starch on a small plate and, taking one slice of fish at a time, press the fish in the sweet potato starch until all sides are fully coated. Shake off the excess starch. Transfer the fish to a clean plate and repeat with the remaining fish.

Heat the oil in deep wok over medium-high heat until it reaches 350°F (175°C) on an instant-read thermometer. Gently slide the battered fish into the hot oil, working with a couple of pieces at a time, and cook until they turn a light golden brown, 2 to 3 minutes. The oil will shine and fizzle around the fish. With a spider strainer, gently remove the fish from the oil and drain on a paper towel–lined plate or wire rack set in a rimmed baking sheet to drain. Turn off the heat.

TO SERVE: Divide the soup, Napa cabbage, and fish into serving bowls. Season each serving with 1 tablespoon of the fried garlic, a couple of drops of black vinegar to taste, and fresh cilantro sprigs for garnish.

I'm always skeptical when dish origin stories are linked to powerful, historical figures who miraculously come up with culinary masterpieces in the midst of their conquests for land and influence. This particular one is attributed to 17th century Chinese pirate king Koxinga (sometimes known as Zheng Cheng-gong), who ousted the Dutch colonists from Taiwan. It's said that when the Dutch opposition hid his supply of rice, he made due by feeding his soldiers oysters dipped in sweet potato starch. Thing is, oyster omelets are quite common in China as well, and by now it's hard to pinpoint who exactly came up with this dish, and where.

This recipe is inspired by the omelets at Fort Oyster Omelet 古堡蚵仔煎專賣店 in the Anping district of Tainan. Shaded by giant banyan trees, the shop has been around since 1958 and is the only oyster omelet eatery I frequent, because I'm convinced no one makes it better than they do. Of course, people have disparate opinions on what the texture of a proper oyster omelet should be like. I prefer mine as soft, glassy, and mucus-like as possible. Ivy likes hers a bit firmer, with crisp edges.

Oyster Omelet

蚵仔煎
Ôr Á Tsian

¼ cup plus 2 tablespoons (90 ml) water

3 tablespoons sweet potato starch

1 tablespoon Thai rice flour, such as Erawan (see Notes; optional)

¼ teaspoon fine sea salt

8 to 10 small raw shucked oysters (about 100 g total) or small peeled shrimp

1 tablespoon canola or soybean oil, plus 1 teaspoon more if needed

½ teaspoon Taiwanese rice wine (michiu) or cooking sake

1 scallion, minced

1 large egg

½ cup (40 g) bean sprouts

½ cup (40 g) chopped Taiwanese bok choy (see Notes) or romaine lettuce, cut into 1-inch (2.5-cm) segments

¼ cup (70 ml) Haishan Sauce (page 370)

NOTES:
Taiwanese bok choy is a very specific variety that can occasionally be found at Asian supermarkets. If it's not available, use romaine lettuce or any neutral, crisp lettuce as a substitute. Don't use regular bok choy.

If you want yours on the firm side, add the rice flour. But if you're like me, skip it. It's important to get small, coin-size oysters for this recipe, which might be difficult to source. Plopping in giant blobs of oysters will make this dish extremely clunky. If you truly can't procure small oysters, substitute with fresh, coin-size peeled shrimp.

In a medium bowl, make the batter by whisking together the water, sweet potato starch, rice flour (if using), and salt.

Gently pat the oysters dry with a paper towel. Heat a large, flat-bottomed nonstick frying pan over medium heat and add the oil. When the oil begins to shimmer, add the oysters and rice wine. Cook until the oysters start to firm up, about 2 minutes. Toss in the scallions and cook until their fragrance is released, about 30 seconds.

Crack the egg in the middle of the pan over the oysters and scallions, then break the yolk with the tip of a spatula. When the whites of the egg begin to solidify, about 5 seconds in, quickly whisk the batter again (it has a tendency

(RECIPE CONTINUES)

TAINAN

to clump up otherwise) and pour it immediately into the pan. Sprinkle the bean sprouts on top of the batter, then add the bok choy on top of that. Cover the pan and cook until the batter is jiggly and semitranslucent but firm around the edges, 3 to 4 minutes. Flip the omelet. It might be easier using 2 extremely large spatulas for this, but if it's too difficult to flip, carefully folding it in half will also work (for reference: street vendors make this dish on a flat griddle and use two extremely large bench scrapers to flip over the omelet). If you like the edges of your omelet a bit crispy, swirl in an extra teaspoon of oil around the perimeter of the pan. Cover and cook for another 1 to 2 minutes.

Turn off the heat and transfer the omelet to a plate. Dress with the Haishan Sauce on top. Eat immediately.

This is a steamed, dense rice pudding in a bowl flavored with a delectable spoonful of braised ground pork. Variations on this dish exist throughout East and Southeast Asia, though there are multiple permutations just within Taiwan itself. Hakka communities, for example, make theirs starchy white and plain, dressed with just a small dollop of diced bean curd and cubes of salty, preserved daikon on top. The rendition next to my mom's childhood home in the center of Tainan is almost a mocha color, darkened by a hefty amount of the braising liquid. My recipe straddles a good middle ground between the two and is inspired by the puddings from Ivy's hometown in Tainan's Madou District, which are lightly flavored, but not overwhelmingly so. It's meant to be either a fortifying breakfast or a savory afternoon snack.

Savory Rice Pudding

碗粿
Uánn Kué

FOR THE TOPPING:

1½ teaspoons canola or soybean oil

¼ pound (115 g) ground pork

2 tablespoons soy sauce

1½ tablespoons Taiwanese soy paste (store-bought or homemade; page 366)

1 tablespoon white sugar

1 tablespoon Taiwanese rice wine (michiu) or cooking sake

¼ cup (20 g) fried shallots (store-bought or homemade; page 368)

2 medium dried shiitake mushrooms

1 large soft-boiled egg, peeled

FOR THE RICE PUDDING:

1¼ cups (165 g) Thai rice flour, such as Erawan

½ teaspoon fine sea salt

½ teaspoon white sugar

¼ teaspoon ground white pepper

¼ cup (70 ml) Everyday Garlic Soy Dressing (page 367)

MAKE THE TOPPING: In a medium pot set over medium-high heat, add the oil. When it's hot and shimmering, add the ground pork. Cook and stir until the pinkish color of the meat is gone, about 2 minutes. Add the soy sauce, soy paste, sugar, rice wine, shallots, dried shiitake mushrooms, and 1½ cups (355 ml) water. Bring to a boil, then add in the soft-boiled egg. The water won't cover the egg completely and that's okay; just rotate it occasionally in the liquid. Cover the pot and simmer over low heat until the pork is tender, 40 minutes to 1 hour. If you find the liquid is reducing too fast and beginning to caramelize, add up to ¼ cup (60 ml) water at a time.

Turn off the heat and reserve ¼ cup (60 ml) of the braising liquid. Remove the shiitake mushrooms and the egg from the pot. Cut the mushrooms in half so you have 4 pieces total. Cut the egg into quarters. Set everything aside for later.

SPECIAL EQUIPMENT:
4 small 8-ounce ceramic soup bowls

PHOTOGRAPHY NOTE:
This dish is traditionally steamed in these blue-rimmed bowls and eaten with flat spoons made of bamboo. The bowls, which are made in Taiwan with Taiwanese clay, date back to the 1950s and '60s and were used for both eating and drinking.

(RECIPE CONTINUES)

MAKE THE RICE PUDDING: In a medium bowl, combine the rice flour, salt, sugar, white pepper, the reserved braising liquid, and 1 cup (240 ml) water. Mix very thoroughly until the rice flour has completely dissolved.

In a medium saucepan set over high heat, bring 2 cups (470 ml) water to a rapid simmer. Turn off the heat and remove the saucepan from the stove. Pour the rice milk into the saucepan and stir constantly with a balloon whisk until it thickens and gets creamy like a chowder, about 30 seconds. The liquid should easily coat the back of a spoon. If it gets thick and is the texture of a cake batter, that's okay, too.

Divide the rice pudding among 4 bowls. Top each bowl with 2 tablespoons of the braised ground pork, a slice of the egg, and half of a shiitake mushroom.

Fill a large wok partially with water and bring to a rolling boil over high heat (for steaming tips, see page 38). Arrange the rice puddings in a tiered bamboo steamer. Cover and lower the bamboo steamer basket into the wok. Steam for 30 minutes, replenishing with boiling water in the bottom of the wok if needed.

Turn off the heat and immediately remove the bowls from the steamer. Do not eat immediately; it needs to cool down in order to fully solidify. The pudding should be slightly warmer than room temperature, but not piping hot. Dress each bowl with the Everyday Garlic Soy Dressing and enjoy. The puddings can be stored in the refrigerator for 1 to 2 days. To reheat, steam over medium-high heat for 10 to 15 minutes.

MAKES 4 BOWLS

How to Make the Rice Pudding Batter with Raw Rice Kernels

1   cup (200 g) basmati rice

½   teaspoon fine sea salt

½   teaspoon white sugar

¼   teaspoon ground white pepper

¼   cup (60 ml) reserved braising liquid (from the topping instructions on page 101)

SPECIAL EQUIPMENT:
high-speed blender or food processor

Place the basmati rice in a fine-mesh strainer, and rinse under running water. Transfer to a medium bowl and add enough water to cover at room temperature for at least 4 hours or overnight in the refrigerator.

Drain the rice in a sieve. Transfer the rice to the blender, and add the salt, sugar, white pepper, the reserved braising liquid, and ¾ cup (175 ml) water. Blend on high speed until it's smooth and milky, about 1 minute. To test if it's smooth enough, dip your index finger into the liquid and rub it against your thumb. The rice powder should be fine; if it's still gritty like coarse sand, it isn't blended well enough.

In a medium saucepan set over high heat, bring 1¾ cups (415 ml) water to a rolling boil. Turn off the heat and remove the saucepan from the stove. Pour the rice batter into the saucepan and stir constantly with a balloon whisk until it thickens and gets creamy like a chowder, about 30 seconds. If it gets thick and is the texture of a cake batter, that's okay, too. Divide among 4 bowls. Add the toppings and steam according to the directions above.

Fried Shrimp Rolls

蝦 卷
Xiā Juǎn

蝦 卷
Hê Kńg

NOTES:
1 pound (450 g) shell-on shrimp will yield about ½ pound (225 g) peeled shrimp.

Bean curd sheets are sold dried, refrigerated, or frozen. They should be as thin as a piece of paper (in Taiwan, they're like tissue paper). They're also sometimes shaped like large, folded half-moons. If you get this type of sheet, just cut it directly into rough triangles. If you've procured tougher bean curd sheets that don't soften after you've moistened them with a cloth, soak them in room-temperature water for a couple of minutes until they're pliable. Do not use fresh bean curd sheets.

(RECIPE CONTINUES)

These deep-fried seafood rolls are said to have been popularized in 1965 by a man named Chou Chin-Ken 周進根 in the Anping district of Tainan. A fish ball vendor by trade who sold shrimp rolls on the side, he became so known for the latter that he eventually rebranded his shop Chou's Shrimp Rolls 周氏蝦捲, now a prominent restaurant chain with locations throughout the country. Traditionally, the shrimp rolls are wrapped with caul fat—the lacey membrane that insulates the stomach of a pig. They're dipped in a flour batter and then deep-fried at a high heat until crisp, light, and golden brown. The fat netting is the secret to a juicy roll, but because caul fat isn't easily accessible, my recipe uses bean curd sheets instead. For directions on how to make it with caul fat, see page 107.

½	pound (225 g) peeled and deveined shrimp, minced (see Notes)
¼	cup (20 g) minced Taiwanese flat cabbage or green cabbage
¼	cup (20 g) minced celery
2	ounces (60 g) ground pork
1	large egg, white and yolk divided
1	scallion, minced
1	teaspoon Taiwanese rice wine (michiu) or cooking sake
1	teaspoon toasted sesame oil
3	tablespoons tapioca starch or cornstarch, plus more for dusting
1	teaspoon white sugar
¾	teaspoon fine sea salt
⅛	teaspoon ground white pepper
	Packet of bean curd sheets (see Notes)
4	cups (1 L) canola or soybean oil
½	teaspoon wasabi paste
1	tablespoon Everyday Soy Dressing (page 367)

To make the shrimp roll filling, pat the shrimp completely dry with a paper towel. In a bowl, combine the shrimp, cabbage, celery, ground pork, egg white, scallion, rice wine, sesame oil, tapioca starch, sugar, salt, and white pepper. Stir everything together with chopsticks in one direction until the mixture is very sticky, 1 to 2 minutes. Cover and put it in the refrigerator to firm up for 1 hour.

Take the bean curd sheets and cut them into 5 squares, about 8 × 8 inches (20 × 20 cm). Stack them on top of one another and cut across the diagonal to form 10 isosceles triangles. Moisten the sheets by laying a damp kitchen cloth on top of them for 30 seconds.

Lightly dust your work surface with tapioca starch. Put one triangle on your work surface with the top pointing away from you. The base should be the closest side to you. With a small pastry brush, brush a line of egg yolk on the left and right border of the triangle, so it looks like an upside-down V. With a

spoon, lay a row of filling, about 40 g, horizontally alongside the base of the triangle measuring 3 inches (7.5 cm) long and 1 inch (2.5 cm) wide. Leave a pinky-wide gap at the bottom. Fold in the bottom corners toward the center, and tightly roll the triangle away from you like it's a burrito. Repeat with the remaining triangles and set aside on a tapioca starch–dusted plate.

In a large wok, heat the oil over medium-high heat until it reaches 325°F (160°C) on an instant-read thermometer. With tongs, carefully lower the shrimp rolls into the hot oil, and cook until they are golden brown and crisp on all sides, 3 to 4 minutes. Remove the rolls with tongs and drain over a paper towel–lined plate or a wire rack set in a rimmed baking sheet to drain.

In a small bowl, make a dipping sauce for the shrimp rolls by adding a small dollop of wasabi paste on top of the Everyday Soy Dressing. Enjoy the rolls while they're still hot.

MAKES 6

How to Make the Shrimp Rolls with Caul Fat

These caul fat–wrapped rolls are a tad larger than the versions made with bean curd sheets on the previous page, which is why this recipe makes six shrimp rolls instead of ten. The net volume for the filling, however, is exactly the same.

¼ cup plus 3 tablespoons (105 ml) water

½ cup (60 g) cake flour

½ cup (60 g) tapioca starch or cornstarch

3 tablespoons canola or soybean oil

½ teaspoon baking powder

5½ ounces (around 150 g in total weight) caul fat

Fried Shrimp Roll filling (page 104)

1 tablespoon Everyday Soy Dressing (page 367)

½ teaspoon wasabi paste

In a medium bowl, mix together the water, cake flour, tapioca starch, oil, and baking powder.

Cut the caul fat into 6 squares, about 6 × 6 inches (15 × 15 cm). Lay a row of shrimp filling, about 60 g, on the bottom of the square measuring 4 inches (10 cm) long and 1 inch (2.5 cm) wide. Leave a pinky-wide gap at the bottom. Fold the sides inward and roll the square away from you like it's a burrito. Repeat with the remaining squares and set aside.

In a large wok, heat the oil over medium-high heat until it reaches 350°F (175°C) on an instant-read thermometer.

Give the batter a stir again. With your fingers, dunk a roll into the batter, let the excess drip off, and drop it into the hot oil. Cook until the roll is golden brown and crisp on all sides, 5 to 7 minutes. Remove the roll with tongs and drain over a paper towel–lined plate or a wire rack set in a rimmed baking sheet to drain. Repeat with the remaining rolls.

Crystal Meatball

A crystal meatball is essentially a type of dumpling, but instead of wheat, the wrapper is made with a collection of starches that give it a uniquely soft and gelatinous quality. Texture-wise, the exterior is actually surprisingly similar to a boba, just oversize and stuffed with meat. It's said to have been invented in 1898 in the city of Changhua in central Taiwan, when a flood hit and caused a shortage of food supplies. A man by the name of Fan Wan-Chu 范萬居 decided to make ends meet by grinding sweet potato into powder, molding it into a wrapper, and stuffing bamboo shoots inside. Today, there are regional variants all over the island, and this particular recipe is from Tainan, where the stuffing is exclusively just pork. Unlike the meatballs from Changhua, which are glassy and translucent, Tainan's version leans more on the opaque side and is heavier on the rice flour.

Because there's no gluten in the dough, the raw batter is gooey, sticky, and has no structure whatsoever. The vendors' answer to this is speed. They basically take a quick scoop of batter, plop in the fillings, and put the whole thing in a steamer in one sleek movement. If you look closely at some of the crystal meatballs sold in Tainan, you can actually see ridges on the exterior from the indents of the chefs' fingers. This recipe is designed so that the individual dumplings are shaped in small sauce trays, so you can take your time without worrying about them disintegrating in your hands.

SPECIAL EQUIPMENT:
8 small, round sauce bowls, about 2½ ounces each—the same type of trays they serve soy sauce in at sushi restaurants; stand mixer (optional)

NOTE:
These can keep in the refrigerator for 1 to 2 days, though it's best to eat them on the same day. To reheat, just steam them again over medium-high heat for 10 minutes.

(RECIPE CONTINUES)

FOR THE FILLING:

- 5 ounces (140 g) pork tenderloin
- 5 ounces (140 g) ground pork
- 2 tablespoons fried shallots (store-bought or homemade; page 368)
- 1 tablespoon soy sauce
- 1 tablespoon sweet potato starch
- 1 tablespoon Taiwanese rice wine (michiu) or cooking sake
- 1½ teaspoons white sugar
- ½ teaspoon fine sea salt
- ½ teaspoon ground white pepper
- 1 garlic clove, minced

FOR THE WRAPPER:

- 1 cup (130 g) Thai rice flour, such as Erawan
- ¼ teaspoon fine sea salt
- ½ cup (80 g) sweet potato starch
- ½ cup (60 g) tapioca starch

Canola or soybean oil, for brushing

FOR THE SAUCE:

Everyday Garlic Soy Dressing (page 367) and/or Haishan Sauce (page 370)

MAKE THE FILLING: Cut the pork tenderloin into ½-inch- (1-cm-) thick chunks, about 1 inch (2.5 cm) long. In a large bowl or the bowl of a stand mixer, combine the sliced pork tenderloin, ground pork, fried shallots, soy sauce, sweet potato starch, rice wine, sugar, salt, white pepper, and garlic. Mix thoroughly with chopsticks in one direction until the meat is very sticky, about 5 minutes. (Alternatively, churn in a stand mixer on low speed with

the dough hook attachment for 2 minutes.) Cover and put in the refrigerator for at least 30 minutes or up to overnight.

MAKE THE WRAPPER: In a medium bowl, combine the rice flour, salt, and ⅔ cup (155ml) water. Whisk until the flour dissolves and the liquid looks like milk.

In a medium saucepan set over high heat, heat 2 cups (470 ml) water until it starts boiling. Reduce the heat to low and pour in the rice batter. Mix continuously with a balloon whisk until it begins to solidify and turn into a thick batter, 30 seconds to 1 minute. The texture will be reminiscent of a cake batter or a really dense frosting. When the batter begins to form stiff peaks on the whisk, turn off the heat, and immediately remove the pot from the stove. Let it cool until the batter is just slightly warmer than room temperature, about 30 minutes.

In a medium bowl, mix together the sweet potato starch and the tapioca starch. Fold the starches into the warm batter with a silicone spatula and mix until they are completely dissolved. (Alternatively, transfer to a stand mixer and knead with the paddle attachment for 2 minutes on high speed.)

With a pastry brush, coat the inside of 8 small, round sauce bowls with the oil. Take the filling out of the refrigerator.

Dip a small silicone spatula in water, scoop out a portion of the batter with it, and plaster on a thin but even layer in a sauce bowl. Take a handful of the meat filling, about 43 g, and put it in the center of the bowl. Scoop another portion of the rice batter out and plaster it over the meat, covering it completely. Dip your fingers in water and shape the rice batter so that it forms a smooth, round dome. Use a finger to peel any excess batter off the edge of the bowl. The dome should only be about 2 inches (5 cm) in diameter and about 1 inch

(2.5 cm) tall. If the dough is getting too sticky, wet your hands again. Smooth off the top with your fingers so that it shines. We don't want an extremely thick layer of dough, so shape it so that the skin is relatively thin. The rice batter is actually quite forgiving, so you can manipulate it as much as you want. If you still think it's too thick, just pinch off some of the batter and smooth it out again with your hands.

Arrange the bowls in a tiered bamboo steamer and cover. Partially fill a large wok with water and bring to a rapid boil over medium-high heat (for steaming tips, see page 38). Carefully perch the bamboo steamer on top. Steam for 30 minutes, replenishing with boiling water in the bottom of the wok if needed.

When the time is up on the steamer, turn off the heat, and gently take the bowls out. Brush a thin layer of oil on top of each meatball to keep it glistening. Dress with a dollop of Garlic Soy Dressing or Haishan sauce (or both—many restaurants do a blend) and enjoy immediately.

How to Make the Wrapper with Raw Rice Kernels

½ cup plus 2 tablespoons (125 g) basmati rice

¼ teaspoon fine sea salt

½ cup plus 2 tablespoons (100 g) sweet potato starch

¼ cup plus 3 tablespoons (55 g) tapioca starch

SPECIAL EQUIPMENT:
high-speed blender or food processor; stand mixer (optional)

Rinse the basmati rice in a fine-mesh sieve under running water. Transfer the rice to a medium bowl and add enough water to cover. Let sit at room temperature for at least 4 hours or overnight in the refrigerator.

Drain the rice in a sieve. Transfer the rice to a blender and add the salt and ½ cup (120 ml) water. Blend on high speed until milky, about 1 minute. It will be a rather thick but smooth paste.

In a medium saucepan set over high heat, bring 2 cups (470 ml) water to a rolling boil. Reduce the heat to low and pour in the rice batter. Mix continuously with a balloon whisk until it begins to solidify and turn into a thick batter, 30 seconds to 1 minute. The texture will be reminiscent of a cake batter or a really dense frosting. When the batter begins to form stiff peaks on the whisk, turn off the heat, and remove the pot from the stove immediately.

Let it cool until the batter is just slightly warmer than room temperature, about 30 minutes. In a medium bowl, mix together the sweet potato starch and the tapioca starch. Fold the starches into the warm batter with a silicone spatula until they are completely dissolved. (Alternatively, transfer the batter and the starches to a stand mixer, and knead with the paddle attachment for 2 minutes on high speed.) Continue as directed on the previous page.

Coffin Bread

棺材板
Guān Cai Bǎn

棺柴枋
Kuann Tshâ Pang

Coffin bread was invented in 1959 by Hsu Liu-I 許六一, a scrawny man with bold eyebrows, in the heart of a once bustling food center in Tainan called Sakariba 沙卡里巴. His original prototype was a chowder of chicken liver and squid encased in deep-fried toast. An archeology professor saw the creation and told Lin-I it reminded him of a coffin, and a new dish was born. Over the years the liver has been replaced by roughly diced pieces of chicken breast. In Taiwan, coffin bread is a dish that's considered by many to be dated or, at best, retro, though you can still find it scattered throughout select night markets in the south.

3	cups (710 ml) canola or soybean oil
2	slices white toast, each about 1 inch (2.5 cm) thick
2	garlic cloves, minced
1	ounce (30 g) squid, cleaned and sliced into rings
1	ounce (30 g) chicken breast, diced
¼	cup (30 g) peeled and diced carrots
¼	cup (30 g) frozen green peas
¼	cup (30 g) whole canned corn kernels, drained
¼	cup (60 ml) whole milk
½	teaspoon fine sea salt
¼	teaspoon white sugar
⅛	teaspoon ground white pepper, plus more to taste
1	tablespoon tapioca starch or cornstarch

In a large wok, heat the oil over medium-high heat until it reaches 350°F (175°C) on an instant-read thermometer. Gently slide in the two pieces of toast and deep-fry until the bread is light golden brown on both sides, 1 to 2 minutes. Remove the toast with tongs and set aside on a paper towel–lined plate or a wire rack set in a rimmed baking sheet to drain. Turn off the heat.

Discard all but 1 tablespoon of the oil in the wok (you can save it for another use). Warm the oil over medium-high heat. Add the garlic and cook, stirring, until fragrant, about 20 seconds. Add the squid and chicken breast, and cook until the chicken is no longer pink, about 1 minute. Add the carrots, peas, and corn kernels, and quickly mix it together for about 10 seconds. Pour in the milk and ½ cup (120 ml) water and bring everything to a boil. Season with the salt, sugar, and white pepper, adding more to taste.

Meanwhile, in a small bowl, make a slurry by mixing the tapioca starch and 1 tablespoon water. Reduce the heat to medium until the liquid is at a brisk simmer, drizzle in the slurry, and stir until it thickens, about 30 seconds. It should look like a chowder now. Turn off the heat and set aside.

With a paring knife, cut a large square opening in each piece of deep-fried toast. Set the lid aside, or if you'd like you can leave one side of the lid still hinged to the toast, like a door. Scoop out the center of the bread but be careful not to pierce through the bottom (the toast is meant to hold the chowder, not just frame it). Fill each hollow piece of toast with chowder and enjoy immediately.

Why Is Taiwanese Food So Sweet?

There's a deep love for sugar in Taiwan, and the farther south you travel, the sweeter the food gets. I've had sausages that taste like candy, and fish soup so saccharine that someone tasting it for the very first time could easily mistake it for dessert.

"When we make spring rolls, we stir-fry the ingredients inside the roll with nothing but sugar," brags Yen Wei, the food stylist for this cookbook, who was born and raised in Tainan.

"Not even a pinch of salt?" I ask, skeptical.

She shakes her head. "No salt," she says, beaming proudly.

The Taiwanese love for sugar originates from Tainan, the island's first city and the birthplace of the country's sugar industry. It was an industry jump-started by the Dutch East India Company in 1628, which recruited farmers from China to plant sugarcane in the area because Chinese-style sugar was, at that time, considered superior and commanded a higher price. By the 1720s, Taiwan was producing more sugar than any other island in the world (that is, according to a 2022 paper by Guanmian Xu, a professor of history at Peking University).

When Taiwan became a Japanese colony, dozens of sugar factories were set up and equipped with modern machinery. Sugar became such a dominant part of the economy that sugarcane growers made up one-third of all rural households in Taiwan. Most of the sugar they produced was shipped to Japan. In 1946, when the Nationalists took over Taiwan, sugar was turned into a public monopoly, but sugar production plummeted because Taiwan could no longer compete on the international market.

While Taiwan is no longer an international sugar superpower, sugar is an ingredient that remains dominant in our cuisine at large, for better and for worse. In fact, some food critics say that Taiwanese food has gotten excessively sweet over the years because chefs and vendors have played into this stereotype. Sugar, these food critics stress, should be an accent to bring out the natural flavors of the ingredients—not an overpowering force.

Taiwanese Spring Roll

潤餅
Rùn Bǐng

潤餅篋
Jūn Piánn Kauh

A medley of meat and vegetables seasoned with a generous sprinkle of sweet peanut powder, these rolls are tied to the annual Tomb Sweeping Festival—a spring holiday when families gather at their ancestors' graves for some spring cleaning. The dish is left on the grave for the deceased to partake in as the family pays their respects, and then brought back home for the living to eat afterward.

Now, due to regional variations, there's fierce debate on what proper Taiwanese spring rolls should be stuffed with. The recipe below is based on what Ivy grew up with in Tainan, which was her dad's absolute favorite. Feel free to get creative with leftovers from your refrigerator.

½ pound (225 g) pork tenderloin, cut into matchsticks	6 ounces (170 g) bean curd (dòu gān 豆乾) or extra-firm tofu, cut into matchsticks
1½ tablespoons soy sauce	1 cup (100 g) thinly sliced carrots, cut into matchsticks
2 teaspoons toasted sesame oil	1 cup (100 g) thinly sliced celery, cut into matchsticks
1 teaspoon Taiwanese rice wine (michiu) or cooking sake	1 cup (100 g) thinly sliced jicama, cut into matchsticks (optional)
4 large eggs	½ pound (225 g) shredded green cabbage
¼ cup (60 ml) canola or soybean oil, divided	½ pound (225 g) peeled and deveined shrimp
6 ounces (180 g) Oil Noodles (uncooked; page 363) or 3 ounces (85 g) dried lo mein noodles (see Notes)	16 Spring Roll Wrappers (recipe follows)
½ cup (100 g) lima beans or edamame beans, fresh or frozen	Garlic Puree (page 367)
Fine sea salt	Sweet Peanut Powder (page 369)

NOTES:

Fresh ramen noodles are another great alternative to homemade Oil Noodles. They can be found in the refrigerated section in many Asian specialty stores.

Spring rolls that are offered to the ancestors will inevitably get a bit soggy after an afternoon out in the hot humidity. To revive them, some families will gently pan-fry them before enjoying.

(RECIPE CONTINUES)

In a medium bowl, combine the pork tenderloin, soy sauce, sesame oil, and rice wine, and marinate for 15 minutes.

In a small bowl, whisk the eggs and 2 tablespoons water. Strain the mixture through a fine-mesh sieve; this part is important and will make sure the eggs come out uniform and not clumpy. Brush ½ teaspoon of the oil on a nonstick frying pan, then set the heat to medium. When the pan is hot, pour in half the egg mixture and tilt the pan so that the egg forms a thin and even film, then immediately cover the pan with a lid. Cook until the egg completely solidifies, 1 to 2 minutes. Take off the lid, and when the egg is cool enough to handle, gently peel it off the frying pan and transfer it to a cutting board. Brush ½ teaspoon of the oil in the pan again, return the heat to medium,

and repeat the process with the remaining egg mixture. Roll each egg disc into a burrito and cut it into thin ¼-inch (6-mm) strips.

Heat a medium pot of water over high heat until it comes to a rolling boil. If using fresh Oil Noodles, drop them in the boiling water for 2 to 3 minutes. If using dried lo mein noodles, cook according to the package instructions. Remove the noodles with a slotted spoon, and transfer them to a clean plate, reserving the water in the pot. Drizzle oil over the noodles to coat and toss to combine so they don't stick together.

Bring the reserved water to a boil over high heat again and add the lima beans and a pinch of salt. Cook until al dente, about 2 minutes. Turn off the heat, drain in a fine-mesh sieve, and transfer to a large plate or sheet pan.

Heat a wok over medium heat, and swirl in 1 teaspoon of the oil. When the oil is hot, add the bean curd and cook, stirring, until slightly brown on the edges, 1 to 2 minutes. Season with a pinch of salt. Transfer to the plate, keeping the ingredients separated.

With the heat still set over medium-high, heat another 1 teaspoon of the oil, add the carrots into the wok, and cook, stirring until vibrant and slightly softened, 1 to 2 minutes. Season with a pinch of salt and transfer to the plate. Swirl in 1 teaspoon of the oil again and add the celery to the wok. Cook and stir until bright and translucent, 1 to 2 minutes. Season with salt and transfer to the plate. Add 1 teaspoon of the oil, add the jicama, another pinch of salt, and stir until cooked through, to 2 minutes. Transfer to the plate. Swirl in 1 teaspoon of the oil, and add in the cabbage. Cook, add another pinch of salt, and stir until the cabbage is soft and wilted, 3 to 4 minutes. Transfer to the plate. Swirl in 1 tablespoon of the oil and add the shrimp and a pinch of salt. Cook until the shrimp are completely pink and cooked through, 2 to 3 minutes. Transfer to the

plate. Finally, add the last tablespoon of oil. Add the marinated pork and cook, stirring often, until no longer pink and completely cooked through, about 2 minutes. Turn off the heat and transfer the pork to the plate.

Assemble the spring rolls when the fillings are cool enough to handle. Because the wrappers are so thin, each individual roll will require two. Place 1 spring roll wrapper on a clean surface, and lay a second wrapper on top of it, leaving a 1½-inch (4-cm) gap on the top. Spread a small dollop of garlic puree in an even row on the bottom half of the wrapper, then add a little bit of each of the cooked ingredients on top on the puree. Sprinkle the peanut powder on top (the standard is about 2 tablespoons of peanut powder per roll, but add however much you want).

To wrap, fold the left and right sides inward toward the filling. Keeping the sides folded, crease the bottom of the spring roll up and over the filling, and tightly roll it away from you like it's a burrito. Divide the filling among the rest of the spring rolls. You will have 8 rolls in total. Enjoy immediately.

Spring Roll Wrapper

Traditionally, these wrappers are cooked and made on a griddle, not over the stove. To make it easier for everyone, this recipe is designed to work on a nonstick pan, and because these wrappers are so delicate, each spring roll will need at least two sheets to keep everything together.

2 cups plus ½ tablespoon (480 ml) water	½ teaspoon fine sea salt
2½ cups (300 g) bread flour	

In a large bowl, combine the water, bread flour, and salt, and whisk thoroughly until the batter is smooth and there are no lumps. Cover and let it rest at room temperature for 1 hour.

Heat a nonstick 8-inch (20-cm) frying pan over medium heat. Do not add oil to the pan. When the pan is hot, dip a wet pastry brush into the batter, and quickly brush a thin layer of batter all around the frying pan in a circular motion, going over it 3 to 4 times until it forms a visible disc. As it cooks, it will start to turn opaque and pearly white, 1 to 2 minutes. Turn off the heat, and when the wrapper has cooled down, peel it off the frying pan with chopsticks or your fingers. Repeat until the batter is completely used up.

NOTE:
The wrapper will stick to the pan if there's any leftover, crusted batter on it, so always clean the pan after each round. Be conscientious of the heat. If the pan starts smoking, it's too hot. The wrapper can be slightly crispy on the edges, but it should not be toasted.

TAINAN

午餐

Lunch
Break

Cost-Performance Value

"Good food with high CP value," writes douni, a user on a popular Taiwanese online bulletin board called P.T.T. in reference to a bowl of noodles in Guanmiao, Tainan. "It's a large bowl of about [$1] with four to five slices of meat on top of noodles." The post is dated May 17, 2006, and reads like a very standard food review dissecting the best eats of the area. It continues: "The mackerel soup has the highest CP value in town."

First, a translation: CP value is shorthand for cost-performance value, an economics term that has been awkwardly co-opted into an online slang here in Taiwan. All it really means is the best bang for your buck. So when someone says, "That soup dumpling restaurant has a really high CP value!" it means the soup dumplings are really worth the price. Or "The beef noodle soup is tasty, but has a low CP value": the beef noodle soup is tasty, but it's too expensive. Initially used to describe deals on cars and electronics, the term began showing up in people's posts about food in 2010, and it hit a climax two years later when it was used liberally by nearly every food blogger on the island. It's so overused that there are now CP value–themed restaurant listicles and CP value scores given to the best take-out deals in Taipei. So the fact that the aforementioned post dates to 2006 is actually quite extraordinary. It's one of the first online posts that uses the term CP value in relation to food.

In Taiwan, recognition as a place with a high CP value is the loftiest compliment an eatery can get, which says a lot about what modern diners prioritize. It's not so much about the finesse of a dish, how well the staff is treated, or where the ingredients are sourced; the most important criterion for Taiwanese diners is whether the food is worth the money. While quality is occasionally factored in, a dish can taste mediocre but be really cheap and generously portioned and still be considered to have high CP value. And if on the really rare occasion it's pricey, it had better be one of the best dining experiences of all time. Of course, getting the best bang for your buck is universally valued, but what's problematic about Taiwan's love for high cost-performance value is that even though performance can mean a lot of different things, the expectation is that the cost generally remains low.

Thankfully, in recent years, CP value has come under fire from critics who argue it's overused and glosses over the amount of time and effort it takes to create a spectacular dining experience. "I want to remind everyone that there are other aspects to pay attention to," influential Taiwanese food blogger Liz Kao wrote on her blog *Self-Taught Gourmet* in 2012. She cites atmosphere, the taste of the food, and the values of the proprietor as elements worth considering, and that when restaurants are judged solely through the lens of CP value, the act of eating becomes "monotonous and boring." I staunchly agree; not everything remarkable has to be cheap to be worthwhile, and the relentless pursuit of a good deal encourages a culture of large, low-quality lunch bowls while the quality of the ingredients and the working conditions of the staff are forced to take a back seat.

With that said, many of the dishes in this chapter are timeless and popular lunch staples precisely because of their so-called high CP value. Priced extremely

low, they're pushed out with immense speed and efficiency during the lunch rush. These dishes are specifically designed so that most of the cooking is done beforehand. Five-spice-dusted pork chops are deep-fried ahead of time and double-fried to order. The soup for beef noodle soup is made the night before. Oyster vermicelli stew is left simmering all day and scooped out to order. But as I've cooked my way through these recipes many times in the course of writing this book, I've been baffled by how inexpensive these dishes are

in spite of inflation and rising food costs. Because while a lot of them are technically easy to put together, the prep work takes a lot of time and care.

So whether you're a seasoned connoisseur of Taiwanese food or a novice attempting these flavors for the first time, cook the recipes in this chapter with the awareness that each serving is sold for less than $5, and marvel along with me at the resiliency and finesse of the underappreciated chefs who sling these dishes out on a daily basis.

Also known as xiao long bao, soup dumplings were not invented in Taiwan. They're from Shanghai and the surrounding province of Jiangsu, but I've included them because it was Din Tai Fung—a soup dumpling powerhouse headquartered in Taipei—that introduced this dish to the world. The progenitor of the chain, Yang Bing-Yi 楊秉彞, was born in the Chinese province of Shanxi at the start of the Chinese Civil War, and in 1948 he decided to move to Taiwan and meet up with his extended family. He opened a soup dumpling shop about a decade later, and the rest is history. Din Tai Fung now has more than 160 locations across the world and is still very much a hit here on the island after all these years because its emphasis on light and sweet flavors melds well with Taiwanese sensibilities.

The trick to getting the soup into the delicate dumpling is the gelatinized broth, which is extracted by boiling fresh pigskin for many hours. When the stock cools down, it turns into a solid jelly-like substance, but dissolves immediately back into soup once it's hit again with hot steam in the steamer.

Soup Dumplings

小籠包
Xiǎo Lóng Bāo

FOR THE FILLING:

7   ounces (200 g) ground pork

2   tablespoons Scallion and Ginger Water (recipe follows)

1½ teaspoons soy sauce

1½ teaspoons toasted sesame oil

½   teaspoon fine sea salt

½   teaspoon white sugar

½   teaspoon Taiwanese rice wine (michiu) or cooking sake

⅛   teaspoon ground white pepper

¾   cup and 2 tablespoons (200 ml) Jelly Stock (recipe follows)

FOR THE WRAPPERS:

¾   cup plus 2 teaspoons (110 g) all-purpose flour

2   tablespoons (15 g) bread flour

¼   teaspoon fine sea salt

¼   cup (60 g) water

FOR THE DIPPING SAUCE (PER SERVING):

1   tablespoon black vinegar

1½ teaspoons soy sauce

1   ½-inch piece fresh young ginger (5 g), peeled and sliced into thin matchsticks (see Note)

SPECIAL EQUIPMENT:
perforated parchment paper; stand mixer (optional)

NOTE:
Young ginger is less intense and slightly sweeter than regular, mature ginger. You can mimic its subtlety by soaking peeled, sliced pieces of regular ginger in water for 30 minutes.

MAKE THE FILLING: In a bowl, combine the ground pork, Scallion and Ginger Water, soy sauce, sesame oil, salt, sugar, rice wine, and white pepper. Stir vigorously with chopsticks in one direction until everything is mixed thoroughly and sticky, 1 to 2 minutes. Add the cooled down Jelly Stock (it absolutely has to be room temperature; if it's warm, it will cook the meat), and mix again until everything is incorporated. It's going to be quite wet but will firm up in the refrigerator. Cover and refrigerate for at least 4 hours or overnight. The filling will solidify into a jelly; it will look a bit like head cheese.

MAKE THE WRAPPERS: In a mixing bowl, combine the all-purpose flour, bread flour, salt, and water. Mix until it forms a shaggy dough. Bring it

(RECIPE CONTINUES)

together with your hands, transfer to a clean work surface, and knead until smooth and shiny, about 5 minutes. (Alternatively, knead in the bowl of a stand mixer with the dough hook attachment on low speed until it comes together, about 2 minutes.) Cover the dough and let it rest until very soft and pliable, at least 2½ hours at room temperature or overnight in the refrigerator.

Roll the dough into a long cylinder, about 1 inch (2.5 cm) thick. Pinch off 25 equal portions, about 7 g to 8 g each. Cover with plastic wrap and let them rest for 10 minutes.

Flatten each dough into a round disc with your palm. If you are right-handed, arrange a small rolling pin horizontally on the table and put the disc just above it, slightly left of center. Hold the disc with your left hand and move the rolling pin up with your right hand, stopping right before you hit the very center of the disc. Rotate the disc counterclockwise as you flatten it with the rolling pin to maintain the round shape of the disc, making sure the edges are thinner than the center. Shape the disc so it's about 3 inches (7.5 cm) in diameter. If you are left-handed, flip everything over so that you are rotating the disc clockwise with your right hand. The wrappers should feel soft, like earlobes. Cover the finished wrappers with plastic wrap so they don't dry out.

To wrap, put a wrapper in the palm of your left hand, and put 1 tablespoon (about 17 g) of filling in the middle. Cup the wrapper with your left hand and pinch the edges together with your thumb and index finger of your right hand, gently pulling the dough as you work around the dumpling in a counterclockwise motion. At the same time, rotate the dumpling clockwise with your left hand, using your left thumb to press the filling down as you go. Pinch the top of the dumpling closed and repeat with the remaining wrappers. If you're

left-handed, reverse everything over so that you are holding the wrapper in your right hand.

Line a tiered bamboo steamer basket with perforated parchment paper, and arrange the dumplings inside, leaving about two fingers' worth of space between each dumpling. Don't overcrowd them. You can steam them in batches if you don't have enough steamers.

Partially fill a large wok with water and bring to a rolling boil over high heat (for steaming tips, see page 38). Cover and lower the steamer baskets into the wok. Steam over high heat for 6 minutes if you're just using 1 steamer. If you're stacking 2 steamers on top of each other, steam for 7 minutes. Turn off the heat and remove the bamboo steamers from the wok.

MAKE THE DIPPING SAUCE: In a small tray, combine the black vinegar and soy sauce. Add the sliced ginger on top. Enjoy the dumplings with the sauce.

Scallion and Ginger Water

¼	cup (60 ml) water	1	scallion, chopped
1	1-inch piece fresh ginger (10 g), peeled and sliced		

SPECIAL EQUIPMENT:
small blender or immersion blender

In a small blender, combine the water, ginger, and scallion. Blend on high speed for 15 seconds.

Jelly Stock

1   pound (450 g) fresh pig skin

½   pound (225 g) pork bones

½   pound (225 g) bone-in chicken thighs, legs, or wings

½   yellow onion, peeled and halved

1   scallion (20 g), tied into a knot

1   1-inch piece fresh ginger (10 g), unpeeled and sliced

1   whole star anise

1   tablespoon Taiwanese rice wine (michiu) or cooking sake

In a large pot, combine the fresh pig skin, pork bones, and chicken. Cover with at least 1 inch (2.5 cm) water and bring to a boil over high heat. Reduce the heat to medium and simmer for 5 minutes. Drain the skin and bones in a colander, and rinse quickly under running water to get rid of excess scum.

In a large pot, bring 5 cups (1.2 L) water to a rolling boil over high heat. Put the pig skin, pork bones, chicken, onion, scallion, ginger, star anise, and rice wine into the boiling water, and bring to a boil again. Reduce the heat to low and simmer uncovered until it reduces in half, 2 to 3 hours. Turn off the heat and strain the stock through a fine-mesh sieve. Discard the solids. Let it cool down completely to room temperature. There will be a transparent layer of fat that settles on top. Scrape as much of that off as possible. Let cool down completely to room temperature before use.

Beef Noodle Soup

紅燒牛肉麵

Hóng Shāo Niú Ròu Miàn

In the aftermath of the Chinese Civil War in the late 1940s, 1.2 million soldiers of the Republic of China and their dependents retreated from China to Taiwan after defeat by the Communist Chinese. They were stationed in military villages across the island—provisional housing structures that were haphazardly put up because, for years, they believed they would eventually reclaim the mainland and head back home.

That never happened. And as the temporary villages slowly became more permanent, a new culinary culture began to emerge. People from the eastern Chinese coast of Jiangsu and Shanghai were natural champions of red-braising, a slow-cooking technique that combines soy sauce, rock sugar, and meat to create an alluring, reddish glisten. The Cantonese were masters of soup and could extract copious amounts of flavor from bones and leftover cuts of meat. Folks from Sichuan brought over their technique for making spicy, fermented broad bean paste from scratch, and northerners capitalized on the eventual influx of wheat imports from the States and began slinging out robust batches of homemade noodles. From the confines of these military households, a new, wonderful fusion cuisine was born, and all of the above were thrown together into what we know today as beef noodle soup, a dish undeniably made in Taiwan.

"They used a lot of spices back then to mask the flavor of the beef, because the quality of the beef was poor," chef Hung Ching-Lung 洪金龍 tells me. Hung is a five-time beef noodle soup competition winner and owner of his eponymous restaurant, Chef Hung 洪師父, a multinational beef noodle soup chain. Over the years, he's trained hundreds of beef noodle soup chefs around the world and estimates that there are more than 10,000 specialists in Taiwan alone. He tells me that for decades, beef noodle soup was a humble street food dish, slung out in less-than-sanitary conditions at the periphery of these military villages. It had its turning point in 2005, when former Taiwanese president Ma Ying-Jeou—then the mayor of Taipei—launched an annual city-wide beef noodle soup festival and competition, which elevated the industry and dish into an international icon. Today, most of the beef used for this dish is imported from countries like America and Australia, and because the quality of the beef is so high now, the mark of a great chef is a really clean soup with a minimal amount of spice. This recipe is my adaptation of the one that chef Hung gives to his students. He prefers a pure beef bone broth base, but notes that the variations are endless because every restaurant has their own secret recipe. Hung says the key is procuring a really high-quality cut of beef, making a flavorful broth, and everything else is just an accessory. "When you're making beef noodle soup, the only competition is yourself, not other chefs," he stresses.

(RECIPE CONTINUES)

- 2 teaspoons coarse salt
- 2 pounds (900 g) whole boneless beef shank
- 1 tablespoon canola or soybean oil
- 1 1-inch piece fresh ginger (10 g), unpeeled and sliced
- 4 scallions, white and green parts separated
- 3 garlic cloves, smashed and peeled
- 2 tablespoons coarse raw sugar, such as demerara
- 1½ tablespoons dried fermented black beans (dòu chǐ 豆豉)
- 1½ tablespoons fermented broad bean paste (dòu bàn jiàng 豆瓣醬)
- 8 cups (2 L) Bone Broth (page 357, but use beef bones instead of pork) or low-sodium chicken broth
- ¼ cup plus 1 tablespoon (75 ml) soy sauce
- 1 Spice Bag (recipe follows)
- ½ pound (225 g) daikon, peeled and chopped (optional)
- ½ large carrot (50g), peeled and chopped (optional)
- 1 large tomato, quartered
- 1 yellow onion, peeled and halved
- ½ pound (225 g) Taiwanese bok choy or regular bok choy, chopped into 1-inch (2.5-cm) segments
- 1 pound (450 g) fresh wheat noodles or 7 ounces (200 g) dried wheat noodles

Fresh cilantro sprigs (for garnish)

Rub salt evenly all over the beef shank. Cover the beef and let it rest for at least 2 hours or overnight in the refrigerator. This will tenderize and draw out flavor from the meat.

In a large pot, combine the beef shank with enough water to cover. Bring the water to a rolling boil over high heat. Reduce the heat to medium, and simmer for 5 minutes. Turn off the heat. Drain and transfer the beef to a colander in the sink. Rinse the beef under cool running water to get rid of any scum. When the beef is cool enough to handle, chop into bite-size 2-inch-(5-cm-) thick chunks.

Set a large pot over medium-high heat and swirl in the oil. When the oil is hot, add the ginger, the white parts of the scallions, and the garlic, and cook, stirring often, until aromatic, about 20 seconds. Add the sugar, fermented black beans, and fermented broad bean paste, and cook, stirring, until the sugar begins to melt, another 30 seconds. Immediately add in the beef shank, mixing continuously with a wooden spoon to make sure the shank is coated evenly with sauce, about 1 minute. Pour in the bone broth and soy sauce, then add the spice bag, daikon, carrots, tomato, and onion. Cover the pot and bring the soup to a rolling boil. Reduce the

heat to low, and slowly simmer with the lid slightly ajar until the beef is fork-tender, 1½ to 2 hours.

Fill a medium pot with water and bring it to a rolling boil over high heat. Quickly blanch the bok choy for 30 seconds. Ladle it out with a spider strainer and set aside for later.

In the same pot of boiling water, cook the fresh wheat noodles until al dente, about 3 minutes. If using dried noodles, cook according to package instructions. Turn off the heat and drain in a colander. Rinse immediately under running water and shake to dry.

Check the meat; the beef is done when a knife can pierce through the meat with little to no resistance. Turn the heat off. With tongs, pick out only the beef chunks and set aside. Strain the broth through a fine-mesh sieve into a clean pot, discarding the spice bag, the aromatics, and vegetables.

Mince the scallion greens. Divide the noodles among serving bowls. Arrange a handful of beef and the bok choy on top of the noodles and ladle the hot broth over. Garnish with the green parts of the scallions and cilantro.

Spice Bag

In Taiwan, spices are procured at the local Chinese medicine shop. The staff will sell specific aromatics à la carte, or create a blend for you based on what dish you're making. This is the personal blend that I use for everything, but feel free to tweak it according to what you have. Star anise, though, is mandatory—it adds an earthy complexity to dishes. Sichuan red peppercorns give dishes a tangy brightness, dried citrus peels provide sweetness, and cloves add warmth. If whole, high-quality spices are difficult to procure, feel free to substitute 1 teaspoon of five-spice powder for the spice bag and add it directly into the braising liquid. Blooming the spices per the instructions below is optional, and most Taiwanese people don't do it, but I find that it's a really lovely way to coax the flavor out of old spices. And a general rule of thumb when storing high-quality spices is to keep them in your refrigerator; they'll last a lot longer that way.

1 tablespoon canola or soybean oil

1 small cassia or cinnamon stick, about 2 inches (5 cm) long

3 whole star anise pods

3 bay leaves

3 whole cloves

1 Chinese black cardamom pod, also known as tsaoko

1 dried tangerine or mandarin orange peel, about the size of a quarter

1½ teaspoons whole Sichuan red peppercorns

1 teaspoon whole white peppercorns

½ teaspoon whole fennel seeds

In a wok set over low heat, swirl in the oil. When it begins to shimmer, add the cassia stick, star anise pods, bay leaves, cloves, black cardamon pod, tangerine peel, Sichuan red peppercorns, white peppercorns, and fennel seeds. Cook and stir around frequently until it smells lovely, 1 to 2 minutes. Turn off the heat, transfer the spices to a clean plate, and wait until they cool down completely. In a large tea bag or sachet, combine the spice mix ingredients, and tie the bag closed. Use immediately.

Cows Are Friends, Not Food

For generations, long before the industrialization of Taiwan, agrarian households treated cows like friends and esteemed members of the family. Because bovines labored in the field along with farmers and literally did all the heavy lifting—tirelessly moving dirt and crops with plows and carts—many people developed a sentimental attachment to their oxen. Eating beef was so taboo at that time that children were told the act of doing so would make them dumb, or that the police would throw them in jail if they were caught. Some swore a bowl of beef was a ticket straight to hell.

As an ingredient, beef was first introduced into the Taiwanese diet at the turn of the 20th century when the Japanese colonists arrived. But it didn't really catch on because it was new (even for the Japanese) and mostly reserved for the elite class. Just two decades prior, the emperor of Japan had lifted a 1,200-year-old ban on meat in an earnest yet misguided attempt to catch up to Western civilizations. He was convinced Westerners were taller and had better physiques specifically because they ate meat.

In 1949, when the Chinese Nationalist government came to Taiwan from China, the Chinese refugees who moved over introduced more beef-centric dishes to the island, like beef noodle soup and braised beef shank. But because of rampant segregation and resentment between the Chinese newcomers and the local population, their food was largely ignored at first and consumed only by the rich, political elite. In fact, most people in Taiwan didn't start eating beef en masse until the 1980s, during a period of rapid economic growth and industrialization known as the Taiwan Miracle—jump-started by a $4 billion economic stimulus package from the American government. American culture and cuisine were glorified, and cheap steak houses began to pop up at night markets around the country. That made all the difference. It was in these spaces that, for the first time in Taiwan's history, beef became affordable and accessible to the average person.

While cows are no longer eschewed as an ingredient, remnants of the taboo can be found in modern-day society. I have friends who just don't eat or cook beef when they're at home, because they were raised by relatives who grew up in the countryside. Many of the late-night beer restaurants will happily swap out beef for lamb without asking why if you request it, and today there's still a large segment of beef noodle soup restaurants—especially in southern Taiwan—that purposefully have pork trotters on their menu for the older crowd who still can't bring themselves to eat their friends.

Turkey Rice

雞肉飯
Jī Ròu Fàn

雞肉飯
Ke Bah Pñg

A simple bowl of shredded, poached poultry over rice, this is the one and only turkey dish in Taiwanese cuisine. In fact, turkeys are a bit of an enigma on our island. You can't buy the birds at any market—only restaurants serve turkey—and as a North American species, they simply aren't well suited to Taiwan's hot, subtropical climate. Many sources say the Dutch colonists introduced turkeys to Taiwan sometime in the 17th century, but the prevailing theory is that US Air Force troops stationed near the southwestern city of Chiayi in the 1950s jump-started the industry with their Thanksgiving cravings. Whether or not that's true isn't actually verifiable. However, the American presence in Taiwan did happen to coincide with the beginning of the island's large-scale turkey production.

Now, turkeys in Taiwan are exclusive to restaurants for a couple of reasons. First: The industry is heavily centralized by the Taiwanese Turkey Association, which orders turkey eggs in bulk from abroad, hatches them in a centralized nursery, distributes the turkeys across farms in Taiwan, and then ships them directly to restaurants. Second: Because the turkeys here in Taiwan are bred to be absolutely massive, they wouldn't fit in a standard home kitchen anyway. A Taiwan-raised turkey weighs an enormous 55 pounds (25 kg); for context, the average weight of a turkey at an American Thanksgiving table is just 15 pounds (7 kg). And so, for that reason, I've scaled down the proportions of this recipe considerably while keeping true to its spirit. This is a dish that really respects the product, dressing it with shallot-infused fat and turkey broth with a small hit of soy sauce, sugar, and salt.

- 1 tablespoon coarse salt
- 1 4-pound (1.8-kg) skin-on, bone-in turkey breast or whole chicken
- 1 2-inch piece fresh ginger (20 g), unpeeled and sliced
- 4 scallions, tied into a knot
- 2 tablespoons soy sauce
- 1 tablespoon white sugar
- ½ teaspoon fine sea salt
- ⅛ teaspoon ground white pepper
- ¾ cup (180 ml) Shallot Oil (page 368, made with turkey, goose, or duck fat), melted
- Cooked short-grain rice, also known as sushi rice, for serving
- 1 cup (80 g) fried shallots (store-bought or homemade; page 368)
- 8 to 10 thin slices yellow Japanese pickled daikon, also known as takuan (optional)

NOTE:
This can also be made with shredded leftover turkey or chicken. To make the sauce, just use low-sodium chicken broth instead of making the turkey bone stock from scratch.

Rub the salt over the turkey breast. Cover and refrigerate for at least 6 hours or overnight.

In a large stockpot, combine the salted turkey breast, ginger, scallions, and enough water to cover the turkey by 1 inch (2.5 cm). Bring to a rolling boil over high heat, skimming foam from the surface as needed. Turn off the

heat, cover the pot with a tight-fitting lid, and let the turkey sit until an instant-read thermometer inserted into thickest part of the breast registers at least 165°F (75°C), about 40 minutes.

Transfer the turkey to a cutting board. When cool enough to handle, shred the turkey with a fork or your hands, removing and discarding the skin while reserving the bones. Transfer the shredded meat to a baking dish, ladle a bit of broth over it, cover with aluminum foil, and put it in the oven on the lowest setting to keep warm.

Return the turkey bones to the stockpot. Simmer over low heat, uncovered, for 1 hour. Strain the stock through a fine-mesh sieve into a clean pot and discard the solids. Reserve 2 cups of the turkey stock (470 ml)

for the sauce, and store the remaining stock for another use.

In a small pot, make the sauce by combining the reserved turkey stock with the soy sauce, sugar, salt, and white pepper. Bring to a rapid boil over medium-high heat, stirring until the sugar is completely dissolved. Turn off the heat.

To serve, divide the cooked rice into servings bowls. Divide the melted shallot oil on top of the rice, then add the shredded turkey. Spoon a couple of tablespoons of the warm sauce over the turkey. Garnish each bowl with a light-handed sprinkle of fried shallots and a slice of the yellow Japanese pickled daikon, if using. Enjoy immediately.

Oyster and Pork Intestine Vermicelli Stew

大腸蚵仔麵線

Tuā Tīg Ôr Á Mī Suànn

The Taiwanese equivalent of a hearty pot of gumbo, this lovely noodle stew used to be a lunch staple for farmers in the countryside, who would keep a pot of it perpetually simmering over a warm stove. They'd thicken the soup with a slurry of starch to make it more filling and ladle spoonfuls of freshly poached oysters and braised pork intestines on top to serve. The secret ingredient here is the really skinny strands of wheat vermicelli known as red mī suànn 紅麵線. Mi suann—so thin that some varieties can be threaded through the eye of a needle—can be found across the strait in the Fujian province of China as well, but what's unique about the red versions in Taiwan is that the noodles are steamed at a high temperature for up to seven hours until they take on a light caramel color. This steaming process denatures the protein in the noodles so that they can be boiled for a long time without completely disintegrating in the broth. It prevents them from shooting past al dente, which is really important, considering that cooks will sometimes leave the noodles simmering in the soup for hours. These noodles are very difficult to find outside Taiwan, so I designed this recipe to replicate their texture, color, and resiliency. My version here, which requires baking the noodles at a low temperature for an hour instead of steaming them, isn't an exact analogue; true red mi suann is a lot stretchier. But true to form, these noodles can be simmered for a long period of time without falling apart. This recipe includes both oysters and intestines as toppings, but feel free to use either or none.

3   ounces (85 g) Japanese somen noodles or any dried wheat thin noodle, at least 1 mm thick (see Notes)

20 shucked small oysters, about 6 ounces (170 g) in total weight

½   teaspoon Taiwanese rice wine (michiu) or cooking sake

6   tablespoons (60 g) sweet potato starch or cornstarch, divided

4   cups (1 L) Bone Broth (page 357) or low-sodium chicken stock

½   cup (75 g) sliced bamboo shoots, canned or fresh, cut into matchsticks (see Notes; optional)

1   tablespoon fried shallots (store-bought or homemade; page 368)

½   cup (10 g) bonito flakes

1½ tablespoons soy sauce

1   teaspoon fine sea salt, plus more to taste

½   teaspoon white sugar

¼   pound (115 g) Braised Intestines (page 80)

Garlic Puree (page 367)

Black vinegar

Chili sauce, such as Lee Kum Kee chili garlic sauce or Huy Fong sambal oelek (for garnish)

Fresh cilantro sprigs (for garnish)

Ground white pepper

(RECIPE CONTINUES)

Preheat the oven to 300°F (150°C).

On a rimmed baking sheet, spread the noodles out into an even layer, and bake until they are slightly off-white, about 30 minutes. Take the baking sheet out of the oven and give it a gentle shake. Bake again until the noodles are a very light brown, about another 30 minutes. Remove the baking sheet from the oven. When the noodles are cool enough to handle, snap them in half into 4-inch (10-cm) segments.

Bring a medium heavy pot of water to a rolling boil over high heat, and cook the noodles until soft, about 1 minute. They will turn a bit darker in the water and will be a very light reddish-orange hue. Drain in a colander and set aside.

In a small bowl, combine the oysters with rice wine and marinate for 10 minutes. Drain through a fine-mesh sieve, and lightly dab the oysters with paper towels so they aren't too wet. Put 3 tablespoons of the sweet potato starch on a small plate and, working in batches, dredge the oysters in the starch so that they're completely coated. Set the coated oysters aside on a clean plate.

Prepare an ice water bath on the side. Bring a small pot filled halfway with water to a rolling boil over high heat and add the oysters. Cook until they have firmed up, 2 to 3 minutes. Use a spider strainer to transfer the oysters to the ice water bath to cool completely, about 20 seconds. Drain well through a fine-mesh sieve and set aside.

In a medium pot over high heat, add the bone broth and bring to a rolling boil. Add the cooked noodles, bamboo shoots, and fried shallots. Reduce the heat to medium so that the broth is at a brisk simmer, stir, and cook until the bamboo shoots have softened, about 3 minutes. Crush the bonito flakes with your hands or a spoon so that they break off into small flecks, and mix them in. Season with the soy sauce, salt, and sugar, adding more salt if you'd like. In a small bowl, make the slurry by mixing the remaining 3 tablespoons sweet potato starch with 3 tablespoons water. Stream the mixture into the soup, and stir until it thickens, about 30 seconds. Turn the heat off.

To serve, divide the noodle soup into small serving bowls, and top with oysters and the braised intestines. Dress each serving with a dollop of garlic puree, black vinegar, and chili sauce, to taste. To finish off, add fresh cilantro sprigs and a couple of light shakes of ground white pepper.

NOTES:

If you can actually get your hands on a batch of proper red mi suann noodles from Taiwan, know that they are extremely salty and have to be blanched and then rinsed thoroughly under running water before use or else they will ruin the dish. Some of the larger Asian supermarkets have an instant version of mi suann labeled "dried thin noodle" from a brand called Go Cha, designed specifically for an oyster vermicelli stew. Those noodles don't have to be baked or blanched and can be added directly to the soup.

Bamboo shoot quality really varies, especially outside Taiwan. Taste them before you add them in; if they're bitter or stringy, blanch them in boiling water first. When Ivy shops for bamboo, she looks for tender shoots with fat bottoms and smooth edges.

Taiwan Is So Convenient

In February 1980, 7-Eleven, or Seven—as we affectionately call it here—made its debut on the island. My father remembers being so enticed by its glassy doors, fluorescent lights, and neat aisles that he felt moved to apply for a job there. He wasn't alone in his fascination with the brand. Kids thought the shop was the coolest thing on the block, with its bold orange-and-green logo that outshone even the busiest street corner in the city and an interior where every inch was oversaturated with light. The youth were drawn in by novelty, and stayed for the oversize Slurpees and strange, squeaky American hot dogs.

But the older generation was skeptical and bewildered by its popularity. While the modern convenience store was a revelation in the United States, Taiwan already had its own version called the kám á tiàm 咁仔店—the Taiwanese equivalent of a bodega but without a front wall or air-conditioning. These corner shops, which still exist to this day, were already stacked floor-to-ceiling with an overflow of pantry items and kitchen essentials. With the exception of fresh produce, they had everything a household could want or need. Plus, prices at 7-Eleven were simply exorbitant in comparison.

And so, 7-Eleven bled money for about half a decade until they decided to shift gears. The strategy was to add ready-made food to their repertoire; they began to sell hot tea eggs, oden (Japanese-style fish cakes), and rice balls to appeal to local palates. Slurpees were eventually phased out. Tables and chairs were installed, along with coffee machines, which jump-started the coffee culture in the country. Back in the 1980s, Seven was one of the few places where people could buy a cup of coffee, and that made all the difference.

7-Eleven slowly became a regular hangout for idle and retired folks, who went there to sip exotic cups of caffeine and take refuge in the free air-conditioning. The hours were extended around the clock, and aisles were stuffed with alcohol, sanitary items, and more ready-made meals. And as more women began to join the workforce and eschew traditional housewife duties, the convenience store became an increasingly central part of the community.

Today, if you stop a person on the street in the city and ask them what the greatest thing about living in Taiwan is, they'll most likely say, "It's convenient ah." Convenience culture is at the crux of modern Taiwanese society. 7-Eleven remains the dominant brand, trailed closely by a Japanese chain called Family Mart. And while America was the progenitor of the convenience store, Taiwan has elevated it to new heights. Taiwan has the second-highest density of convenience stores in the world, just behind South Korea. We have 7-Elevens in rural towns, on top of mountains, and sometimes even perched on the side of random mountain roads. This saturation of the market wouldn't be sustainable in most other industries, but it works in Taiwan because people have become overly dependent on the sheer convenience of the convenience store. It's the hub where we pay our bills, pick up packages, buy tickets, deposit money, make photocopies, order coffee, and hang out with friends. They sell spicy noodles with duck blood, fresh fruit, roasted sweet potatoes, a huge variety of craft beer, condoms, socks, and

disposable underwear. It's a bank, post office, pharmacy, and grocery store all rolled up into a tiny, compact place. Some 7-Elevens in the more rural parts of Taiwan also double as pseudo daycare centers, where kids can safely wait for their parents to pick them up after school under the supervision of staff. And when the occasion calls for it, my friends and I refer to it as Bar 7—a cheap place for us to pick up cold beers, sit down, and chat in the crisp air-conditioning before hitting town.

As for my dad? He never even got an interview. Back then there was a mandatory English test for all employees, and he flunked it. With his convenience store dreams burst, he moved to Los Angeles with my mom shortly thereafter. Though he jokes that he dodged a bullet by not getting a job there, he still feels a strong affinity for the brand. Sometimes when he's back in town—despite the multitude of restaurants and food options all around him—he'll walk into a 7-Eleven and come out with a delightful bundle of rice balls, roasted sweet potatoes, and icy green tea, muttering under his breath, "It's too convenient ah."

There's a cold noodle vendor called Liu Mama's 劉媽媽麵館 in Taipei that's open exclusively from 9:30 p.m. to 9:00 a.m. By virtue of their hours, they serve a distinct class of night owls who crave sesame-drenched noodles with scoops of julienned cucumbers. It sounds bland in comparison to the typical and perhaps more comforting repertoire of greasy late-night skewers, but there's something both fortifying and refreshing about finishing off a really late night with a large plate of cold noodles. These noodles are also very much a popular lunch staple. So popular, in fact, that you can buy them refrigerated and ready-to-eat at all convenience stores across the country.

Cold Sesame Noodles

涼 麵
Liáng Miàn

FOR THE SESAME SAUCE:

- ½ cup plus 1 tablespoon (135 ml) water
- ½ cup (120 ml) soy sauce
- ½ cup (120 ml) rice vinegar
- ¼ pound (115 g) toasted sesame seeds (page 368)
- ¼ cup plus 1 tablespoon (60 g) white sugar
- 1 tablespoon toasted sesame oil, plus more if needed
- ¼ cup (30 g) unsalted roasted peanuts (page 368)

FOR THE NOODLES:

- 2½ pounds (1.1 kg) Oil Noodles (uncooked; page 363) or 19 ounces (540 g) dried lo mein noodles (see Note)
- 1 teaspoon canola or soybean oil, divided
- 2 large eggs
- 1½ medium Japanese cucumbers or any seedless cucumber (150 g), cut into matchsticks
- 1½ large carrots (150 g), peeled and cut into matchsticks

Garlic Puree (optional; page 367)

Chili crisp, any brand (optional)

MAKE THE SESAME SAUCE: In the blender, combine the water, soy sauce, rice vinegar, sesame seeds, sugar, and sesame oil, and process on high speed until completely creamy and smooth, about 1 minute. Add the peanuts, and blend until smooth again, about another 1 minute. If you prefer a runnier consistency, add more sesame oil to taste.

MAKE THE NOODLES: Bring a medium pot of water to a rolling boil over high heat, and cook the Oil Noodles until al dente, 2 to 3 minutes. If using dried noodles, cook according to the package instructions. Prepare a large ice bath to the side. Drain the noodles in a colander, and transfer to an ice bath to cool down completely, about 20 seconds. Drain again, and drizzle ½ teaspoon of the oil over the noodles to coat. Toss to combine so they don't stick together. Set aside for later.

In a small bowl, whisk the eggs and 1 tablespoon water. Strain the mixture through a fine-mesh sieve and into a clean bowl; this part is important and will make sure the egg comes out uniform and not clumpy.

SPECIAL EQUIPMENT:
high-speed blender

NOTE:
Fresh ramen noodles are another great alternative to homemade Oil Noodles. They can be found in the refrigerated section in many Asian specialty stores.

(RECIPE CONTINUES)

Brush the remaining ½ teaspoon oil onto a nonstick frying pan over medium-low heat. When the pan is hot, pour in the egg mixture and tilt the pan so that the egg forms a thin and even film. Immediately cover the pan with a lid and cook for about 1 minute. Turn off the heat and wait until the egg completely solidifies, 30 seconds to 1 minute. When the egg is cool enough to handle, gently peel it off the frying pan with your fingers or chopsticks and place it on a cutting board.

Roll it into a burrito and cut it crosswise into thin ¼-inch (6-mm) strips.

To serve, divide the noodles into serving plates. Neatly arrange some egg strips, sliced cucumbers, and sliced carrots on top of each serving. Dress with the sesame sauce and plop a bit of the garlic puree and chili crisp on top, if using. Stir the sauce into the noodles. Enjoy immediately or serve chilled.

Deep-fried pork loins are a common centerpiece in lunch boxes throughout the island. Marinated in a simple medley of soy sauce, sugar, and a bit of five-spice powder, then coated in a crispy layer of sweet potato starch, they're a great anchor for an afternoon meal.

Fried Pork Chop

炸 排 骨
Zhá Pái Gǔ

糋 豬 排
Tsìnn Ti Pâi

3   boneless pork loins, about 5⅓ ounces (150 g) each or 1 pound (450 g) in total weight

1   tablespoon soy sauce

1   tablespoon Taiwanese rice wine (michiu) or cooking sake

1½ teaspoons white sugar

1   teaspoon toasted sesame oil

¼   teaspoon fine sea salt

¼   teaspoon ground white pepper

¼   teaspoon five-spice powder

1   garlic clove, minced

4   cups (1 L) canola or soybean oil

½   cup (80 g) thick sweet potato starch (see Note)

Cooked short-grain rice, also known as sushi rice (page 360), for serving

Take a meat mallet and pound the pork loins so that they are about ½ inch (1 cm) thick. In a large bowl, combine the pork with the soy sauce, rice wine, sugar, sesame oil, salt, white pepper, five-spice powder, and garlic. Massage the meat until it's thoroughly coated with the sauce. Cover and refrigerate for at least 2 hours or overnight.

In a deep wok over medium-high heat, warm the oil until it reaches 350°F (175°C) on an instant-read thermometer.

Spread the sweet potato starch on a plate and press the pork loins into it until both sides are fully coated. Shake off the excess starch. Transfer the coated pork loins to a clean plate.

Working with one pork loin at a time, gently slide a pork loin into the hot oil and cook until it's light golden brown, turning it over often so both sides are completely submerged, 4 to 5 minutes. Remove the pork from the oil with tongs, and transfer to a paper towel–lined plate or a wire rack set in a rimmed baking sheet to drain. Skim off and discard any leftover crumbs in the oil with the ladle. Repeat with the remaining pork loins.

Bring the oil up to 375°F (190°C) over medium-high heat again and slide in a fried pork loin. Fry until golden brown and until the thickest part of the meat registers 145°F (63°C), 1 to 2 minutes. Transfer to a paper towel–lined plate or a wire rack set in a rimmed baking sheet to drain again. Repeat with the remaining pork loins. Enjoy immediately, served over warm white rice.

NOTE:
Thick sweet potato starch is coarse—similar to panko bread crumbs but a bit finer. Some brands will specify between thick and thin sweet potato starch. If you can only find thin, lightly spritz the starch with some water so that it clumps up and creates small beads.

Railway Bento Box

If you find a person in Taiwan old enough to remember the days when the island was under Japanese rule, chances are they will regale you with glowing stories about the era. It was a time associated with modernity, progress, and economic prosperity. My maternal great-grandfather trained as a doctor in Japan, which remains a deep source of pride for that side of the family. And my father was taught to refer to his mother as *okaasan*, the Japanese word for mother. To this day, loan words from Japan—like *motorcycle*, *bread*, *hospital*, and *baseball*—are scattered throughout the Taiwanese lexicon, all things popularized in Taiwan at the turn of the 20th century with new colonial government. However, the actual act of colonization was far from rosy, and for about seven years, bloody waves of uprisings against the Japanese by the locals—both ethnically Chinese and indigenous peoples—marred the island. These incidents have been largely wiped out of the public consciousness, and this selective amnesia has given way to a view of the past that fixates chiefly on the progress that Japan brought to the island.

One of the most exalted artifacts from that era is our modern railway system, which operates with Japanese synchronicity and precision, and the cuisine that accompanies it. While a primitive trolley system used to transport raw materials was created when Taiwan was under the jurisdiction of the Qing Dynasty, it was the Japanese who commissioned the first passenger trains and connected the island from top to bottom and side to side. With the advent of these trains came a flurry of business opportunities. In 1940, a train ride on the east coast of the island from the city of Hualien to Taitung would take eight dreary hours (today it takes about two). At the train platforms, entrepreneurial merchants would sell lunch boxes packaged in paper-thin wooden boxes and filled to the brim with rice, bamboo shoots, braised pork belly, or fried pork chops. They became such a hit that eventually, in 1949, the Taiwan Railway Administration took matters into their own hands and started producing packaged meals.

When my parents were young, these lunches were served by train staff in round stainless steel boxes, which could be dropped off for recycling afterward. The stations would clean and reuse the boxes, though they were eventually phased out for plastic because people kept on forgetting to return them. Today these train meals—which we call biàn dang 便當—remain a nostalgic symbol of the Japanese era. They can be purchased at most major railway stations across the island at dedicated stalls or bought aboard the trains themselves. The contents have stayed more or less the same—rice topped with slabs of pork, served with braised eggs and mildly seasoned greens, a balanced meal in a box designed to provide nourishment to weary travelers.

Pickled Mustard and Pork Noodle Soup

榨菜肉絲麵

Zhà Cài Ròu Sī Miàn

An import from the lower reaches of the Yangtze River in China likely brought over by Chinese refugees in the early 1950s, this is my go-to order at noodle restaurants across Taiwan. It's a clear noodle soup topped with thin slivers of pork accented with a pinch of sour from the pickled mustard stems. The topping is really minimalistic and held together only by a sparse dash of sugar and salt, but it's so addictive and adaptable that you can put it on top of rice or just a bed of cold noodles.

½ pound (225 g) pork tenderloin, cut into matchsticks	2 tablespoons canola or soybean oil
1 tablespoon soy sauce	2 garlic cloves, minced
2 teaspoons Taiwanese rice wine (michiu) or cooking sake	½ teaspoon white sugar
1 teaspoon toasted sesame oil	1 scallion, white and green parts minced and separated
¼ teaspoon ground white pepper	1 fresh bird's eye chili, thinly sliced (optional)
½ pound (225 g) preserved mustard stem (zhà cài 榨菜) (see Note)	Fine sea salt
1½ pounds (680 g) fresh wheat noodles or 11 ounces (310 g) dried wheat noodles	6½ cups (1.5 L) Bone Broth (page 357) or low-sodium chicken broth

In a medium bowl, combine the pork tenderloin with the soy sauce, rice wine, sesame oil, and white pepper, and mix thoroughly so the pork is evenly coated with sauce. Cover and set aside for 30 minutes.

Rinse the preserved mustard stem under running water. Slice into thin matchsticks. In a small bowl, combine the sliced preserved mustard stem and enough water to cover. Soak for 10 minutes.

Meanwhile, cook the noodles. Bring a medium pot of water to a rolling boil over high heat, add the fresh noodles, and cook until al dente, about 3 minutes. If using dried noodles, cook according to the package instructions. Drain in a colander and divide the noodles into serving bowls. Set aside for later.

Drain the pickled mustard slices through a sieve, discarding the soaking liquid. Squeeze out the excess water, and pat dry with paper towels.

In a wok set over medium-high heat, swirl in the oil. When the oil is hot, add the garlic and cook until fragrant, about 20 seconds. Add the marinated pork and cook until the edges of the pork turn opaque, about 30 seconds.

NOTE:

The salt levels of pickled mustard stems vary wildly by brand. Always wash, soak, and taste before using. If they're saltier than the ocean and make you flinch, you should definitely soak them longer.

PHOTOGRAPHY NOTE:

This bowl is a family heirloom passed down from photographer Ryan's grandmother.

Quickly toss in the sliced mustard stem, sugar, the white parts of the scallions, and the bird's eye chili, if using. Cook, stirring, until the pork is no longer pink and is fully cooked through, about 3 minutes. Taste and season with a pinch of salt if needed. Turn off the heat and divide the toppings evenly over the noodles in the serving bowls.

In a large stockpot, heat the bone broth over high heat until it comes to a boil. Turn off the heat, taste, and add a pinch of salt if you'd like (the pickled mustard stem will add a natural layer of saltiness to the broth, so extra salt is completely optional). Ladle the hot broth into the serving bowls, and garnish with the remaining green parts of the scallions. Enjoy immediately.

Japanese inventor Momofuku Ando is often credited as the creator of instant noodles and introduced the world to a new, magical type of convenience where deep-fried noodles and a flavor packet could be combined with boiling water to form a complete meal. But what stories often fail to mention is that Momofuku—who was born in Taiwan as Go Pek-Hok 吳百福 when the island was under Japanese rule—didn't actually invent the instant noodle. He simply introduced to the world a technique that was already being used in Taiwan.

Old-school Taiwanese instant noodles are these deep-fried egg noodles, usually sold stacked up together in plastic at the wet markets. They're shelf-stable and cooked to order, quickly boiled in broth and accompanied by thin slices of fish cake, some vegetables, and a gently poached egg. Because the noodles are deep-fried, they need only a couple of minutes in hot water to soften up.

Taiwanese Instant Noodles

鍋燒意麵
Guō Shāo Yì Miàn

2½ cups (590 ml) Bone Broth (page 357) or low-sodium chicken stock

¼ cup (5 g) bonito flakes

½ teaspoon fine sea salt, plus more to taste

¼ teaspoon ground white pepper, plus more to taste

1 bundle Deep-Fried Egg Noodles (recipe follows), about 2½ ounces (70 g) in total weight

1 or 2 large shell-on shrimp

1 ounce (30 g) pork tenderloin, cut into matchsticks

3 slices Japanese fish cake, also known as kamaboko, cut into ⅛-inch (3-mm) thick half-moons (optional)

1 small baby bok choy, halved

1 large egg

1 scallion, minced (for garnish)

In a small pot, add the bone broth and bring to a rolling boil over high heat. Add the bonito flakes, without stirring, and turn off the heat. Steep for 10 minutes. With a fine-mesh ladle, lift out the bonito flakes and discard.

Bring the stock to a brisk simmer over medium heat. Add the salt and white pepper, adding more if you'd like. Add the egg noodles and with chopsticks, neatly arrange the shrimp, pork, fish cakes (if using), and bok choy around and on top of the noodles. Reduce the heat to low. With chopsticks, gently create a hole in the middle of the noodles and crack the egg inside. Cover and wait until egg white is set, the shrimp is pink, and the pork is opaque, 3 to 4 minutes. Turn off the heat and garnish with the scallions. You can either eat directly out of the pot or transfer carefully to a large serving bowl.

NOTE:
Shell-on shrimp is traditional; you can peel the shrimp ahead of time if you'd like.

PHOTOGRAPHY NOTE:
This dish was traditionally cooked and served in the aluminum pot you see in this photograph. The pots are getting increasingly hard to find; very few vendors still use them.

Deep-Fried Egg Noodles

1½ cups (190 g) bread
flour

1 teaspoon fine sea salt

3 large egg whites (90 g)

Tapioca starch or
cornstarch

5 cups (1.1 L) canola or
soybean oil

SPECIAL EQUIPMENT:
stand mixer (optional); pasta machine

In a large mixing bowl, combine the bread flour, salt, and egg whites. Mix to form a shaggy dough. Bring the dough together with your hands and knead until it forms a solid mass and is relatively smooth, about 5 minutes. (Alternatively, knead in the bowl of a stand mixer with the dough hook attachment on low speed until it comes together, about 2 minutes.) Cover with plastic wrap, and let it rest at room temperature for 1 hour.

Set up a pasta machine with the rollers at the widest setting. Unwrap the dough and cut it in half. Flatten one piece of the dough, and feed through the machine. Fold the dough into thirds like a letter and run it through again. Dust the noodle sheet with tapioca starch on both sides. Repeat until the dough is completely smooth and glistening, passing it through the next couple of settings 2 to 3 times until it's 1/16 inch (2 mm) thick. Repeat with the second piece of dough.

Cut the pasta into thin spaghetti noodles and arrange them into 4 separate bundles, about 75 g each. Let the noodles rest for 10 minutes.

In a large wok or a heavy-bottomed pot, heat the oil over medium-high heat to 350°F (175°C).

Put one bundle of noodles in a spider strainer and spread them out so that the noodles are in an even single layer across the strainer, not clumped together. Carefully lower the spider strainer down into the hot oil. The oil will fizz and sparkle and the noodles will instantaneously expand. Flip the spider strainer upside down so that the noodles fall into the oil. If they get stuck, use chopsticks to gently push them out. Cook until the noodles are light golden brown, about 2 minutes. Remove the noodles with the spider strainer, and transfer to a paper towel–lined plate or a wire rack set in a rimmed baking sheet to drain. Repeat with the remaining bundles of noodles, frying one bundle at a time. Make sure the temperature stays at 350°F (175°C) for each round. When the fried noodles have completely cooled down to room temperature, they can be cooked right away, stored in a sealed plastic bag in the pantry for up to 2 months, or frozen for up to 4 months.

This was one of the first dishes I ever learned how to make: chunky nuggets of seasoned pork tenderloin are coated in a sticky mat of fish paste, cooked, and then added on top of a clear rice noodle soup with daikon, carrots, and chunks of Napa cabbage. As a very young child, I was in charge of the fish paste–coated pork; my job was to plop the meat gently into a pot of barely simmering water. Mom would leave a big batch of the cooked nuggets, a big stockpot of soup, and a large bowl of rice noodles on the counter for us to assemble our own bowls with.

Pork Nugget Vermicelli Soup

肉羹米粉
Ròu Gēng Mǐ Fěn

米粉羹
Bí Hún Kenn

FOR THE PORK NUGGETS:

½ pound (225 g) pork tenderloin

2 teaspoons soy sauce

1 teaspoon Taiwanese rice wine (michiu) or cooking sake

1 teaspoon white sugar

¼ teaspoon fine sea salt

⅛ teaspoon ground white pepper

1 tablespoon tapioca starch or cornstarch

½ pound (225 g) Fish Paste (page 361)

FOR THE SOUP:

3 medium dried shiitake mushrooms (10 g)

1 tablespoon canola or soybean oil

5 cups (1.1 L) Bone Broth (page 357) or low-sodium chicken stock

½ pound (225 g) Napa cabbage, chopped into 1-inch (2.5-cm) segments

¼ pound (115 g) carrot, peeled and cut into ½-inch (1-cm) cubes

¼ pound (115 g) daikon, peeled and cut into ½-inch (1-cm) cubes

¼ cup (5 g) bonito flakes

3 ounces (85 g) dried rice vermicelli noodles

1 teaspoon fine sea salt, plus more to taste

1 teaspoon white sugar, plus more to taste

2½ tablespoons tapioca starch or cornstarch

Ground white pepper

Black vinegar

Fresh cilantro sprigs (for garnish)

MAKE THE PORK NUGGETS: Slice the pork tenderloin into 2 × ½-inch (5 × 2-cm) nuggets. In a small bowl, combine the pork nuggets with the soy sauce, rice wine, sugar, salt, and white pepper. Mix thoroughly. Add the tapioca starch, and massage until the starch is completely absorbed and there is no more liquid, about 1 minute. Cover and marinate in the refrigerator for 30 minutes.

Take the pork out of the refrigerator, and add in the fish paste, mixing with your hands so that the pork is evenly coated.

(RECIPE CONTINUES)

Heat a pot of water over high heat until tiny bubbles begin to break on the surface of the water, then turn off the heat. One by one, carefully lower the nuggets into the pot of water. The fish paste will begin to solidify, turn whitish-gray, and form a craggy exterior around the pork. When all the nuggets are in the pot, reduce the heat to medium-high, and bring the liquid to a rapid boil. Cook until all the nuggets float, about 5 minutes. Ladle the pieces out with a spider strainer and set aside on a clean plate. Turn off the heat. The liquid can be reserved for soup or saved for another use. The pork nuggets can be used immediately or stored in the refrigerator for up to 2 days.

MAKE THE SOUP: In a small bowl, cover the dried shiitake mushrooms with water and soak until soft, about 1 hour. If you are in a rush, soak them in boiling water for 30 minutes (though they won't be nearly as flavorful). Remove the mushrooms from the liquid and squeeze out the excess water. Cut off the stems and discard. Thinly slice the mushroom caps and set aside.

In a large stockpot set over high heat, add the oil. When it's hot and shimmering, toss in the sliced shiitake mushrooms and cook, stirring, until fragrant, about 30 seconds. Pour in the bone broth, and add the Napa cabbage, carrots, and daikon. Crush the bonito flakes with your hands or a spoon so that they break off into small flecks and stir them in. Cover and bring to a rolling boil. Reduce the heat to a low simmer and cook until the daikon has turned translucent and is soft, 25 to 30 minutes.

Meanwhile, cook the vermicelli. Bring a medium pot of water to a rolling boil over high heat and add the vermicelli. Cook until al dente, about 1 minute. Drain in a colander and set aside.

Season the stockpot with soup with the salt and sugar, adding more if you'd like. Bring the heat up to medium so that it's at a brisk simmer. In a small bowl, whisk the tapioca starch and 3 tablespoons water to form a slurry. Stream the mixture into the soup, and stir until it thickens, about 30 seconds. Turn off the heat.

To serve, divide the vermicelli into serving bowls and arrange a handful of nuggets on top of each serving. Ladle the hot soup and vegetables on top to cover. Garnish each individual serving with white pepper, a small hit of black vinegar, and some cilantro.

家常菜

Family
Style

The Six-Part Meal

My husband and I sit huddled around our dining table in Taipei with the Notes app pulled up on his phone. "Okay, so I have potatoes, cheese, bagels, and wine written down," he says, checking his shopping list. "What else do we need?"

"Cold smoked salmon!" I say. "And a couple of bags of avocados, please."

He types it all down and squeezes my hand. "Oh, I'm excited," he says, smiling. We're planning our monthly trip to Costco, and it's sincerely one of our most exciting pastimes here in Taiwan.

More than 30 years ago, when my parents first immigrated to Los Angeles from Taiwan, they shared a similar ritual, but instead of avocados and smoked salmon, their list consisted of fresh clams and bags of water spinach. Every week, regardless of the traffic forecast, they would load up the car and drive an hour east from the San Fernando Valley, where we lived, to the San Gabriel Valley just to shop at 99 Ranch Market, a Taiwanese-owned supermarket chain with a lush inventory of Asian goods. My mom and dad would immediately grab two shopping carts and divide up the tasks. My brother would sit in the one manned by my dad, and they'd head straight to the live seafood section, and I would ride with my mom and beeline toward the produce. We'd stay in the store for an hour or two, until both carts were loaded to the brim with everything they craved—squirming live shrimp, large Korean pears, dried rice noodles from a factory in northern Taiwan, and bags of freshly ground fish paste.

I never truly understood the fervor and loyalty my family had to 99 Ranch until I settled full-time in Taiwan with my husband and realized embarrassedly that we had developed a similar relationship with Costco. At first, having constant access to Taiwanese food was delightful; it felt like we'd won the lottery. But after a while we began to crave the creature comforts of Western society—good bread, fresh salads, and solid blocks of cheese. Our friends, who were in a similar situation, recommended Costco as a solution to our cravings. At first we were skeptical; but today, we can probably navigate the store blindfolded and still manage to grab everything we want.

Similarly, for my immigrant parents in Los Angeles who barely spoke any English in the 1990s, processing and cooking their Taiwanese grocery haul was a coping mechanism for being in a strange and faraway land. Good food is transportive, and my mom made a concerted effort to bring our family into the vibrant embrace of Taiwan every single night. Taiwanese family meals are markedly different from what's served in restaurants. There's no deep-frying at home (because lard used to be the traditional oil of choice, and it would take an immense amount of lard to properly fry anything). Dumplings—whether made of rice or wheat—rarely appeared on our dinner table; it was too much effort. Everything was chopped, sautéed, and seasoned in one go with such rough approximation that you'd think my mom was making it up as she went.

She had an unspoken rule of six, and that was that every day, six elements would show up without fail on our table: soup, seafood, meat, vegetables, rice, and fruit. Soup was either a lightly salted broth of pork ribs with cubed daikon or an earthy shiitake mushroom soup stewed with a whole chicken. And seafood was usually a crispy butterflied milkfish belly patted

generously with white pepper, or a steamed whitefish seasoned with a light dash of soy sauce. Meat would often be braised pork belly or her version of three-cup chicken made with Heineken beer instead of Taiwanese rice wine, and the vegetables and fruit were whatever was in season—often water spinach and Korean pears, respectively. A glistening pot of short-grain rice, of course, held everything together; it wouldn't be a complete dinner otherwise. On a more indulgent day, more dishes would appear on the table, like stir-fried rice vermicelli dotted with meaty chunks of shiitake mushrooms or ripped-up chunks of Napa cabbage that were braised and folded in with a little too much dried shrimp. It was here at the family dining table that I began my education in the food of my ancestors, and despite access to a multiplicity of cuisines and ingredients in the cultural rainbow that is Los Angeles, my mother never once strayed from her Taiwanese repertoire.

One would think that because I'm multicultural—born in America to Taiwanese parents—I would be content with the food wherever I am. But as years of living abroad have taught me, the grass is truly always greener. Now that I've been away from California for so long, I dearly miss the crispness of fresh romaine lettuce, a good burger, and the brininess of raw oysters with a wedge of lemon. But if you wrestle me away from Taiwan, I assure you that after a while I would start dreaming of soft pork ribs bobbing in soup and creamy chunks of fresh luffa gourd harvested straight from the vine.

With all that said, this chapter is dedicated to the people of Taiwan who've been away from home for a while. I hope these family-style recipes can transport you back into the embrace of our island, or to childhood memories of a kitchen warmed by a steaming pot of rice and soup. And if you have your own families now, I hope you can pass these flavors down to your loved ones like my mom did with me—a reminder of where we come from and of the sustenance that made us who we are today.

Quick Seafood Congee

海鮮粥
Hǎi Xiān Zhōu

海產糜
Hǎi Sán Muâi

For years I was convinced my mom made this dish up because she was feeling lazy. All she would do was fold in day-old leftover rice with whatever shellfish we had in the fridge, some shiitake mushrooms, minced celery, and fried shallots, cover it up with broth, and call it dinner. On more luxurious days, the seafood included gorgeous, chewy slabs of abalone and fat, fresh clams. It's a one-pot wonder teeming with flavor, and it wasn't until I was an adult that I realized that my mom wasn't actually being innovative or lazy at all; she was just re-creating a childhood dish of hers. While congee is often associated with breakfast, this particular version is available all day long—especially in the south of Taiwan, where my family is from. It was a noted favorite of my maternal great-grandmother, who would stop and eat a bowl of this on her way back home from her morning wet market runs.

1	cup (200 g) short-grain rice, also known as sushi rice
5	medium dried shiitake mushrooms
1	tablespoon small dried shrimp
3	tablespoons canola or soybean oil
1	1-inch piece fresh ginger (10 g), peeled and sliced into thin matchsticks
4	cups (1 L) Bone Broth (page 357) or low-sodium chicken stock
¼	pound (115 g) peeled and deveined small shrimp
¼	pound (115 g) small scallops
¼	pound (115 g) squid, cleaned and cut into rings
1	teaspoon Taiwanese rice wine (michiu) or cooking sake
½	cup (80 g) minced celery
½	cup (40 g) fried shallots (store-bought or homemade; page 368)
½	teaspoon fine sea salt, plus more to taste

Ground white pepper

Cook the rice at least 4 hours before (for instructions on how, see page 360). Transfer to a large bowl, and let it cool down to room temperature. Alternatively, use 2 cups (420 g) cooked leftover rice.

In a medium bowl, cover the dried shiitake mushrooms with water and soak until they're soft, about 1 hour. If you are in a rush, soak them in boiling water for 30 minutes (though they won't be nearly as flavorful). In a small bowl, submerge the dried shrimp in water for 10 minutes. Drain the dried shrimp through a fine-mesh sieve. Remove the shiitake mushrooms from the bowl and squeeze out any excess water. Trim the shiitake stems and discard. Thinly slice the shiitake mushroom caps and set aside.

NOTE:
My mom usually keeps a pot of this simmering in a Tatung steamer all day. The rice will eventually soak up most of the liquid and become really thick; just add a bit of extra broth or water to thin it out.

In a large pot set over high heat, drizzle in the oil. When the oil is hot and shimmering, add the sliced shiitake mushroom, dried shrimp, and ginger and stir until it smells lovely, about 10 seconds.

Pour in the bone broth, cover, and bring the stock to a rolling boil. Add in the shrimp, scallops, squid, and rice wine, and cook, stirring, until the shrimp just begins to turn pink, about 2 minutes. Add the cooked rice and stir constantly so that the rice breaks up into the soup and all the seafood is completely cooked through and opaque, about another 2 minutes. Mix in the celery and shallots. Season with the salt, then taste and add more if you'd like. Turn off the heat and add a dash of white pepper to taste. Enjoy while hot.

Ivy's grandfather owned a rice vermicelli factory in the countryside of Tainan, and she remembers playing elaborate games of hide-and-seek on the premises as a little kid, weaving behind the machinery and ducking underneath the massive bamboo trays that propped the fresh batches of hair-thin noodles in the hot sun to dry. Despite being surrounded by the product all day long, she never got tired of vermicelli. In fact, her nickname as a kid was actually "rice vermicelli," because her relatives knew making a big pot of it would instantaneously bring her joy. The trick here is to blanch the noodles in boiling water instead of soaking them in water for a couple of hours (a common mistake). Blanching softens the noodles so that they can really hold the sauce and ensures they don't turn mushy. When buying rice vermicelli, look for the package with a red and yellow tiger on it. It's made in northern Taiwan and can be procured at most major Asian supermarkets.

Stir-Fried Rice Vermicelli

炒米粉
Chǎo Mǐ Fěn

炒米粉
Tshá Bí Hún

FOR THE PORK:

- ¼ pound (115 g) pork tenderloin, cut into matchsticks
- 2 teaspoons soy sauce
- 1 teaspoon toasted sesame oil
- 1 teaspoon Taiwanese rice wine (michiu) or cooking sake

FOR THE NOODLES:

- 5 medium dried shiitake mushrooms
- 1 tablespoon small dried shrimp
- 2½ tablespoons soy sauce
- ½ teaspoon fine sea salt, plus more to taste
- ½ teaspoon white sugar
- ½ teaspoon toasted sesame oil
- ½ teaspoon black vinegar
- ¼ teaspoon ground white pepper, plus more to taste
- ¼ pound (115 g) dried rice vermicelli noodles, such as Tiger brand
- 2 tablespoons lard or canola or soybean oil
- ½ pound (225 g) Taiwanese flat cabbage or green cabbage, cored and cut crosswise into ½-inch (1-cm) strips
- 1 ounce carrot (30 g), peeled and cut into matchsticks

PREPARE THE PORK: In a small bowl, combine the pork tenderloin with the soy sauce, sesame oil, and rice wine. Marinate for 15 minutes.

MAKE THE NOODLES: In a medium bowl, cover the shiitake mushrooms with water, and soak until they're soft, about 1 hour. If you are in a rush, soak them in boiling water for 30 minutes (though they won't be nearly as flavorful). In a small bowl, cover the dried shrimp with water, and soak for 10 minutes. Drain the dried shrimp through a fine-mesh sieve. Remove the shiitake mushrooms from the bowl and squeeze out any excess water. Reserve 2 tablespoons of the shiitake mushroom soaking liquid and discard the rest. Trim the shiitake stems and discard. Thinly slice the shiitake mushroom caps and set aside.

(RECIPE CONTINUES)

In a medium bowl, make the sauce for the noodles by mixing together the soy sauce, salt, sugar, sesame oil, black vinegar, white pepper, and the reserved shiitake mushroom soaking liquid.

Bring a large pot of water to a rolling boil over high heat, and blanch the dried rice noodles until al dente, about 1 minute. Drain in a colander and set aside.

In a wok over medium-high heat, add the lard. When it's hot and shimmering, add the sliced shiitake mushrooms and dried shrimp, and cook until it smells lovely, about 40 seconds. Add the marinated pork, and stir-fry until the pork is medium-rare and still slightly pink, about 30 seconds. Remove the shiitake mushrooms, dried shrimp, and pork from the wok, but reserve the lard. Increase the heat to high, toss in the cabbage, and stir-fry until wilted and soft, about 1 minute.

Use your spatula to gently push the cabbage to the sides, leaving space in the middle of the wok. Pour the sauce in the center of the wok, and immediately add the rice noodles and carrots on top. Add the cooked shiitake mushrooms, dried shrimp, and pork back into the wok. Toss and stir until the liquid is completely absorbed, 1 to 2 minutes. Taste and add more salt and white pepper if you'd like. Turn off the heat, and transfer everything to a clean serving platter. Enjoy while hot.

Liver is a delicate ingredient that has be handled with immense care or else it'll turn leathery and muddy, which isn't how anyone wants their liver—or any food, for that matter—to come out. The key is making sure the liver is still rosy and tender in the middle. The sweetness from the soy sauce–based marinade really complements the heavy, earthy notes of the offal, and it's especially lovely when accented with thin slivers of quick-pickled daikon and carrots.

Pork Liver Stir-Fry

炒豬肝
Chǎo Zhū Gān

炒豬肝
Tshá Ti Kuann

FOR THE MARINADE:

- ½ pound (225 g) pork liver
- 1 teaspoon white sugar
- ½ teaspoon soy sauce
- ½ teaspoon fine sea salt
- ¼ teaspoon ground white pepper
- ¼ teaspoon five-spice powder (optional)

FOR THE STIR-FRY:

- 1 teaspoon Taiwanese rice wine (michiu) or cooking sake
- 1 teaspoon soy sauce
- 1 teaspoon toasted sesame oil
- 2 tablespoons canola or soybean oil

Quick Daikon and Carrot Pickle (for garnish; page 349)

MARINATE THE PORK LIVER: Slice the pork liver into ½-inch (1-cm) bite-size discs, about 2 inches (5 cm) wide each. Transfer to a fine-mesh strainer and rinse the pieces under running water until the water runs clear. In a medium bowl, combine the liver with the sugar, soy sauce, salt, white pepper, and five-spice powder, if using. Cover and refrigerate for 1 hour.

PREPARE THE STIR-FRY: In a small bowl, make a sauce by combining the rice wine, soy sauce, and sesame oil.

In a wok set over medium-high heat, heat the oil. When it's hot and shimmering, add the liver and cook, stirring gently, until it firms up but is still tender, 2 to 3 minutes. Test to see if it's done by cutting one in half; if it's slightly pink in the center, it's done. Quickly pour the sauce around the perimeter of the wok. Stir until the sauce is absorbed and coats the liver, about 10 seconds. Turn off the heat. Transfer to a serving plate and garnish with slivers of pickled daikon and carrots.

Pan-Fried Milkfish Belly

煎虱目魚肚
Jiān Shī Mù Yú Dù

煎虱目魚肚
Tsian Sat Bàk Hî Tōo

A bony saltwater fish with an impressive range from South Africa all the way to Hawaii, the milkfish has been a culinary constant throughout Taiwan's history. The indigenous Siraya tribe that inhabited southern Taiwan called it mata, their word for eye, after the fish's distinct beady eyes. While the fish has been around since indigenous times, milkfish farming was encouraged during the Dutch occupation of Taiwan in the 17th century as a way to stimulate trade and generate taxes, and the farms relied on the natural estuaries around the south of the island to harvest and collect the juvenile fish. Today the fish is an icon. There's an industry-sponsored milkfish museum in Tainan that brags about the fish's history, and a small coastal district in the same city is home to a giant milkfish statue comprising a gawking baby with a milkfish head called "Milkfish Kid" (which caused controversy after its debut because it turned out to be much uglier than anyone could ever have imagined). Sometimes labeled as bangus, milkfish can be procured at most major Asian supermarkets, though this recipe can be adapted for any fish fillet, like mackerel or salmon.

1	milkfish belly, butterflied, about 7 to 8 ounces (200 to 230 g) in total weight	½	teaspoon coarse salt
2	teaspoons Taiwanese rice wine (michiu) or cooking sake	¼	teaspoon ground white pepper
		¼	cup (60 ml) canola or soybean oil

Place the fish on a plate and add the rice wine, rubbing it in so that the fish is coated in it. Let it rest for 20 minutes.

Place the fish on top of a layer of paper towels. Pat the fish dry with more paper towels. It's important the fish is completely dry or else it won't get crispy. Massage the salt and white pepper on both sides of the fish.

In a flat-bottomed wok or skillet, heat the oil over high heat. When it's hot and shimmering, slide the fish in gently, skin side down. Cover with a lid and cook for 10 seconds (it will splatter and pop, so a lid is absolutely necessary). Reduce the heat to medium and cook until the bottom of the fish is golden brown and crispy, about 2 minutes. Flip the fish over with a spatula and cover the pan. Increase the heat to high and cook for another 10 seconds. Reduce the heat down to medium again (last time, I promise), and fry until the other side is also golden brown, 1 to 2 minutes. Transfer to a clean plate and enjoy immediately.

Luffa Gourd with Clams

絲 瓜 蛤 蜊
Sī Guā Gé Lí

菜 瓜 蚶 仔
Tshài Kue Ham Á

This is a recipe from my friend Acer Wang, who, in case you were wondering, was indeed named after the Taiwanese electronics company. An engineer by day, he's a marvelous cook and showed me his version of this classic luffa dish after a lovely stroll through his neighborhood wet market. Luffas are vibrant, jade-green summer gourds and taste like a cross between a zucchini and a cucumber, though they get quite tough and fibrous as they ripen on the vine. Sometimes they're grown until they're old and stringy and made into sponges for bathing. Keep in mind that luffas are a warm-weather vegetable, so they might be a bit more difficult to source in colder months.

1	pound (450 g) fresh Manila or short-neck clams
2	teaspoons fine sea salt, divided
1½	tablespoons canola or soybean oil
1	½-inch piece fresh ginger (5 g), peeled and cut into matchsticks
3	garlic cloves, minced
1½	pounds (680 g) luffa gourd, peeled and cut into ½-inch (1.5-cm) half-moons
¼	cup (60 ml) low-sodium chicken broth or water
⅛	teaspoon ground white pepper, plus more to taste

In a medium bowl, combine the clams with 1 teaspoon of the salt. Add water to barely cover the clams. Cover and set aside in a cool, dark place, and let rest for at least 2 hours or up to 6 hours. This process purges sand and grit from the clams. Scrub the clams with a brush, drain, and set aside.

Set a wok over medium heat, and swirl in the oil. Add in the ginger and garlic, and cook, stirring until aromatic, about 30 seconds. Add the luffa gourd and the remaining 1 teaspoon salt, and stir-fry until the edges of the luffa begin to brown, 1 to 2 minutes.

Slide the clams into the wok and increase the heat to high. Pour in the chicken broth around the perimeter of the pan. Cover and cook, shaking the wok occasionally until all the clams are completely opened up, 3 to 4 minutes. Pick out and discard any clams that have not opened up. Season with the white pepper, adding more if you'd like. Turn off the heat and transfer the luffa and clams to a rimmed serving plate. Enjoy immediately.

Bitter Melon with Salted Duck Egg

鹹蛋苦瓜
Xián Dàn Kǔ Guā

鹹卵苦瓜
Khôo Kue Kiâm Nn̄g

Bitter melon gets a bad rap, and that's because it's often served out of balance—cooked with too much oil or not enough proper seasoning. The opposite of bitter isn't sweetness, it's saltiness, so the strategy here is to use a generous touch of salt. This is a recipe from my friend Acer Wang, who emulsifies the egg yolk into a creamy sauce first before tossing the whites and melon in.

1	large green or white bitter melon, about 1 pound (450 g) in total weight	2	tablespoons canola or soybean oil
6	cups (1.4 L) water	2	garlic cloves, minced
1	teaspoon fine sea salt	¼	teaspoon salt, plus more to taste
2	cooked salted duck eggs (see Note)	½	teaspoon toasted sesame oil
1	teaspoon Taiwanese rice wine (michiu) or cooking sake	1	scallion, green part only, minced
½	teaspoon white sugar		

Trim off the top and bottom of the bitter melon. Slice it in half lengthwise. Scrape out and discard the soft, pithy center with a spoon. Cut the bitter melon crosswise into thin ⅛-inch (3-mm) half-moons. Prepare an ice bath to the side.

In a medium pot, combine the water and salt and bring to a rolling boil over high heat. Add the bitter melon and cook for 40 seconds. Turn off the heat and use a spider strainer to transfer the bitter melon to the ice water bath to cool completely, about 20 seconds. Transfer the bitter melon to a paper towel–lined plate and drain well.

Peel the cooked salted duck eggs and separate the yolks and whites. In a small bowl, combine the yolks, rice wine, and sugar. Mash and mix it all together with the flat side of a fork. Roughly chop the whites and set aside.

In a wok set over medium heat, add the oil. When it begins to shimmer, add the garlic, and stir-fry until it smells lovely, about 30 seconds. Add the seasoned and mashed egg yolks and cook, stirring constantly, until it gets bubbly and foamy, about 10 seconds. Increase the heat to high, and quickly add the egg whites and bitter melon. Mix until the egg completely coats the bitter melon and the bitter melon softens a bit, 1 to 2 minutes. Season with the salt, adding more to taste. Drizzle in the sesame oil around the perimeter of the pan. Toss in the scallion greens and give it one last good stir to combine. Turn off the heat, and transfer to a clean plate. Enjoy immediately.

NOTE:
Most salted duck eggs in America, which can easily be procured at an Asian supermarket, are already cooked. In Taiwan, we have access to both raw and hard-boiled versions. If you happen to get a raw one, just hard-boil it like you would a normal egg.

Sweet potato leaves grow like weeds here in Taiwan, so much so that I often compost the excess or give them away to friends. They're one of the few things I don't purposefully cultivate in my garden, yet they insist on reincarnating every chance they get. They're a leafy green that's looked down upon, especially among the older generation here in Taiwan, precisely because they were an ingredient that thrived in the toughest of conditions and so were often all people had to eat in times of famine. While the leaves of the sweet potato are indeed attached to actual sweet potatoes, the varieties that are sold at grocery stores and wet markets are bred especially for their leaves. With heart-shaped foliage and hollow stems, they're in the same family as water spinach, which can be prepared exactly the same way.

Sweet Potato Leaves Stir-Fry

炒地瓜葉
Chǎo Dì Guā Yè

炒番薯葉
Tshá Han Tsû Hiòh

2 tablespoons canola or soybean oil

2 garlic cloves, minced

½ pound (225 g) sweet potato leaves with stems attached, tough fibrous parts discarded

1 tablespoon water, plus more if needed

½ teaspoon fine sea salt

Heat a wok over high heat and add in the oil. When the oil is shimmering, add the garlic and stir until fragrant, about 10 seconds. Add the sweet potato leaves, and immediately swirl in the water around the edge of the wok, creating steam. Stir until the leaves are wilted and the stems are soft, 1 to 2 minutes. If it's too dry, add another 1 tablespoon water. Season with the salt and mix thoroughly. Turn off the heat, and transfer to a clean plate. Enjoy immediately.

NOTE:
Street vendors will sometimes dress this dish up with a dollop of Garlic Puree (page 367) and Braised Minced Pork Belly (page 90).

The dish has a unique, briny hit to it, which comes from dehydrated flounder and dried shrimp—both of which impart a fishy, almost fermented shrimp paste–like aroma to the dish. The cabbage is but a conduit for the flavors of the land and sea; sometimes people will even top it off with dried scallops or deep-fried pork rinds if they're feeling fancy. The flounder can easily be found in most Asian supermarkets in the States, though if you really can't find it, a couple of dashes of instant dashi powder will do the trick.

Braised Napa Cabbage

白菜滷
Bái Cài Lǔ

白菜滷
Pèh Tshài Lóo

5   medium dried shiitake mushrooms

1   ounce (30 g) dried tofu skin (optional)

8   small dried wood ear mushrooms

1   tablespoon small dried shrimp

3   tablespoons lard or canola or soybean oil

½   ounce (15 g) dried flounder, sometimes known as dried stockfish, cut into 1-inch (2.5-cm) squares (see Notes)

4   garlic cloves, minced

1   pound (450 g) Napa cabbage, ripped into 2-inch (5-cm) chunks

1   cup (240 ml) Bone Broth (page 357) or low-sodium chicken stock

½   large carrot (50 g), peeled and cut into thin 1 × 2-inch (2.5 x 5-cm) slices

½   teaspoon fine sea salt, plus more to taste

⅛   teaspoon ground white pepper, plus more to taste

SPECIAL EQUIPMENT: mortar and pestle or food processor (optional)

NOTES:
This dish eats on the softer side. The texture is really based on personal preference; if you'd like your cabbage a bit firmer, cook it for a shorter amount of time.

Dried flounder (biǎn yú 扁魚) is also sometimes labeled as brill fish, dà dì yú 大地魚, or ròu yú 肉魚. Chinese medicine stores might also have it in stock, sometimes in powdered form. If you can only get your hands on the powder, substitute it 1:1 by weight and add it directly into the cabbage mixture.

In medium bowl, cover the dried shiitake mushrooms with water and soak until they're soft, about 1 hour. If you are in a rush, soak them in boiling water for 30 minutes (though they won't be nearly as flavorful). In a large heatproof bowl, cover the dried tofu skin, if using, with boiling water and soak for 30 minutes. In another medium heatproof bowl, cover the wood ear mushrooms with boiling water and also soak for 30 minutes. In a small bowl, cover the dried shrimp with water and soak for 10 minutes.

Drain the dried shrimp through a fine-mesh sieve. Drain the tofu skin and chop it into 1 × 2-inch (2.5 × 5-cm) segments. Drain the wood ear mushrooms and with a knife or scissors, trim off and discard any tough, craggy bits. If they're larger than a half dollar, cut them in half. Remove the shiitake mushrooms from the bowl and squeeze out any excess water. Trim the shiitake stems and discard. Thinly slice the shiitake mushroom caps and set aside.

In a wok set over low heat, add the lard. When the lard is hot and shimmering, add the dried flounder. Fry the dried flounder pieces, stirring often, until they turn golden brown and begin to crisp up like bacon, about 4 minutes. Be very careful to make sure not to burn them; they will turn bitter. Remove the fried flounder from the wok and drain it on a paper towel–lined plate, reserving the oil in the wok. When the flounder is cool enough to

(RECIPE CONTINUES)

handle, transfer it to a mortar and pestle or food processor, and crush the fried flounder pieces into a powder (or alternatively, place it in a plastic bag, and crush it into fine pieces with your hands).

Heat the reserved oil over medium-high, and add the dried shrimp, sliced shiitake mushrooms, and garlic, stirring until fragrant, about 20 seconds. Toss in the Napa cabbage, and stir-fry to combine, about 2 minutes. Pour in the bone broth, the crushed flounder powder, the wood ear mushrooms, and the dried tofu skin, if using. Bring the liquid to a rolling boil. Stir again, cover, and reduce the heat to low. Simmer, stirring occasionally, until the Napa cabbage is soft and wilted, 10 to 12 minutes. Add in the carrots and cook, covered, for another 3 minutes. Turn off the heat and season with salt and white pepper, adding more if you'd like. Enjoy while hot.

Shallow-frying the tofu before coating it in sauce creates a fun dichotomy of textures; the tofu is firm on the outside but soft on the inside, and is then draped in a delectable sweet and savory concoction of soy sauce, sugar, and sesame oil. There are so many variations of this dish throughout Asia—with chili peppers, with a lot more scallions, or with a heaping dollop of oyster sauce, though Taiwanese households keep it rather toned down.

Red-Braised Tofu

紅燒豆腐
Hóng Shāo Dòu Fu

紅燒豆腐
Âng Sio Tāu Hū

- 1 box (350 g) firm tofu
- ¼ cup (60 ml) canola or soybean oil
- ¼ cup (60 ml) water
- 2 tablespoons soy sauce
- 2 teaspoons coarse raw sugar, such as demerara
- ½ teaspoon toasted sesame oil
- ¼ teaspoon fine sea salt
- 1 1-inch piece fresh ginger (10 g), peeled and sliced
- 1 scallion, cut into 1-inch (2.5-cm) segments
- ¼ cup (25 g) thinly sliced carrots, cut into matchsticks

Gently pat the tofu with a paper towel to get rid of excess moisture. Slice the block of tofu in half lengthwise. Cut the block crosswise into 5 slices so there are 10 pieces total.

In a wok over high heat, pour in the oil, and heat it up until wisps of smoke begin to appear. Gently slide in the sliced tofu. Cook, flipping the tofu slices over occasionally with a spatula, until both sides develop a very light golden brown crust, 2 to 3 minutes on each side. Turn off the heat and transfer the fried tofu on top of the paper towel–lined plate to drain. Reserve 1 tablespoon oil and discard the rest.

In a small bowl, make the sauce by mixing together the water, soy sauce, sugar, sesame oil, and salt.

Heat the reserved 1 tablespoon oil in the wok over medium heat. When the oil begins to shimmer, add the ginger and cook until fragrant, about 30 seconds. Gently slide in the cooked tofu, and pour the sauce around the perimeter of the wok. The liquid will begin to gently bubble and thicken around the tofu. Cook and reduce, flipping the tofu around multiple times, about 5 minutes. When there is still a bit of liquid in the wok, increase the heat to high and add the scallions and carrots. Toss until everything is evenly mixed together, about 10 seconds. Turn off the heat, and transfer to a clean serving plate. Enjoy immediately.

Tribute Ball Soup

貢丸湯
Gòng Wán Tāng

摃丸湯
Kòng Uân Thng

"The meat should be so fresh that it quivers," says Huang Shih-Kai 黃世凱, as he pounds the pork with two large batons. "We use the hind leg of the pig." Huang is the third-generation proprietor of a local meatball brand called Hai Rei Meatballs 海瑞摃丸, based in the northern city of Hsinchu. The city is known for their tribute balls, or gòng wán 貢丸, a Taiwanese meatball so incredibly elastic and rubbery that you can actually play Ping-Pong with it. *Gong* means tribute, but it's also an alliteration of the Taiwanese word for "to pound" (kòng 摃) and how it got its name. In the late 1940s, Huang's grandfather and the brand's namesake Hai-Rei started off on a street corner selling rice vermicelli noodles and would give out a meatball soup to pair as part of a lunch set. He eventually became so well-known for his homemade meatballs that he pivoted his entire business to making them. "Back then, each serving just had one meatball because it took so long to make them," Shih-Kai explains. He says that, in those days, a single person could churn out only about ten pounds (4.5 kg) of the meatballs before calling it a day. It was imperative to source the slab of pork before postmortem rigidity set in and stiffened the meat, and the chef would have to immediately pound the pork with a wooden mallet until it broke all sense of resistance and melted into a bright pink slime. Today—thankfully—there are machines for this. This recipe isn't Huang's grandfather's but a version developed to cater to the average home cook. Egg white strengthens the texture of the meatball and gets it to a similar level of elasticity as the traditional version.

FOR THE MEATBALLS:

1 pound (450 g) pork tenderloin

2 ounces (60 g) pork back fat

1½ teaspoons fine sea salt

2 large eggs, whites only

1 garlic clove, chopped

1½ tablespoons white sugar

1 teaspoon toasted sesame oil

¼ teaspoon ground white pepper

¼ cup (60 ml) ice water

FOR THE SOUP:

8 cups (2 L) water

2 teaspoons fine sea salt, plus more to taste

⅛ teaspoon ground white pepper, plus more to taste

¼ cup (40 g) minced celery (for garnish)

MAKE THE MEATBALLS: Cut the pork tenderloin into 1-inch (2.5-cm) cubes. Transfer them to a large resealable plastic bag, press so that it's flat and in a single layer, and freeze until the pork is partially frozen, about 2 hours. Finely mince the pork back fat and transfer it to a small resealable plastic bag, press so that it's flat and in a single layer, and freeze until it's partially frozen, about 2 hours. Freeze the paddle attachment of the stand mixer, if using, as well.

SPECIAL EQUIPMENT:
food processor; stand mixer with paddle attachment (optional)

(RECIPE CONTINUES)

In a food processor, combine the partially frozen pork tenderloin with the salt. Pulse on high speed until it becomes a pink sludge, about 1 minute. If the sludge gets stuck, use a spoon to loosen up the mixture around the blades and then keep blending. The final consistency will look unsettlingly similar to the pink slime that chicken nuggets are made out of. If you still see visible chunks of meat, keep blending. Add the egg whites, garlic, sugar, sesame oil, and white pepper, and pulse until all the ingredients have completely incorporated inside, about another 1 minute. Don't get lazy with the blending; it's really important to get a really smooth and shiny paste with an almost latex-like sheen. Add in the ice water and pulse until it's completely incorporated in, about 1 minute. Cover with plastic wrap and refrigerate to keep cold.

Transfer the partially frozen pork back fat to a cutting board and mince it very finely again.

With a silicone spatula, mix the fat into the chilled pork paste until the fat is distributed evenly throughout, about 2 minutes. Alternatively, churn in a stand mixer on low speed with the frozen paddle attachment for 1 minute ("You want to aerate it," says Shih-Kai).

MAKE THE SOUP: In a medium pot, bring the water to a simmer over medium heat until tiny bubbles begin to break on the surface of the water. Immediately turn off the heat.

Shape the pork sludge mixture into twenty even meatballs, about 30 g each, and add the meatballs to the water as you make them. You can do this with a wet spoon, with really wet hands, or by picking up a large handful of the pink sludge with one hand and pushing it through the space between your index finger and thumbs (strange, but really effective!).

When all the meatballs are in, increase the heat to high and bring the liquid to a rolling boil. Reduce the heat down to medium, and simmer until the meatballs are completely cooked through, 5 to 7 minutes. To check if they're cooked through, cut a meatball in half. If it's still pink in the middle, it has to be cooked longer. Turn the heat off, and season with the salt and white pepper, adding more to taste.

To serve, ladle 4 to 5 meatballs with some soup into a small bowl, and garnish with the celery.

This recipe is inspired by directions from Yuting Yeh, who grew up in Taiwan and moved to the States in her teens. I met her through the Taiwanese Home Cooking group on Facebook, a small yet prolific corner of the internet where the Taiwanese diaspora congregates to share their culinary creations, and where she used to be an administrator. "I was craving a safe and inclusive space with a sole focus on the food from Taiwan," she tells me. Indulging in recipes from home has been a way for her to stay connected to the island, and she often calls up her grandmother for advice. This hearty soup is a regular staple throughout most Taiwanese households around the world. Daikon and pork are the bare minimum, though Yuting says she'll occasionally add corn and carrots to bulk it up.

Daikon and Pork Soup

蘿蔔排骨湯
Luó Bo Pái Gǔ Tāng

菜頭排骨湯
Tshài Thâu Pâi Kut Thng

- 1 pound (450 g) spare pork ribs, cut into 1-inch (2.5-cm) chunks
- 1 pound (450 g) medium daikon, peeled and cut into 1-inch (5-cm) oblique chunks
- 1 tablespoon Taiwanese rice wine (michiu) or cooking sake
- 2 scallions, tied into a knot
- 1 1-inch piece fresh ginger (10 g), unpeeled and sliced
- ½ tablespoon fine sea salt, plus more to taste
- Ground white pepper, plus more to taste
- Toasted sesame oil
- Fresh cilantro sprigs (for garnish)

In a medium pot, combine the spare pork ribs and enough water to cover, and bring to a rolling boil over high heat. Reduce the heat to medium, and briskly simmer for about 5 minutes. Turn off the heat. Drain the pork ribs in a colander in the sink. Rinse the ribs under cool running water, getting rid of any scum.

In a large pot over high heat, bring 7 cups (1.6 L) water to a rolling boil. Add the pork ribs, daikon, rice wine, scallions, and ginger. Cover and cook until the liquid comes to a boil again, then reduce the heat to low and keep it at a gentle simmer until the ribs are soft and tender, about 40 minutes. Season with salt and ground white pepper, adding more if you'd like. Remove and discard the ginger and scallions before serving.

Divide into soup bowls and enjoy while hot. Add a couple of drops of sesame oil and fresh cilantro sprigs to taste.

PHOTOGRAPHY NOTE:
These hand-painted tiles were loaned to us by the Museum of Old Taiwan Tiles in Chiayi. They were in vogue from 1915 to 1935 and exclusive to wealthy families.

Indigenous Taiwan:
The People Before Us

Aeles Lrawbalrate guides me through our daily walk in the forest, and the first thing we're doing today is spelunking in the caves near her house. Large, dramatic clusters of elephant ears have sprouted at the entrance, and we giddily snap photos of each other from inside the cave, our bodies backlit but dimly illuminated by the neon green glow of the sunlight hitting the leaves. Once we've had our fun, it's time to procure our groceries for the day. The caveat is that there are no stores; we're foraging from the forest around us. We pick up handfuls of dark, heart-shaped leaves wrapped around the trunk of a nearby paper mulberry tree. The plant's name is dangaw, the Rukai word for betel leaf. Peppery and herbaceous, it's lovely in a sausage or as an accent in a pork dumpling. We stumble across unruly clusters of citrus and a chandelier of prickly wild bitter melon dangling from the forest canopy. "I have a food map in my head of the forest," Aeles says, smiling. "Before, we all did."

In 2017, I lived with Aeles for a month as a volunteer, working as a helper at her restaurant, Dawana 達瓦娜家園, in southeastern Taiwan. A chef, restaurant owner, activist, and grandmother, she belongs to the Rukai people, one of 16 officially recognized Austronesian indigenous groups in Taiwan. The term *Rukai*, though, is a bit simplistic; it was given to them by the former Japanese occupants of Taiwan, and is but a broad categorization for a bunch of tribes with similar linguistic qualities.

In actuality, Aeles belongs to the Taromak tribe, a mountainous civilization whose history is rooted in what they call the Kindoor mountains (Kěn dù ěr shān 肯杜爾山) on the east coast of Taiwan in modern-day Taitung County. But like most indigenous groups in Taiwan, their culture and way of life have been brutally ravaged by colonialism over the years. In 1923, the Japanese came and dragged them down from their ancestral villages. In 1949, the Chinese arrived and mandated that they learn Mandarin and stop speaking their mother languages. The colonialists set up Christian churches and told them their rituals and shamans were the work of the devil. "Colonialism almost destroyed my culture," Aeles says. "Food is our last line of connection."

Aeles grew up with an intimate understanding of her culture. Her father—who is in his mid-90s—used to run barefoot in the mountains between neighboring villages as a messenger with just a burning torch for light. Her mother was the last shaman of the tribe, and Aeles would oftentimes wake up to a house full of people with ailments looking for her mother, who would in turn prescribe them plant medicines from the forest. Aeles tells me she didn't inherit her mother's shamanic powers. Her sister did, though, but she has eschewed the calling because she converted to Christianity.

Through Aeles, I'm taught the original culture of Taiwan, which has been largely obscured over the centuries by waves of immigration and what she unabashedly calls "brainwashing." She shows me the Roxburgh

sumac trees in the hills, whose fruit used to be a substitute for salt because, as a mountainous tribe, they didn't have access to the ocean. During our breaks, we make hair wreaths with ferns. Her son, Cegaw, hunts as a hobby, and he introduces me to his peers across neighboring territories.

The indigenous peoples of Taiwan are Austronesian, and they share a linguistic, cultural, and culinary heritage with the people of Austronesia—a wide umbrella that encompasses Madagascar, the Philippines, Indonesia, New Zealand, and Hawaii. In fact, there's a popular migration theory called the "Out of Taiwan Model," which suggests that the Austronesian language originated in and radiated out of Taiwan around 10,000 to 6,000 BC. Aeles often likes to point out that her language is more mutually intelligible with Tagalog and the Māori languages than it is with any Chinese dialect. And the similarities also show up in the food. Many of the crops that the early Polynesians brought with them on canoes also have a long history in indigenous Taiwan, like taro, sugarcane, paper mulberry, and sweet potato (the latter of which, contrary to popular belief, wasn't introduced to Taiwan by the Chinese but

was actually brought to Taiwan by ancient Polynesians who had traveled to South America). The people here also share similar cooking styles with their Austronesian cousins, like lowering hot rocks into large pits and putting food wrapped in leaves on top of the rocks, burying everything with soil, then finally uncovering it in a couple of hours for a hearty, warm feast. When I visit Aeles to take photos of her food for this book, I notice a freshly dug pit in the ground in front of her restaurant, built for the very same purpose. "I'm afraid people will think it's unsanitary," she says sheepishly. I reassure her to the contrary.

Over the years, I've had many long conversations with Aeles about the preservation of indigenous cuisine and knowledge. Indigenous food provides direct insight into the physical land of Taiwan and the fauna and flora that made us who we are. Aeles's mission is to teach the world about her culinary culture, and there's an urgency to it, especially as Taiwan continues to be conflated with China. "I want my cuisine to be decolonized," she says. "Our cuisine is our connection to nature."

Abai

Abai

阿拜

Ā Bài

During the short month that I lived with Aeles, I came to appreciate and crave the nurturing simplicity of an abai—a parcel of millet, glutinous rice, and fatty ground pork tied up and steamed in two layers of leaves. We regularly ate it for lunch, though it's traditionally reserved for special occasions. "The women will make this during the harvest festivals and weddings while the men go out and hunt," says Aeles. The secret ingredient is an indigenous Taiwanese leaf known as fake garlic (*Trichodesma khasianum*), an edible papery film that tastes exactly like raw garlic, which is then enveloped in the fragrant embrace of the shell ginger—a nonedible, glossy leaf that imparts a gorgeous, ginger-like fragrance to the dish. This is one of the few dishes still out there that gives a snapshot of what precolonial Taiwanese cuisine was like. The island had hundreds of varieties of millet, a staple carb that has now fallen out of vogue with the mainstream. Wild boar was a common protein, and native leaves were often foraged and used for food. Unfortunately, fake garlic and shell ginger leaves aren't easily accessible outside Taiwan, so here I'm using cabbage and dried bamboo leaves. If you can get your hands on a large leafy variety of chard instead of cabbage, so much the better. The dark green hue of steamed chard is the exact same color as fake garlic leaf.

¾	cup plus 2 tablespoons (175 g) hulled millet
½	cup (100 g) long-grain glutinous rice, also known as sticky rice
½	pound (225 g) ground pork
1½	teaspoons soy sauce
1¼	teaspoons fine sea salt, divided
1	garlic clove, peeled and minced
⅛	teaspoon ground white pepper
½	cup (40 g) peeled and shredded kabocha squash, with a box grater on the coarsest side
1	large green cabbage, enough for 5 large leaves; or 5 large chard leaves, at least 8 × 8 inches (20 × 20 cm)
15	bamboo leaves or 5 large shell ginger leaves
	Cotton twine, for wrapping

In a fine-mesh sieve, combine the millet and glutinous rice, and wash under running water. Transfer to a large bowl, and soak with enough water to cover for at least 4 hours at room temperature or overnight in the refrigerator.

In a medium bowl, mix the ground pork with the soy sauce, ¼ teaspoon of the salt, garlic, and white pepper. Cover and marinate in the refrigerator for 30 minutes or up to overnight.

Drain the millet and rice mixture in a sieve, transfer to a large bowl, and combine it with the shredded kabocha squash and the remaining 1 teaspoon of salt. Mix thoroughly.

Bring a large pot of water to a rolling boil over high heat. Add the cabbage leaves, and cook until they are soft and pliable, about 30 seconds. Turn off the heat. Remove the cabbage leaves from the pot, and rinse under running water. Shake to dry, and transfer the leaves to a large paper towel–lined plate.

Add the bamboo leaves in the same pot of boiling water, and blanch for 30 seconds. Remove and wash thoroughly under cool running water. Pat the leaves dry with paper towels. Cut off 1 inch (2.5 cm) from the top and bottom of each leaf.

If the cabbage leaves are really thick, place a cabbage leaf flat on the cutting board with the protruding rib facing up. Take a paring knife and shave part of it off so that it's no longer protruding and rather flat. Flip it over and overlay ½ cup, about 93 g, of the millet, glutinous rice, and kabocha squash mixture in a pile on the bottom half of the cabbage leaf. Create a little indent in the pile and add 3 tablespoons (about 45 g) of the ground pork in the middle of the seasoned millet and rice. Mound the millet and rice over the pork so that it's covered.

Fold the left and right sides of the cabbage inward toward the filling. Keeping the sides folded, crease the bottom of the cabbage up and over the filling, and tightly roll it away from you like it's a burrito. Repeat with the rest of the cabbage leaves and filling. You will have 5 rolls in total.

Cut the cotton twine into 5 pieces, about 4 feet (1.2 m) long per piece.

Take 1 bamboo leaf and place it vertically on the table, with the protruding rib of the leaf touching the table. Take 1 more vertical-facing bamboo leaf (also with the protruding rib touching the table), and lay half of it to the right of the first bamboo leaf, with the left edge of the second leaf lined up on the midrib of the first leaf. Take a third leaf and overlay it vertically in the middle of the two leaves. It should look like a rounded rectangle. Place the cabbage roll vertically in the center of middle leaf. Fold the left and right sides of the rectangle toward the center so that cabbage is covered and crease the top and bottom edges down to form a tight rectangular parcel.

Take some cotton twine and loop it around the parcel 4 to 5 times, applying tension with each turn. Tie the loose ends together with a standard bowknot (like how you tie your shoelaces). Repeat. You will have 5 parcels in total.

Arrange the parcels in a tiered bamboo steamer and cover. Partially fill a large wok with water (for steaming tips, see page 38). Bring the water to a rapid boil over high heat and place the steamer on top. Steam for 50 minutes, replenishing the bottom of the wok with boiling water if needed. Turn off the heat. To eat, peel the bamboo leaves off the parcel and enjoy immediately. The steamed parcels can be frozen for up to 2 months. To reheat, steam them over high heat for 30 minutes.

As an indigenous chef who gets invited to events all over Taiwan and throughout Austronesia, Aeles is often hounded with questions about edible native plants. Over the years she's been waging an informal campaign to promote the betel leaf (*Piper betle*)—a local plant that's distributed across the southern part of the island and can also be found throughout Southeast Asia. Her mother, who was the last shaman of the tribe, used to prescribe it as a remedy for women dealing with urinary tract infections. She'd boil a pot of it and instruct the patient to squat over it. "It's a natural disinfectant," says Aeles. A heart-shaped, glossy vine in the same family as black pepper, it's a punchy herb that adds dimension to whatever it's paired with. Unfortunately, in Taiwan, the betel leaf has quite a bit of stigma attached to it. While it's not related to the betel nut—a psychoactive and highly addictive substance that's chewed for the high it imparts—at all, it's the leaf wrapper that the betel nut is sold in, and so there's a fear of using it as a culinary ingredient. Aeles stresses that the betel leaf is edible without danger. Used frequently in Southeast Asian cooking as well, it imparts a peppery aroma to everything. Aeles loves folding it into pork dumplings or stuffing it into this sausage. This is an adaption of her recipe for betel leaf sausage, which she smokes over an open fire.

Smoked Betel Leaf Pork Sausage
Drangaw Drete

荖葉香腸
Lǎo Yè Xiāng Cháng

1½ pounds (680 g) pork shoulder

½ pound (225 g) pork back fat

1½ ounces (45 g) fresh or frozen betel leaf, finely minced

2½ teaspoons fine sea salt

2½ teaspoons white sugar

Natural hog casing, soaked in warm water for 30 minutes and rinsed thoroughly

2 tablespoons dark brown sugar

2 tablespoons loose-leaf black or green tea, any type

1 tablespoon all-purpose flour

Canola or soybean oil, for pan-frying

Cut the pork shoulder and pork back fat into 1-inch (2.5-cm) cubes, and transfer to a large bowl. Combine and massage in the betel leaf, salt, and sugar with your hands. Transfer everything to a large resealable plastic bag (or two), press the meat so that it's flat and in a single layer, and refrigerate for 4 hours or up to overnight. Put the bowl and paddle of the stand mixer, the meat grinder attachment, and kidney plate in the freezer.

Move the bag of seasoned pork shoulder and pork back fat from the refrigerator to the freezer, and chill until it's partially frozen, about 1 hour. With the meat grinder fitted with the kidney plate or the coarsest grinding plate you have, grind the meat mixture on medium speed.

SPECIAL EQUIPMENT:
stand mixer with meat grinder (preferably with kidney plate); sausage stuffer attachment

NOTE:
Use about ½ teaspoon of oil for each sausage. You can also grill the sausages, which is how it's traditionally done.

(RECIPE CONTINUES)

FAMILY STYLE

Transfer the ground meat to the bowl of a stand mixer outfitted with the chilled paddle attachment and mix at low speed until the meat is super sticky, 2 to 3 minutes. (Alternatively, use pair of large chopsticks and stir the meat repeatedly in one direction until very sticky, about 5 minutes.) To test if it's sticky enough, press a small patty of meat into your palm. Hold your palms out, facing down on the table. The meat should continue to stick to you.

With the sausage stuffer attachment, stuff the sausage into the natural hog casing, and twist into 5-inch (12-cm) links, keeping them relatively thin, about 1 inch (2.5 cm) in diameter. With a toothpick, poke holes to release the air bubbles out of the sausages.

Line a wok with an 8 × 8-inch (20 × 20-cm) piece of aluminum foil, and sprinkle the dark brown sugar, flour, and black tea on top of the foil. Place a steamer rack on top of the mixture. Turn your extraction fan to the highest setting. Set the heat to medium, and when the wok begins to smoke, carefully arrange the sausages on top of the steamer rack. Immediately cover the wok with a tight-fitting lid and continue smoking for 5 minutes. Turn off the heat and leave the sausages in for 2 to 5 minutes, depending on how smoky you want your sausage to be.

Uncover and remove the sausages from the wok. Cook immediately, or store any extras in freezer for up to 2 months. To cook the sausages, set a skillet over medium-low heat, and drizzle in oil (see Note). When the oil is hot, add the sausage and cook, turning occasionally, until the thickest part of the sausage registers 160°F (70°C) on a thermometer, 10 to 15 minutes. Turn off the heat, remove from skillet, and rest for 5 minutes before enjoying.

Pigeon Pea and Pork Soup

Karidrang

樹豆排骨湯

Shù Dòu Pái Gǔ Tāng

Native to the Indian subcontinent, pigeon peas were introduced to Taiwan during the Japanese colonial era and naturalized by our indigenous communities. Even though the ingredient has been here for generations by now, it's a legume that's still largely exclusive to indigenous Taiwanese cuisine. Aeles associates it with the cozy, cold winter mornings of her childhood. Her mother would wake up and start warming a large pot of soup, and then they would go about their day. "She would put a wood log underneath the pot, and when we came back home in the evening, we would find a steaming hot bowl of pigeon pea soup," she says. As a crop, pigeon pea was embraced because it's a natural, living fertilizer. The plant is a nitrogen-fixer, which means it takes nitrogen out of the air and fixes it in the soil. And it's also incredibly resistant. In the Rukai language, the word for pigeon pea means dry. "It's a drought-tolerant food. I don't need to water it. It can grow on slopes and survive," Aeles tells me. Seasoned with a generous handful of ginger, this comforting soup is also considered by people in the tribe to be a natural aphrodisiac. "It gives you energy," says Aeles with a sly smile. This recipe uses pork ribs as the meat of choice, but Aeles prefers to cook pigeon peas with wild game, hunted and brought to her by her community.

1 cup (200 g) dried pigeon peas	1 2-inch piece fresh ginger (20 g), unpeeled and sliced
1½ pounds (680 g) spare pork ribs, cut into 1-inch (2.5-cm) chunks	½ tablespoon fine sea salt, plus more to taste

Wash the pigeon peas by rinsing them in several changes of water. In a medium bowl, soak them with enough water to cover for at least 4 hours or overnight in the refrigerator. Drain in a fine-mesh strainer and set aside.

In a medium pot set over high heat, combine the pork ribs with enough water to cover. Bring to rolling boil, reduce the heat to medium, and briskly simmer for about 5 minutes. Turn off the heat. Drain the pork ribs in a colander in the sink. Rinse the ribs under cool running water to get rid of excess scum.

In large pot set over high heat, bring 7 cups (1.6 L) water to a rolling boil. Add the blanched pork ribs, pigeon peas, and sliced ginger. Cover and bring to a boil again. Reduce the heat to low, gently simmering until the ribs are fork-tender and the peas are al dente, about 1 hour. Season with salt, adding more to taste. Serve while hot.

PHOTOGRAPHY NOTE:
The snake engraving on the spoon depicts a venomous pit viper known as the hundred-pace snake 百步蛇, so named because it's said that if you get bitten by one, you'll have only one hundred steps left before death. The snake is the revered totem animal of Aeles's tribe.

Hakka Taiwan: Hakka Mama

Chung Kuo Ming-Chin 鐘郭明琴 is a delightful force of nature whose cooking skills are so legendary that CEOs, the literati, food critics, and minor celebrities have been known to drive for hours to her hidden mountainside adobe just for a home-cooked meal. On paper, she's a housewife, widow to esteemed Hakka writer Chung Tieh-Min 鍾鐵民—who was known for his playful prose celebrating agrarian life—and mother to Chung Shun-Wen 鍾舜文, a well-known painter whose works of art include botanical sketches, cat portraits, and flat landscape renderings of the countryside.

But of course, Mama Chung is so much more than all that. She's a masterful chef and gardener who's able to whip up a symphony of dishes by herself without breaking a sweat. A petite little woman with large round eyes and a gray bob haircut, she has the ability to entertain a small crowd of complete strangers with her wit and charisma. As my team and I are getting settled in the dining room in preparation for the photo shoot, she jumps onto a stool and tries to pull a plate of steamed pork with preserved daikon greens out of her pressure cooker, wobbling so precariously that her daughter, Shun-Wen, rushes over to stabilize her. "These dishes are really simple," Ming-Chin says, grinning, as she steps down and plants her feet on solid ground. We all let out a collective sigh of relief. "Hakka cuisine is all about the original flavor of the ingredients."

Of course, it's really not as simple as she makes it out to be. Her preserved daikon greens have been aged for nine years. She sources all her meat from a local butcher who raises only Taiwanese black pigs—which she swears by because of their higher fat content—and she grinds all the meat herself with just a heavy cleaver. Her cooking vessel of choice is a large round-bottomed wok, with a thick patina that she's been nurturing for more than two decades. And to top it off, she grows most of her own vegetables and fruit.

"When I cook, it's all about feeling," she says as she fries up lunch for us. "Measuring is too troublesome."

When I ask her to describe Hakka cuisine to me, she stresses its simplicity. "Hokkien-speaking people have a lot of color in their dishes. Hakka is more rustic. We do a lot of stir-frying," she says.

The Hakka people are a migratory group with Chinese ancestry whose settlements were concentrated in the hills of southern China. Renowned for their self-sufficiency, they make up about 15 percent of Taiwan's population, and many arrived during the first major wave of Chinese immigration to the island. When they came, they went straight to the hills—a terrain that they were already very familiar with. Mama Chung and her daughter live in Meinong, a small village just northeast of Kaoshiung, and they're stewards of a chunk of land where they have their own fruit trees and an expansive vegetable patch. To us visitors, it

feels like they truly live in Eden—far removed from the fumes and smog of our flatland cities.

We're clearly not the only people who feel that way. Over the years, Mama Chung's home has become quite a tourist attraction. Shun-Wen tells me a story of how one day, she and her mom catered for a massive group of 70 who rolled up to their house in a giant bus. They put out tables in the living room and courtyard, and Mama Chung cooked everything outside with an enormous wok. Somehow they managed, and everyone left with their bellies full and happy.

"The three of us just sat there on the couch at the end of the day, completely out of breath and exhausted," says Shun-Wen. "Me, Mom, and our little dog."

Hakka Stir-Fry

客家小炒
Kè Jiā Xiǎo Chǎo

Hag' Ga´ Seu' Cau'

Walk into any Hakka restaurant in Taiwan and chances are this dish will be on the menu. In fact, Hakka stir-fry is so ubiquitous that it's practically a cliché. Mama Chung made this dish for me as a favor, and stressed that it's not something she makes often at home because it's mostly a restaurant dish. A quick stir-fry composed of squid, pork, tofu, and bean curd, it's easy enough to throw together once you get your shopping in order, though dried squid and bean curd (dòu gān 豆乾) will likely have to be procured at an Asian specialty market. It's said that this dish is a by-product of the harsh agricultural living conditions of the Hakka diaspora. They didn't have access to ample amounts of meat, and whenever they did, they would offer it up to the gods and ancestors. When the rituals were over, they'd throw together a stir-fry with what was left on the altar, and thus this scrappy dish was born.

1½ ounces (40 g) whole dried squid	½ teaspoon white sugar
¼ pound (115 g) skin-on pork belly	¼ teaspoon ground white pepper
½ pound (225 g) bean curd (dòu gān 豆乾)	2 tablespoons lard or canola or soybean oil
2 tablespoons soy sauce	¼ pound (115 g) celery ribs, cut into thin matchsticks
1 tablespoon Taiwanese rice wine (michiu) or cooking sake	3 garlic cloves, minced
½ teaspoon toasted sesame oil	3 scallions, green parts only, cut into 1-inch (2.5-cm) segments
½ teaspoon fine sea salt	

In a medium bowl, soak the dried squid with enough water to cover. Cover and refrigerate for at least 4 hours or overnight.

Cut the pork belly into thin ⅛-inch (3-mm) slices, about 1 inch (2.5 cm) wide. (If it's difficult to cut, place it in the freezer for 15 minutes to firm up.)

Remove the squid from the bowl and rinse it under running water, discarding the soaking liquid. Transfer to a cutting board, and with the squid head pointing right, cut the squid crosswise against the grain into ¼-inch (6-mm) strips. It's important to cut the squid against the grain or else it will curl up when you cook it.

Cut the bean curd in half through its equator and slice into ¼-inch (6-mm) strips.

In a small bowl, combine the soy sauce, rice wine, sesame oil, salt, sugar, and ground pepper, and mix well to make a sauce.

Heat the lard in a wok over medium-high heat and add the bean curd. Cook, stirring, until lightly browned on both sides, about 3 minutes. Transfer the bean curd to a clean plate, reserving the lard. Heat the reserved lard over high heat and add the sliced pork belly and squid. Cook, stirring, until the edges of the pork are opaque, about 1 minute. Return the bean curd to the wok and add the celery and garlic. Pour the sauce around the perimeter of the pan, and quickly stir until everything is mixed together, the celery is tender, and the pork is completely cooked through, 1 to 2 minutes. Add the scallions, and quickly toss to incorporate, about 10 seconds. Turn off the heat, and transfer to a clean plate. Enjoy immediately.

There's an effortless quality to Mama Chung that I adore. She has a jar of de-hydrated preserved daikon tops that she says she's been aging for nine years. And when she opens it for us to smell, it's earthy, medicinal, and sweet—without a hint of rot or musk.

"What's the minimum amount of time you have to age it for?" Ivy asks her.

"Three years," Mama Chung answers, with a twinkle in her eye.

Of course, aging a jar of greens for a minimum of three years and up to a decade is an unattainable standard for us mere mortals. But to be fair, most of her life is. She likes to sprinkle her preserved daikon tops on top of fatty pork she grinds herself with just a cleaver and mixes it with a bit of salt. That's all thrown into the pressure cooker, and out comes a marvelously seasoned block of juicy pork, held together by the complexity of the preserved greens. For accessibility reasons, I've replaced the preserved daikon tops with dried preserved mustard greens (méi gān cài 梅干菜), which are fermented and aged in a similar fashion.

Some other key differences between this recipe and Mama Chung's: She doesn't add starch, because the pork she uses, from Taiwanese black pigs, is extremely fatty and doesn't need starch to seal the juices in. She also doesn't use soy sauce because she prefers to let the natural flavor of the pork shine.

½ cup (20 g) dried salted preserved mustard greens (store-bought or homemade; see page 348)

1 pound (450 g) coarsely ground pork

1 tablespoon tapioca starch or cornstarch

1 teaspoon soy sauce (optional)

1 teaspoon fine sea salt

In a small bowl, soak the preserved mustard greens in room-temperature water for 1 hour. Rinse the greens thoroughly under running water to get rid of any dirt or grit. Pat dry with paper towels or run through a salad spinner to dry. Mince the greens finely.

In a heatproof medium bowl, combine the ground pork, tapioca starch, soy sauce (if using), and salt, and quickly massage the seasoning into the meat, about 10 seconds. Put the dried preserved mustard greens on top (see Note), transfer the bowl to a steamer, and cover.

Partially fill a large wok with water (for steaming tips, see page 38). Bring the water to a rapid boil over medium heat and place the steamer on top. Steam for 20 minutes. Enjoy immediately.

Steamed Preserved Greens and Pork

蘿 蔔 苗 蒸 肉
Luó Bo Miáo Zhēng Ròu

蘿 蔔 苗 蒸 肉
Loˇ Ped Meuˇ Ziinˊ Ngiugˊ

NOTES:

Mama Chung prefers to arrange the preserved greens on top of the pork, but if you'd like, you can massage the greens directly into the ground pork before steaming.

You can procure mei gan cai from Asian specialty markets or online, where it's sometimes labeled as "dried marinated mustard" or "dried mustard leaf." Make sure to buy the salted version, not the sweet one.

Pan-Fried Noodle Cake

麵 線 煎
Miàn Xiàn Jiān

麵 線 煎
Mien Xien Jien´

This is remarkably straightforward: thin, salty wheat noodles are boiled, pressed in a mold overnight, and then shallow-fried in lard until the edges are crispy and firm. Traditionally made with thin, hand-pulled wheat noodles made in Taiwan, this recipe uses Japanese somen as an approximation because Taiwanese wheat vermicelli is difficult to find. They're quite similar; Japanese somen is just a few hairs thicker. For these directions, Mama Chung insists on lard as the frying oil of choice. She says she's experimented with alternatives like soybean, peanut, and sesame oil, but none of those taste quite right. Traditionally, this dish is served plain without sauce or seasoning, but that's because it's designed to be a carb on a lush dinner table spread, paired with a hearty soup and saucy stir-fries.

½ pound (225 g) Japanese somen noodles or any dried thin wheat noodle, at least 1 mm thin	5 tablespoons lard, divided, plus more if needed (see Note)
	Everyday Garlic Soy Dressing (optional; page 367)

Bring a medium pot of water to boil over high heat. Add the noodles and cook according to package instructions. Drain in a colander and shake dry.

Line a rectangular glass food storage container with enough parchment paper to cover the bottom and the long sides. Add the cooked noodles to the container and fold the excess parchment paper over the noodles. With a spatula or the back of a spoon, use your weight to press the parchment paper down firmly on the noodles to compress them. The noodle cake will be roughly 1 inch (2.5 cm) thick. Put a heavy object on top and refrigerate for at least 4 hours or overnight to set.

Remove the noodle cake from the pan. Transfer it to a cutting board and cut it into eight even rectangles.

Heat a wok over medium-high heat and add 3 tablespoons of the lard. When the lard is hot, slide in the noodle cake rectangles and pan-fry, shaking the wok so that the noodles don't stick, until the bottoms are crispy and dark golden brown around the edges, 3 to 4 minutes. Swirl in the remaining 2 tablespoons lard around the perimeter of the wok. Flip the rectangles over one by one, and cook until the other side is also crispy, another 3 to 4 minutes. If it starts to burn, add a little bit more oil. Turn off the heat and enjoy immediately. This dish is quite plain, but that's because it's meant to be paired with other dishes. To eat alone, enjoy with the Everyday Garlic Soy Dressing as a dip.

SPECIAL EQUIPMENT:
8 × 4-inch (20 × 10-cm) rectangular glass food storage container or baking pan with sides

NOTE:
Mama Chung swears by lard as the oil of choice for this dish, but a good substitute is to start off with 3 tablespoons of canola oil and then add 2 tablespoons of toasted sesame oil at the end.

熱
炒

Beer Food

Hot and Noisy
with a Crate of Cold Beers

More than half a decade ago, my friend Chris started corralling people for group dinners at the rooftop of Baxian Grill 八仙碳烤, a rèchǎo 熱炒 restaurant at the edge of the largest park in Taipei. Perched on short plastic stools with a large yellow crate of emerald-green Taiwanese beer bottles on the side of the table, we'd spend hours there, indulging in plates of fat clams licked with rice wine, a casserole of basil-laden chicken, fried rice with slivers of pork, and tender fiddleheads mixed with ginger. Chris's dinners were a gathering place where many of Taiwan's English-speaking writers, academics, and journalists congregated. It was over beers and these greasy plates that I met many of the people who are my friends today, because it's difficult not to bond over great food and alcohol.

Rechao offers all the sensory joys of a night market but without the need to push through the masses, and deserves the same unilateral, unitalicized recognition as Japan's izakayas and Hong Kong's dai pai dong. Used both as a verb and a noun, the literal translation of rechao is "hot stir-fry." The term refers to a distinct genre of semi-outdoor, dinner-only eateries serving up plates of food cooked over the inferno of a giant wok. These establishments are usually situated on street corners or right by busy intersections and are marked by bright red or yellow lanterns strung up like Christmas lights. And at every table, conversations are punctuated by clinking bottles of cold Taiwanese lagers.

"The first thing people want to do when they get home from work is crack open an ice-cold beer," says Hu Nei-Ta 胡內達, the co-owner of Fat Man Eatery 胖子小吃部, another rechao restaurant in Taipei. Fat Man Eatery was started by his father, Hu Ching-Chung 胡慶忠, who traded a lucrative former life as a casino owner for the restaurant industry. The elder Hu started off with just a street stall, but because of his natural charisma and his wife's incredible cooking, he eventually expanded into a rechao restaurant. Today, his adult son has taken over the chef's toque, and I'm interviewing him in his restaurant in the middle of the day during off-hours.

The younger Hu lays down the facts for me: A master rechao chef should be armed with a repertoire of anywhere between 100 and 200 dishes he can whip up at any time. He must be able to conjure a dish in less than one minute and be fluent in the arts of stir-frying, braising, roasting, and deep-frying, and be able to multitask and toggle between all the skills. "And why do you cook all the food in a giant wok?" I ask, expecting Hu to wax poetic about the merits of wok-frying. Perhaps he would get into how the hot flames impart a smokiness to the food, or how the round carbon steel surface ensures that the food is cooked evenly.

"Because it's fast. If you're too slow, you're wasting my time," he responds, without missing a beat.

While Taiwanese food as a whole is usually light on both salt and heat, rechao food is a glaring exception. Chili peppers (albeit the most mild of varieties) are scattered in a lot of the dishes, and everything is seasoned heavily with salt and ground white pepper. Fresh seafood is another defining characteristic of the genre; many of the more prominent rechao businesses will have live seafood tanks where patrons can handpick the fish and shellfish they want to eat.

Now, dining by the side of the street has always been a Taiwanese pastime, but the modern rechao came into existence in the 1980s when large, industrial gas-powered burners were introduced across the island. Most of the food is baptized by fire over giant flames, which adds a delicious, slightly scorched quality to every single dish. Beer, the defining beverage of the experience, is poured into small shot glasses and refilled by petite, pretty beer ladies who go table to table offering patrons whatever brand of beer they've been paid to promote. And it works: rechao restaurants account for nearly 45 percent of all beer sales in the country.

Beer is a universal social lubricant, and while the Taiwanese have a reputation for being rather reserved and unabashedly polite, it's at the rechao table where our true selves come out. I've seen grown men face-plant across multiple tables after hours of drinking, and belly-deep laughter so intense that beer snorts out of the nose. I've seen rows of flushed, rosy cheeks and tables of strangers cheering at each other for no reason other than it's the end of the week. As with any culture, food and enough alcohol binds people together, and the rechao experience in Taiwan—hot, noisy, and messy, in all its glory—remains my all-time favorite.

Taiwan is a subtropical country teeming with ferns hanging out from the cracks of buildings, in between the nooks of banyan trees, and all over the hillsides. While ferns aren't a daily part of our cuisine, they're regularly fried up at rechao restaurants across the island. I'm partial to the tender shoots—also known as fiddleheads—of the bird's nest fern, which is actually (and hilariously) a popular houseplant all around the world but grows wild here on the island. The shoots are usually fried with the pickled seeds of the bird lime tree (*Cordia dichotoma*), which adds a delicious hit of brininess to the dish. But because these seeds are next to impossible to procure outside Taiwan, I've substituted them with fermented black beans, which have a similar effect.

Stir-Fried Fiddle-heads

炒過貓
Chǎo Guò Māo

炒蕨貓
Tshá Kuè Niau

½	pound (225 g) any edible fern, tender shoots only		1	1-inch piece fresh ginger (10 g), peeled and cut into matchsticks
6	cups (1.4 L) water		2	tablespoons dried fermented black beans (dòu chǐ 豆豉)
1	teaspoon fine sea salt, plus more to taste		½	teaspoon Taiwanese rice wine (michiu) or cooking sake
1	tablespoon canola or soybean oil		½	teaspoon white sugar
			½	teaspoon toasted sesame oil

Break off any tough or fibrous parts off the fern and trim so that each piece is about 2½ inches (6 cm) long.

In a medium pot over high heat, combine the water and salt and bring to a rolling boil. Add the fern and cook about 20 seconds. Quickly drain in a colander and shake to dry.

In a wok, heat the oil over medium heat. When the oil is shimmering, add the ginger and fermented black beans, and cook, stirring, until it smells lovely, about 1 minute. Increase the heat to high, and immediately add the fern, rice wine, sugar, and sesame oil. Toss until the fermented black beans are evenly distributed across the dish and the sugar has dissolved, 5 to 10 seconds. Taste and add a pinch more salt if you'd like. Turn off the heat, and transfer to a serving plate. Enjoy while hot.

A sizzling pot of diced chicken, the *three* in three-cup chicken refers to soy sauce, black sesame oil, and rice wine, though not in the same proportions, and definitely not a cup of each. Add a bit of sugar, and the combination of the aforementioned ingredients creates a versatile nutty, salty, and sweet concoction that can also be reused on mushrooms, calamari, or even eggplant. A kiss of fresh Taiwanese basil—a local variety that's most similar to Thai basil but with light anise overtones—rounds out the dish and gives it a lovely brightness. While this dish can be traced to the Jiangxi province of China, the biggest difference is that the Taiwanese renditions incorporate a generous handful of basil.

Three-Cup Chicken

三 杯 雞
Sān Bēi Jī

三 杯 雞
Sam Pue Ke

¼   cup (60 ml) Taiwanese rice wine or cooking sake

3   tablespoons plus 1 teaspoon soy sauce

2   tablespoons water

1   tablespoon coarse raw sugar, such as demerara

¼   teaspoon ground white pepper

2   tablespoons lard or canola or soybean oil

6   garlic cloves, smashed

1   2-inch piece fresh ginger (20 g), unpeeled and cut into ¹⁄₁₆-inch (1.5-mm) slices

2   pounds (900 g) skin-on, bone-in chicken thighs, chopped into 2-inch- (5-cm-) thick pieces (see Note)

2   cups (40 g) fresh Thai basil

1   red jalapeño pepper or any fresh medium chili, deseeded and sliced into thin rings (optional)

1   to 2 tablespoons black sesame oil

In a small bowl, make the sauce by mixing together the rice wine, soy sauce, water, sugar, and white pepper.

In a wok, heat the lard over medium heat. When it begins to shimmer, add the garlic and ginger, and cook until they are lightly brown and the edges of the ginger begin to curl, 2 to 3 minutes. Turn off the heat and remove the garlic and ginger, reserving the oil in the wok. Set the garlic and ginger to the side.

Increase the heat to high and add the chicken. Sear until the chicken is well browned on all sides, 3 to 5 minutes. Pour in the sauce, bring to a boil, and return the ginger to the wok. Cover and reduce the heat to medium-low. Gently simmer until the chicken is cooked through and the sauce has reduced to a treacly, sticky glaze, 12 to 15 minutes.

Uncover the wok and increase the heat to high so the sauce begins to bubble vigorously. Return the garlic to the wok, and quickly toss in the basil and jalapeno pepper, if using. Mix to combine, and drizzle the black sesame oil over the chicken. Turn off the heat, and transfer to a clean plate. Enjoy immediately.

NOTE:
Free-range, bone-in chicken is traditional, but it's totally okay to make this with boneless chicken thighs for general ease. Boneless chicken will cook a bit faster than bone-in chicken, so be sure to watch the meat closely and check it at about the 10-minute mark. Dark meat is mandatory, or else the dish will come out dry and stringy.

BEER FOOD

Fried Rice

炒飯
Chǎo Fàn

炒飯
Tshá Pn̄g

One of my favorite pastimes is watching short videos of old-school chefs making fried rice in giant woks—a mesmerizing feat of strength and timing with volcanic fire spewing out from a gas range. The large flames impart a unique smokiness to kernels of rice, and it's immensely satisfying to watch. My gas stove in Taiwan has more or less that same high-fired intensity, which is great for making a beautiful plate of fried rice but also makes it difficult for me to maintain a slow and low simmer. So when I inquired about replacing my Taiwanese-style stove with a much more expensive American-style range at my local appliance store, the owner—bless his heart—looked at me with horror and said, "Why would you do that? Do you want food with no flavor?" This recipe can be made without a gas stove, of course, but it's imperative that you start with a batch of slightly dried-out rice and pour the soy sauce around the perimeter of the pan so that the rice doesn't steam with the excess liquid. Also, don't be afraid of lard; it's the difference between a decent plate of fried rice and a plate that tastes exactly like it does on the streets of Taiwan.

1	cup (200 g) short-grain rice, also known as sushi rice
3	ounces (85 g) pork tenderloin, cut into matchsticks
3	tablespoons soy sauce, divided
½	teaspoon toasted sesame oil
2	large eggs
¼	cup (60 ml) lard or canola or soybean oil, divided
½	teaspoon fine sea salt, plus more to taste
½	teaspoon ground white pepper, plus more to taste
1	scallion, minced

Cook the rice at least 4 hours before or overnight (for instructions on how, see page 360).

Remove the rice from the cooking pot and transfer it to a large bowl. Let it sit at room temperature before use, and break it up with your hands so that there aren't any lumps. Alternatively, you can use 2 cups (420g) leftover cooked rice.

In a small bowl, combine the pork tenderloin with 1 tablespoon of the soy sauce and the sesame oil. Marinate the pork at room temperature for 15 minutes.

In a small bowl, whisk the eggs until smooth.

In a wok set over high heat, add 2 tablespoons of the lard. When it begins to shimmer, add the eggs and scramble quickly. Remove the eggs from the wok when just about done, about 15 seconds. Transfer to a clean bowl.

NOTE:

If you're comfortable with the idea, ditch the spatula for a large stainless steel cooking ladle. A spatula can cut through the kernels of rice, which might make the dish sticky. Mix and toss the rice with the rounded back of the ladle.

Reduce the heat to medium and add the remaining 2 tablespoons lard in the wok. Add the pork and stir-fry until medium-rare and the edges are opaque, about 30 seconds.

Add the cooked rice, salt, and white pepper, then immediately increase the heat to high. Pour the remaining 2 tablespoons soy sauce around perimeter of the pan. Vigorously stir and toss the rice until the wok begins smoking.

Return the scrambled eggs to the wok and add the scallions. Toss again to combine. Taste and add more salt or ground white pepper if needed. Turn off the heat, and transfer to a clean large plate.

BEER FOOD

Sometimes referred to in Mandarin as melon seeds from the sea, fresh clams are one of nature's most delectable treats. Salty with sweet honeydew undertones, a good batch of clams doesn't need much seasoning, if any at all. When I'm shopping at the wet market, I look for trays of clams that have their feet hanging out and are actively squirting water at passersby. Of course, an active mollusk isn't necessarily indicative of freshness, but I like judging them in this way because it makes my shopping trip that much more entertaining. The key to putting this dish together is layering in the seasoning. Add the soy sauce too early and you'll get a really bitter, almost burnt aftertaste. But drizzle it in halfway and you'll get a nice synthesis of flavors that really highlights the soft brininess of these ocean gems.

Stir-Fried Clams with Basil

塔香蛤蜊

Tǎ Xiāng Gé Lí

炒蚶仔

Tshá Ham Á

- 1½ pounds (680 g) fresh Manila or short-neck clams
- 2 teaspoons fine sea salt
- 2 tablespoons canola or soybean oil
- 1 1-inch piece fresh ginger (10 g), unpeeled and sliced
- 3 garlic cloves, sliced
- 1 scallion, white and green parts minced and separated
- 1 tablespoon Taiwanese rice wine (michiu) or cooking sake
- 1 teaspoon coarse raw sugar, such as demerara
- 2 teaspoons soy sauce
- 1½ cups (30 g) fresh Thai basil
- 1 red jalapeño pepper, or any fresh medium chili, sliced (optional)

In a medium bowl, combine the clams with the salt. Add water to barely cover the clams. Cover and set aside in a cool, dark place, and rest for at least 2 hours or up to 6 hours. This process purges sand and grit from the clams. Scrub the clams with a brush, drain, and set aside.

Heat the oil in a wok over medium heat. When the oil is hot, add the ginger, garlic, and white parts of the scallion, and stir it all together until aromatic, about 30 seconds.

Slide in the clams and increase the heat to high. Add the rice wine and 1 tablespoon water. Cover and cook until all the clams have partially opened up, about 2 minutes. Remove the lid, add the sugar, and pour the soy sauce around the perimeter of the wok. Once all the clams have opened up, quickly fold in the basil, red jalapeño pepper, and the scallion greens. Toss well until everything is evenly mixed together, about 5 seconds. Remove from the heat, pick out and discard any clams that have not opened up, and enjoy immediately.

Poached Squid with Five-Flavor Sauce

五味透抽
Wǔ Wèi Tòu Chōu

五味透抽
Gōo Bī Thàu Thiu

Taiwanese five-flavor sauce is an elegant medley of ketchup, soy paste, sugar, rice vinegar, and black vinegar, and is said to have originated in the seafood restaurants of Beitou, a mountainous district in northern Taipei. Essentially our take on cocktail sauce with distinct sweet and sour notes, it's designed to pair with cold seafood that's a bit on the chewier side, like squid, abalone, calamari, and shrimp. Just blanch whatever you're eating quickly in hot water, chill, and pour the sauce over. It's really that easy!

FOR THE SQUID:

1   1-inch piece fresh ginger (10 g), unpeeled and sliced

1   scallion, tied into a knot

2   teaspoons Taiwanese rice wine (michiu) or cooking sake

2   medium cleaned squid, about 1 pound (450 g) in total weight

FOR THE FIVE-FLAVOR SAUCE:

2   tablespoons ketchup

2   teaspoons Taiwanese soy paste (store-bought or homemade; page 366)

2   teaspoons white sugar

1   teaspoon rice vinegar

½   teaspoon black vinegar

¼   teaspoon fine sea salt, plus more to taste

1   scallion, green part only, minced

1   garlic clove, minced

1   ½-inch piece fresh ginger (5 g), peeled and minced

1   fresh bird's eye chili, minced (optional)

MAKE THE SQUID: Prepare an ice water bath on the side. In a medium pot, combine the ginger, scallion, rice wine, and 4 cups (1 L) water, and bring to a rolling boil over high heat. Add the squid, and cook until they turn completely white, 40 seconds to 1 minute. Turn off the heat and use a spider strainer to transfer the squid to the ice water bath to cool completely. Remove the squid from the ice bath and cut them into ½-inch (1-cm) rings. Transfer to a serving plate.

MAKE THE FIVE-FLAVOR SAUCE: In a small bowl, whisk together the ketchup, soy paste, sugar, rice vinegar, black vinegar, salt, and 2 tablespoons water. Stir in the scallion greens, garlic, ginger, and bird's eye chili, if using. Taste and add more salt if you'd like.

To serve, pour the sauce over the squid, or serve it in a small bowl to the side as a dip. This dish can be served immediately or chilled for up to 4 hours in the refrigerator and served cold.

Taiwanese Booze

Taiwan Beer 台灣啤酒

A crisp lager that graces the tables of every beer restaurant and the liquor section of every convenience store in the country, Taiwan Beer has been the island's bestselling brand for more than a century (though part of its success is because it was a monopoly for most of its history). Established in 1919 during the Japanese colonial era as Takasago Beer, it was taken over by the Taiwan Tobacco and Liquor Corporation when the Nationalist government arrived in Taiwan in 1945 and rebranded as Taiwan Beer. While the company stopped monopolizing the alcohol and spirits industry in 2002, it has remained many people's default beer of choice, not only out of nostalgia but because, all things considered, it's a pretty damn good lager. Made with barley, hops, yeast, water, and local short-grain rice, it's an extremely light-bodied brew with sweet, refreshing notes. It also just pairs really well with late-night plates of greasy, wok-fried food. What's not to love?

Kaoliang 高粱

Produced mostly on the Taiwanese island of Kinmen, kaoliang is Taiwan's high-proof booze of choice. It's a strong liquor with an alcohol range of 38 to 58 percent that's made from distilled and fermented sorghum. For some—myself included—it's an acquired taste. As with any extremely high-proof alcohol, the experience of sipping kaoliang can be like drinking straight rubbing alcohol, but I've come to appreciate it in recent years after my husband taught me how to properly enjoy it: Take it in very slowly, ideally in a small chilled shot glass. If you sip it slowly enough, you might be able to pick up on the subtle sweetness of the liquor—spicy with hints of licorice. But hey, if you're just looking for a good time, go ahead and do shots. That's what most folks do with it on the weekends anyway.

Gently poaching a slab of pork belly in water and slicing it into thin pieces is a technique from Sichuan, but here in Taiwan it's dressed with soy paste (a condiment unique to the island) and a very light touch of mild chili oil, because people here aren't super keen on spicy notes. Overcooked pork is disappointing, so the foolproof way to do this is to put the pork belly in water, bring it to a boil, let it simmer very briefly, and then turn off the burner and let the residual heat slowly cook the meat.

Garlic Sliced Pork

蒜泥白肉

Suàn Ní Bái Ròu

1   pound (450 g) pork belly (see Note)

2   scallions, tied into a knot

1   1-inch piece fresh ginger (10 g), unpeeled and sliced

¼   cup (60 ml) Everyday Garlic Soy Dressing (page 367)

½   teaspoon toasted sesame oil

¼   teaspoon chili crisp or chili oil, any brand (optional)

1   medium Japanese cucumber or any seedless cucumber

Minced garlic (for garnish; optional)

In a medium pot, combine the pork belly with enough water to cover. Add the scallions and ginger and bring the water to a rolling boil over high heat. Cover with a tight-fitting lid, reduce the heat to medium, and simmer for about 5 minutes. Turn off the heat and leave the pork in the pot until the thickest part of the belly measures 145°F (60°C) on an instant-read thermometer, 20 to 30 minutes. Drain in a colander, briefly rinse under running water to get rid of any muck that has accumulated on top, and let it cool down completely to room temperature.

In a small bowl, make the sauce by mixing together the Everyday Garlic Soy Dressing with the sesame oil and chili crisp, if using.

Trim the edges off the cucumber and cut it how you'd like—slice it into thin matchsticks or cut it into 4 even sections and slice lengthwise with a sharp knife into paper-thin strips. Arrange the cucumber beautifully on a serving plate.

Cut the cooked pork into ⅛-inch (3-mm) slices. Artfully arrange the pork on top or around the cucumber and pour the sauce on top. Feel free to go fancy with the plating. Some places will wrap each individual piece of pork belly over a slice of cucumber or vice versa, like a taco. Garnish with the garlic if you'd like. Get creative. This dish is usually served at room temperature.

NOTE:
Skin-on pork belly is typical, but you're more than welcome to take the skin off if you want.

BEER FOOD

Shacha Beef with Water Spinach

沙茶牛肉
Shā Chá Niú Ròu

沙茶牛肉
Sa Te Gû Bah

Brought over by Teochew immigrants from Chaozhou in the mid-20th century, shacha is a gritty, dark brown condiment made with blended small dried shrimp, dehydrated olive flounder, shallots, and garlic. It pairs especially well with red meat, and this quick, tasty stir-fry made with beef and water spinach is a mainstay at many of the outdoor beer restaurants in the country. You might also find it made with lamb instead—a remnant of the old days when beef was taboo. The hollow stems of the water spinach take a bit longer to cook, so toss those in first before folding in the leafy bits.

¼ pound (115 g) beef tenderloin or flank steak

½ teaspoon Taiwanese rice wine (michiu) or cooking sake

2 teaspoons soy sauce

2 teaspoons tapioca starch or cornstarch

2 tablespoons canola or soybean oil, divided

2 garlic cloves, minced

2 tablespoons shacha sauce, such as Bullhead Barbecue Sauce (for homemade, page 371), divided

½ pound (225 g) water spinach, cut into 2-inch (5-cm) segments, stems and leafy parts separated

2 tablespoons water

⅛ teaspoon fine sea salt (optional)

Slice the beef thinly into 1 × 2 inch- (2.5 × 5 cm-) thin strips, about ⅛ inch (3 mm) thick. (If the beef is difficult to cut, place it in the freezer for 15 minutes to firm up.) In a medium bowl, combine the sliced beef, the rice wine, soy sauce, and tapioca starch. Mix and marinate for 15 minutes.

In a wok over medium heat, heat 1 tablespoon of the oil. Add the garlic, and stir-fry until aromatic, about 30 seconds. Add the beef and 1 tablespoon of the shacha sauce, and cook, stirring, until the beef is medium-rare and covered with sauce and garlic, about 1 minute. Remove the beef from the wok and set aside.

Increase the heat to high and swirl the remaining 1 tablespoon oil into the wok.

Add in the stems of the water spinach and water, and cook, stirring, until soft, about 30 seconds. Add the leafy parts of the water spinach. Cook, stirring, until soft, another 30 seconds. Return the beef back to the wok with the remaining 1 tablespoon shacha sauce. Toss and combine until the beef is cooked through, about 30 more seconds. Taste and add salt if desired. Turn off the heat. Serve and enjoy immediately.

Dry-Fried Green Beans

乾煸四季豆

Gān Biān Sì Jì Dòu

The secret to getting perfectly blistered spears of string beans is deep-frying them in a vat of hot, bubbly oil first, and then mixing them with the earthy aromatics last. Cook them right and they'll come out an electrifying shade of green. This dish is likely of Chinese provenance because of its use of numbing peppercorns and chili peppers, and the uniquely Taiwanese spin on it is the addition of small dried shrimp, which gives it an extra layer of umami.

1 ounce (30 g) preserved mustard stem (zhà cài 榨菜) (see Note)

1 tablespoon small dried shrimp

1 pound (450 g) string beans, trimmed

2 cups (470 ml) canola or soybean oil

3 garlic cloves, minced

1 ½-inch piece fresh ginger (5 g), peeled and minced

2 to 4 dried red chili peppers, such as chiles de arbol, chopped into ½-inch (1-cm) chunks

2 scallions, minced

½ teaspoon whole Sichuan red peppercorns (optional)

2 ounces (60 g) ground pork

2 teaspoons soy sauce

1 teaspoon Taiwanese rice wine (michiu) or cooking sake

½ teaspoon white sugar

½ teaspoon fine sea salt, plus more to taste

½ teaspoon rice vinegar

Briefly rinse the preserved mustard stem under running water. Cut into matchsticks, and in a small bowl, combine the sliced mustard stems with enough water to cover. Soak for 10 minutes. In another small bowl, combine the dried shrimp with enough water to cover and soak for 10 minutes.

Drain the mustard stems, squeeze out the excess water, and pat dry with paper towels. Mince finely and set aside for later. Drain the dried shrimp, transfer to a cutting board, and mince finely. Set aside for later.

Make sure the string beans are dry. If they're not, pat them completely dry with paper towels or run through a salad spinner (this part is really important or else oil will splatter everywhere later).

In a wok, heat the oil over high heat until it reads 375°F (190°C) on an instant-read thermometer. Lower half the beans into the hot oil and deep-fry until the skin is wrinkled and slightly blistered, about 5 minutes. With a spider strainer, immediately transfer the fried string beans to a paper towel–lined plate to drain. Repeat with the remaining batch of string beans. Turn off the heat.

NOTE:
The salt levels of pickled mustard stems vary wildly by brand. Always wash, soak, and taste before using. If they're saltier than the ocean and make you flinch, you should definitely soak them longer.

Reserve 2 tablespoons of the oil in the wok, and safely discard the rest. Heat the oil over medium heat, add the minced preserved mustard stem, and stir-fry until they are slightly brown around the edges, about 30 seconds. Add the garlic, ginger, dried red chili peppers, scallions, Sichuan red peppercorns (if using), and the dried shrimp, and cook, stirring often, until it smells lovely, about 30 seconds. Add the ground pork, and stir until the edges are opaque, about 20 seconds. Add the deep-fried string beans, and drizzle in the soy sauce and rice wine around the perimeter of the wok. Season with the sugar and salt. When the pork is completely cooked through and slightly crispy around the edges, drizzle in the rice vinegar around the perimeter of wok. Taste and add more salt if needed. Toss well. Turn off the heat and serve.

Preserved Daikon Omelet

菜脯蛋
Cài Pú Dàn

菜脯卵
Tshài Póo Nn̄g

(store-bought or homemade; page 351)

Conceptually, an omelet with a late-night beer isn't the most natural pairing, but it works well in this context because the omelet is dotted with a generous helping of salted preserved daikon, which gives it a piquant punch. Unlike a Western omelet, which is elegantly pan-fried with a reasonable amount of butter, this rendition is shallow-fried in quite a bit of oil, which helps it expand into a fluffy disc. The recipe is inspired by instructions from Phaedra Fang, a curator at the National Taiwan Museum. She learned how to cook from her mother, and this omelet used to be a staple on their dinner table and sometimes even the next morning, when the leftovers would be folded into porridge or paired with toast. "My mother was the rare homemaker who actually made three full meals a day," she says. For Phaedra, sharing her mother's recipe with the world is a way to keep her memory alive.

1 ounce (30 g) preserved radish, also known as salted daikon (store-bought or homemade; page 351)

3 large eggs

2 scallions, finely minced

½ teaspoon soy sauce

¼ teaspoon ground white pepper

3 tablespoons lard or canola or soybean oil, divided

Briefly rinse the preserved radish under running water. In a small bowl, combine the preserved radish with enough water to cover. Soak for 10 minutes. Drain, squeeze out the excess water, and pat dry with paper towels. Dice the radish into small ⅓-inch (8-mm) cubes and set aside for later.

Crack the eggs into a large bowl, and add the scallions, soy sauce, and white pepper. Whisk thoroughly until no lumps remain. Set aside.

In a wok over medium heat, add 2 tablespoons of the lard. Add the diced preserved radish, and cook, stirring, until fragrant and the edges are slightly browned, about 2 minutes.

With a spatula, remove the preserved radish from the wok, and stir it into the egg mixture so that it's evenly incorporated.

Add the remaining 1 tablespoon of lard into the wok and increase the heat to medium-high. Pour the egg mixture with the preserved radish in. The edges of the omelet will begin to foam up and solidify, like a puffy ring, and the middle will be a bit raw. Stir the middle gently with chopsticks and cook until the middle is barely set (it will still be a bit runny), about 30 seconds. Shake the wok back and forth so that the omelet is loose. Flip the omelet over

NOTE:
The salt levels of preserved radish vary wildly by brand. Always wash, soak, and taste before using. If it's saltier than the ocean and makes you flinch, you should definitely soak it longer.

with a large spatula or, with one sharp and smooth motion, thrust the pan forward, upward, and then back so that the omelet flips over. Reduce heat to medium-low and cook until the center of the omelet is cooked through, 20 to 30 seconds. Transfer to a clean plate and enjoy immediately.

Sweet and sour is a universal flavor combination, and using fruit as the acid of choice is a really common technique in East Asia. Southern China, for example, has chunks of chicken thighs sautéed in an orange-juice slurry, which eventually evolved into the American-Chinese deep-fried orange chicken we all know and love today. Here in Taiwan, we use pineapples instead of oranges and shrimp instead of chicken. To finish off, this dish is often garnished with rainbow sprinkles for a pop of color—though toasted sesame seeds are traditional and admittedly a bit more demure.

Pineapple Prawns

鳳梨蝦球

Fèng Lí Xiā Qiú

FOR THE SHRIMP:

- 1 pound (450 g) peeled and deveined large shrimp (see Notes)
- 1 teaspoon Taiwanese rice wine (michiu) or cooking sake
- ½ teaspoon fine sea salt
- 1 egg white
- 1 tablespoon tapioca starch or cornstarch
- ½ teaspoon toasted sesame oil
- 4 cups (1 L) canola or soybean oil

FOR THE SAUCE AND GARNISH:

- ¼ cup (60 g) Kewpie mayonnaise
- 1½ teaspoons rice vinegar
- 1 teaspoon white sugar
- ½ teaspoon fine sea salt
- 10½ ounces (300 g) fresh pineapple, peeled, cored, and cut into 1-inch- (2.5-cm-) wide wedges (see Notes)
- Rainbow sprinkles or toasted white sesame seeds (for garnish; page 368)

MAKE THE SHRIMP: Pat the shrimp completely dry with paper towels. In a large bowl, combine the shrimp, rice wine, and salt. Mix to combine, then add the egg white. Mix to combine again, and add the tapioca starch and sesame oil. Massage the marinade into the shrimp with your hands. Cover and chill in the refrigerator for at least 20 minutes.

In a large wok over medium-high heat, heat the canola oil until it registers 350°F (175°C) on an instant-read thermometer. Add in half of the shrimp, and fry, stirring so they don't clump together, until they curl and turn pink, about 1 minute. With a spider strainer, transfer the shrimp to a paper towel–lined plate, and drain thoroughly. Repeat with the remaining shrimp. When the shrimp is cool enough to handle, gently pat off any excess oil with more paper towels.

MAKE THE SAUCE: In a small bowl, mix together the Kewpie mayonnaise, rice vinegar, white sugar, and salt.

In a large mixing bowl, combine the fried shrimp and sauce, and mix thoroughly so that the shrimp is completely coated. Transfer to a serving plate, and artfully arrange the pineapple on the perimeter of the plate. Garnish with rainbow sprinkles.

NOTES:

If you're buying shell-on shrimp, 2 pounds (900 g) will yield about 1 pound (450 g) of peeled shrimp.

Canned pineapples will work as well; just make sure to drain before use.

Rainbow sprinkles are a popular garnish in the south of Taiwan. For northerners, it's considered a bit tacky.

BEER FOOD

夜市

Night
Market

Once Upon
a Night Market

Every year when my family and I arrived in Taiwan for winter vacation, I could feel and smell the mustiness of the subtropical country before I could see it. The humidity would grip my body like plastic wrap the moment I stepped out of the airplane and onto the jet bridge, and compared to the doldrums of suburban Los Angeles, Taipei felt like the background of a wonderful, lucid dream. I began to associate the gas fumes of scooters, the bright paper lanterns, and the push and pull of the crowds around me with feelings of immense, blissful joy. I'd beg to be escorted through a night market immediately upon arrival and would saunter in wide-eyed, one hand clenching Mom's hand and the other clasping a skewer pierced into a half-eaten sweet Taiwanese sausage.

For visitors and people who live outside Taiwan, there's a distinct romanticism associated with our night markets that has remained stuck in perpetuity, even as the conditions surrounding the markets have shifted dramatically with time. A collection of open-air evening bazaars scattered across our island nation, the night markets are, for many people around the world, the gateway into Taiwanese cuisine. It's hard not to salivate in the presence of crispy kernels of chicken tossed with shimmery leaves of bright green basil, or of sweet and savory sausages grilled to order, or vibrant orange sweet potato balls submerged in hot oil and pressed against the edge of a wok until they puff up, glassy and translucent. It's all an olfactory and visual delight, and today, night markets are inadvertently one of the most influential transmitters of Taiwanese soft power.

"It used to be so packed, you could barely move your arms," Taipei culture writer Jason Cheung 張哲生 tells me as he escorts me through Shilin Night Market, which was once the most popular night market in the country. Today, the market isn't so packed. There's a bit of foot traffic, but there aren't any lines. Some spots in the market barely have any people. A lone spring roll vendor hangs out in the corner, and his back straightens up immediately as we approach him and order a roll. He says that business has suffered immensely with the pandemic border closures, but even before that, the rate of customers was already steadily declining.

To understand why traffic in Taiwan's night markets has waned considerably, you must consider their history. Night markets were birthed at the edges of temples, composed of informal congregations of opportunistic peddlers who relied on the magnetism of these religious places. People would gather on a regular basis at the temples to pay their respects to the gods, and vendors would swarm in from all directions to sell their wares on shoulder poles or simple pushcarts. The bazaars eventually became semipermanent fixtures at many of the more popular temples around the island, and reached a climax in the 1980s and '90s at the height of Taiwan's economic prosperity. It's here where the perception of night markets is stuck in time—dense, bright streets packed with people, where vendors are one-dish specialists and have been perfecting the same food for generations.

Indeed, there was a romantic rowdiness to the night market in those days. And the food was marvelous. I still remember walking in the 1990s and early 2000s through an ocean of family-owned stalls. My brother and I would fish for live goldfish with paper nets or pop balloons with darts in exchange for stuffed animals. We'd indulge in barbecued squid (a rarity these days), and I could swear the stinky tofu was stinkier back in the day.

There was a dark side, though. Night markets were highly unregulated, full of counterfeits and people operating without licenses. Many would sell their goods on large picnic blankets on the ground. The police sometimes conducted random checks, but you'd hear about them before you saw them—a chorus of people screaming "police" ripping down the market streets. Merchants would hurriedly wrap up all their goods in their blankets, fling them behind their shoulders, and run for dear life. And if that sight wasn't terrifying enough, the markets were also—and still are, to a certain extent—controlled by local neighborhood mafia groups who bullied stallkeepers for protection fees. It was messy and raw, but that was part of the appeal.

Eventually, in the mid-2000s, the government swooped in, and initiatives to clean up the loud, dirty, and unsettling side of the night markets—though born out of good intentions—began to strip the markets of their signature grit. At Shilin Night Market, a bright, fluorescent underground basement was built out in 2011 in an attempt to contain many of the food vendors and tidy up the street. The project flopped. "We're not Singapore," Cheung, who was staunchly against the initiative, tells me. "It's so sterile." Some markets became heavily produced, with uniforms, trade shows, and tacky performances.

From a business side, wildly successful stalls became franchises, and with franchises came gentrification. As Taipei expanded and people's standards of living rose, so did the noise complaints. Many large markets were forced to downsize, and family-owned stalls began to be replaced with chains. "I think the quality is pretty much the same. But the diversity of food options has gone down," Cheung muses. "When you go to Taiwan's old streets, you'll see that the food is repetitive. They're duplicates of one another."

This isn't to say the Taiwanese night market is dead. Far from it. There are still a handful of thriving ones, like Raohe and Ningxia Night Market in Taipei. And on a good day, these markets are reliably swollen with rivers of people, many looking for a quick meal on the way home from work, others on leisurely strolls, determined to snack around. And if you look hard enough, you might be able to spot the actual temple that birthed the night market, a living remnant of bygone days.

The recipes in this chapter encompass some of the most timeless dishes of Taiwan's night markets—dishes that have persisted across the generations. They're all designed to be eaten on the go, slathered with an appropriate amount of sauces or spices. These are snacks designed to propel you through the evening but keep you wanting more.

Fried Stinky Tofu

臭豆腐
Chòu Dòu Fu

臭豆腐
Tshàu Tāu Hū

SPECIAL EQUIPMENT:
large disinfected pickle jar and pickling weight (see Note on page 348)

NOTES:
Amaranth comes into season during the summer and can be procured at specialty Asian grocery stores. It's sometimes vaguely labeled as Chinese spinach and comes in both green and red varieties. The plant also grows wild all around the world in temperate and tropical climates, but please forage responsibly.

The brine that the tofu is soaked in should be discarded, but the mother brine can be used indefinitely. Just filter out the solids and combine it with freshly made brine.

(RECIPE CONTINUES)

Stinky tofu is indisputably the most misunderstood dish in Taiwanese cuisine. Falsely thought to be a malodorous block of fermented tofu bobbing in a moldy cauldron of meat and miscellaneous vegetables, it's often said to have an odor reminiscent of dirty socks, sewage, or manure. All of that is hearsay, because stinky tofu is really just tofu soaked in a simple pickle brine, and it's only soaked in that brine for less than a week. While it is rather pungent (more of an overripe cheese than manure, to be honest), there's nothing rotten about this dish. The tofu itself isn't fermented and is as hygienic as your average jar of pickles.

The secret is in the pickle brine, which is made out of amaranth soaked in saltwater for a couple of months and up to a half a year. It's the amaranth that's fermented, not the tofu, and it's usually mixed with a blend of miscellaneous greens and herbs like water spinach, red peppercorns, pickled mustard greens, orange peels, winter melon, or bamboo shoots for balance.

My recipe is quite minimalistic in comparison but retains that signature fragrance typical of proper stinky tofu. I've mixed in water spinach for a bit of depth, and the rice water helps speed up the fermentation process by acting as a starter. Like with any fermented dish, it's important to be patient. The brine has to be aged for a minimum of two months before it can be used. I tried it at the one-month mark and found it a bit too salty; this is one of those things that gets better with time.

FOR THE BRINE:
1   cup (200 g) uncooked white rice, any type

10 cups (2.4 L) filtered water, divided

10½ ounces (300 g) amaranth greens

5½ ounces (150 g) water spinach

2½ tablespoons fine sea salt

2   tablespoons Taiwanese rice wine (michiu) or cooking sake

FOR THE TOFU:
1   box (350 g) medium-firm tofu

4   cups (1 L) canola or soybean oil

Everyday Soy Dressing (page 367)

Taiwanese Pickled Cabbage (page 349)

MAKE THE BRINE: Place the rice in a fine-mesh colander and wash it briefly under running water. Transfer the rice to a medium bowl and combine with 2 cups (470 ml) of the filtered water. Stir and let it sit for 10 minutes. In a sieve set over a medium bowl, drain the rice—reserving the soaking liquid only. Save the rice for another use.

Chop the amaranth and water spinach into 4-inch- (10-cm-) long segments. In the pickling jar, add the amaranth, water spinach, salt, rice wine, reserved rice soaking liquid, and the remaining 8 cups (2L) filtered water. Weigh down the amaranth and water spinach with a pickling weight and seal the jar.

Store the jar in a dark and cool place until pungent, a minimum of 2 months.

MAKE THE TOFU: Place the tofu in a large glass food storage container. Open the pickling jar outside or in a well-ventilated room, and strain some of the brine through a mesh sieve and into the glass food storage container, making sure the tofu is completely submerged. Put the lid on and refrigerate for 3 days. Reserve the mother brine for future use.

Heat the oil in a wok over medium-high heat until it reaches 350°F (175°C) on an instant-read thermometer. Remove the tofu from the brine, and gently pat it with paper towels to get rid of any excess moisture. Slice the block of tofu in half lengthwise. Cut the block crosswise into 3 chunks so there are 6 pieces total.

Open a window or turn on the stove's exhaust fan to its highest setting. Gently slide the tofu into the hot oil and cook, stirring constantly, until light golden brown, 3 to 4 minutes. Turn off the heat. Remove the tofu from the wok with a spider strainer and transfer it to paper towel–lined plate to drain, about 1 minute.

Bring the oil up to 375°F (190°C) over medium-high heat again and return the tofu to the wok. Fry quickly until golden brown, about 1 minute. Transfer the tofu with a spider strainer to a fresh paper towel–lined plate again to drain. Enjoy the tofu immediately with a drizzle of Everyday Soy Dressing and pickled cabbage on the side.

Since 1951, Cheng Yi-Chu 鄭一竹 and his family have been whipping up buckets of freshly baked black pepper buns. Pork is mixed with aromatics and a generous dash of pepper, enveloped in a flaky crust, and baked in a tandoor drum enclosed in hinoki wood. "This dish was invented in Taiwan," claims Cheng. A night market staple, the origin of the black pepper bun is often attributed to Fuzhou, the capital of the Fujian province of China. Cheng's great uncle was from there, but Cheng insists that the buns in Fuzhou had only scallions and pork. He says the addition of black pepper in the buns is a flair that's unique to our island.

For practical reasons, this recipe uses an oven instead of a tandoor drum. It's also important to bake the buns on a preheated surface, preferably a pizza stone if you have one. The high temperature will immediately seal the dough and prevent the filling from leaking out during the baking process.

Black Pepper Bun

胡椒餅
Hú Jiāo Bǐng

胡椒餅
Hôo Tsio Piánn

FOR THE FILLING:

- 6 ounces (180 g) pork tenderloin, cut into ½-inch (1-cm) cubes
- 4 ounces (120 g) ground pork
- 2 tablespoons Scallion and Ginger Water (page 126)
- 1 tablespoon Taiwanese rice wine (michiu) or cooking sake
- 1½ tablespoons soy sauce
- 2 teaspoons white sugar
- 1 teaspoon ground black pepper
- 1 teaspoon ground white pepper
- 1 teaspoon toasted sesame oil
- ½ teaspoon five-spice powder
- ½ teaspoon fine sea salt

FOR THE YEAST DOUGH:

- 2 cups (250 g) all-purpose flour
- ½ cup plus 2 tablespoons (150 ml) water
- 2 teaspoons lard or unsalted butter, softened
- 2 teaspoons white sugar
- 1 teaspoon active dry yeast
- ¼ teaspoon fine sea salt

FOR THE OIL PASTE:

- ½ cup (60 g) cake flour
- 2 tablespoons (30 g) lard or unsalted butter, softened

FOR ASSEMBLY:

- 3 scallions, minced
- ¼ cup (20 g) raw white sesame seeds, hulled

MAKE THE FILLING: In a large bowl, combine the pork tenderloin, ground pork, Scallion and Ginger Water, rice wine, soy sauce, sugar, black pepper, white pepper, sesame oil, five-spice powder, and salt. Mix thoroughly with chopsticks in one direction until the pork is very sticky, about 5 minutes. (Alternatively, use a stand mixer, and mix with the paddle attachment on medium speed for about 2 minutes.)

SPECIAL EQUIPMENT:
stand mixer (optional); pizza stone (optional)

(RECIPE CONTINUES)

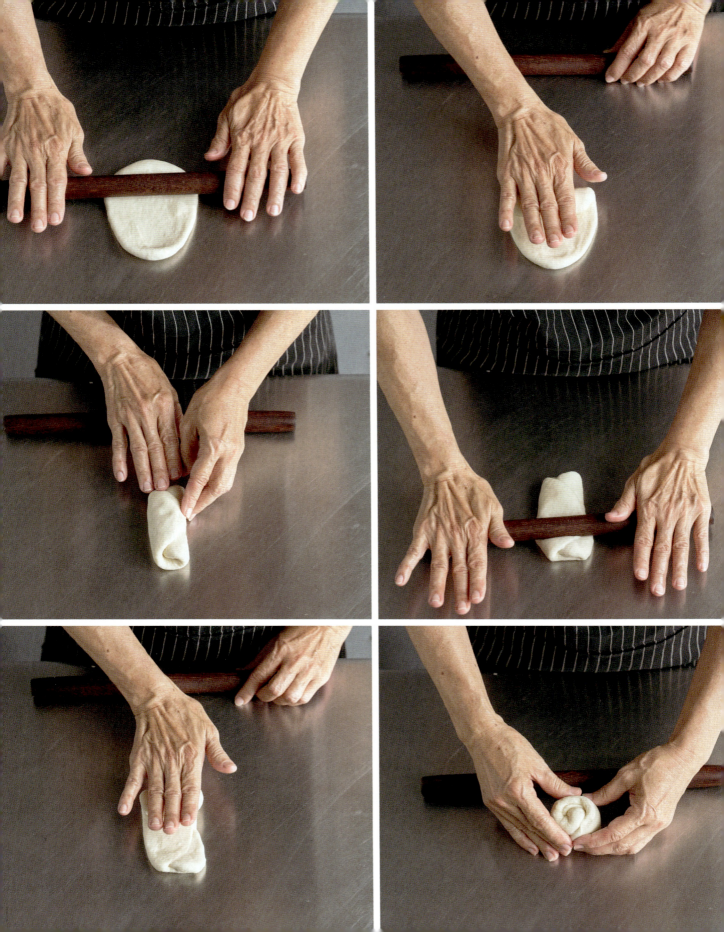

Prepare a parchment paper–lined sheet pan. Form the pork into 6 balls of about 60 g each and arrange on the prepared sheet pan. Cover with plastic wrap and refrigerate until firm, at least 1 hour or up to 4 hours.

MAKE THE YEAST DOUGH: In a large bowl, combine the all-purpose flour, water, lard, sugar, yeast, and salt. Mix together until it forms a shaggy dough, and then bring the dough together by hand. Transfer to a clean work surface, and knead until shiny and smooth, about 10 minutes. (Alternatively, knead in a stand mixer with the dough hook attachment on low speed for 2 minutes.) Transfer the dough to a bowl, cover with plastic wrap, and let it rest at room temperature until slightly puffed up and soft to the touch, about 20 minutes. This isn't a fully leavened pastry, so don't worry about waiting for the dough to double. Lift the dough out of the bowl and transfer it to a clean work surface. With a bench scraper, divide the dough into 6 even pieces, about 70 g each, roll them into balls, and cover with plastic wrap again.

MAKE THE OIL PASTE: In a medium bowl, combine the cake flour and lard, and mix with your hands until it forms a cohesive and smooth paste. Divide and shape into 6 even balls about 15 g each.

ASSEMBLE THE BUNS: Take a yeast dough ball and flatten it with your palm into a 3-inch (7.5-cm) disc. Place an oil paste ball at the center of the disc, and wrap the disc around the oil paste, pinching it closed and rolling it in your hands so it's a smooth, larger ball. Cover with plastic wrap and repeat with all the remaining yeast dough and oil paste balls. Let rest for 10 minutes.

Take a completed ball and, with a rolling pin, flatten it up and down into an elongated oval, about 6 inches (15 cm) long. From the narrow, bottom tip of the oval, roll it

away from you like it's a burrito to form a cigar. Rotate it clockwise 90 degrees so that it's facing up.

Flatten it up and down with a rolling pin again into another long oval, also about 6 inches (15 cm) long. Once again, roll it away from you like it's a burrito. Stand it up on the table like a pillar so that one of the swirled ends points up to the ceiling. Flatten it with your palm into a disc. It will look a bit like a swirly snail shell. Cover with plastic wrap and repeat with the remaining dough balls. Let rest for another 10 minutes.

Preheat the oven to 450°F (230°C). Heat a pizza stone or baking sheet on the lower rack of the oven until very hot, at least 15 to 20 minutes.

Take the pork balls out of the refrigerator.

With a rolling pin, flatten one of the snail shell–shaped dough discs into a flat, round disc, about 4 inches (10 cm) wide. Place a pork ball in the middle, add 1 tablespoon of the scallions, and gently envelop the dough around and over the filling. Pinch the dough together to seal. Cover with plastic wrap. Repeat with the remaining dough and filling.

Pour the sesame seeds onto a small shallow plate. With a pastry brush, brush a thin layer of water on the top of each bun. Dip the smooth side of the bun into the sesame seeds so that the top is evenly coated. Remove the pizza stone or baking sheet from the oven, and quickly arrange the buns on top.

Reduce the oven temperature to 425°F (220°C). Bake the buns on the lower rack for 25 minutes, until the tops are crisp and tan. Remove from the oven and enjoy while hot.

Fried Chicken Cutlet

炸雞排
Zhá Jī Pái

糋雞排
Tsìnn Ke Pâi

Taiwan is a sucker for industry-sponsored food spectacles. We have beef noodle soup competitions, a milkfish museum, and, in 2006, Taiwan's Council of Agriculture decided they were going to host a food festival centered around fried chicken cutlets, a popular night market snack. As part of the initiative, they decided to track down the first known person to sell the dish. So they parsed through chicken wholesale orders over the decades and eventually found a woman known as Auntie Zheng 鄭姑媽 in Taipei, who, according to the records, had been selling the dish for more than 30 years. Auntie Zheng's stall started out at the outskirts of a military village, where she sold cheap sandwiches and hamburgers to residents, but she eventually pivoted to deep-fried chicken breasts when she realized it was a cheaper cut of meat. In Taiwan, juicy morsels of dark meat are usually preferred over white meat because they're much moister; chicken breast is considered an unwanted cut because it has a tendency to dry out. However, Auntie Zheng found out that deep-frying helped the breast retain its moisture, and thus an icon was born.

FOR THE CHICKEN:

2   boneless chicken breasts, butterflied, about 1 pound (450 g) in total weight

2   tablespoons soy sauce

1   tablespoon Taiwanese rice wine (michiu) or cooking sake

2   garlic cloves, minced

2   teaspoons white sugar

½   teaspoon fine sea salt

½   teaspoon ground white pepper

¼   teaspoon five-spice powder

2   tablespoons all-purpose flour

¼   teaspoon baking powder (optional)

6   cups (1.4 L) canola or soybean oil

1   cup (160 g) thick sweet potato starch (see Note)

FOR THE SEASONING:

½   teaspoon chili powder, any type

½   teaspoon ground white pepper

¼   teaspoon fine sea salt

NOTE:
Thick sweet potato starch is coarse—similar to panko bread crumbs but a bit finer. Some brands will specify between thick and thin sweet potato starch. If you can only find thin, lightly spritz the starch with some water so that it clumps up and creates small beads.

(RECIPE CONTINUES)

MAKE THE CHICKEN: With a meat mallet, pound the chicken breasts so that they are about ½ inch (1 cm) thick. In a large bowl, combine the chicken breasts, soy sauce, rice wine, garlic, sugar, salt, white pepper, and five-spice powder, and massage the marinade into the chicken. Cover and refrigerate for at least 2 hours or overnight.

In a small bowl, combine the all-purpose flour and baking powder (if using), and mix thoroughly. Add it to the chicken marinade, massaging it into the chicken so that everything is thoroughly mixed together.

In a wok set over medium-high heat, warm the oil until it reaches 350°F (175°C) on an instant-read thermometer.

Place the thick sweet potato starch on a plate and, working in batches, press the chicken into the starch until both sides are fully coated. Shake off the excess starch.

Working with one chicken breast at a time, gently slide a chicken breast into the hot oil, and cook until light golden brown, turning it over often so both sides are completely submerged, 5 to 6 minutes. Remove the chicken from the oil with tongs, and transfer to a paper towel–lined plate or a wire rack set in a rimmed baking sheet to drain. Skim off and discard any leftover crumbs in the oil with the ladle. Repeat with the remaining chicken breast.

Increase the temperature of the oil to 375°F (190°C) over medium-high heat again and slide in a fried chicken breast. Fry until the chicken is golden brown and until the thickest part of the meat registers 160°F (70°C), about 2 minutes. Transfer the chicken to a paper towel–lined plate or a wire rack set in a rimmed baking sheet to drain again. To check if the chicken is done, pierce one with a chopstick; the juice that runs out should be clear. Repeat with the remaining chicken.

SEASON THE CHICKEN: While the chicken is still hot, season with the chili powder, white pepper, and salt, adding more of each if you'd like. Enjoy immediately.

Taiwanese-style popcorn chicken was popularized in 1975 by a man named Chen Ting-Chih 陳廷智, who proudly hung up a sign on his food stall bragging about how he had allegedly invented it. His boast worked, and he later franchised out his store to more than 3,000 fried chicken vendors on the condition that they buy and use his proprietary spice blend. The dish came at a time when American fried chicken was slowly gaining traction in the country as an exotic offering, but popcorn chicken caught on because it was bite-size, easier to eat on the go, and seasoned with familiar spices. Now, most self-declared inventors of popular Taiwanese dishes are often eventually canonized, but Chen's story doesn't have a happy ending. In 2019, his son and daughter were jailed for lacing the company's popcorn chicken spice blend with non-food grade magnesium carbonate, which has cancerous side effects. I know this isn't the most enticing story, but it's all the more reason to learn how to make this at home.

Popcorn Chicken

鹹酥雞
Xián Sū Jī

鹹酥雞
Kiâm Soo Ke

FOR THE CHICKEN:

- 1 pound (450 g) boneless chicken thighs, cut into 1-inch (2.5-cm) chunks
- 2 tablespoons soy sauce
- 1 tablespoon Taiwanese rice wine (michiu) or cooking sake
- 2 garlic cloves, minced
- 2 teaspoons white sugar
- ½ teaspoon fine sea salt
- ½ teaspoon ground white pepper
- ¼ teaspoon five-spice powder
- 2 tablespoons all-purpose flour
- ¼ teaspoon baking powder (optional)
- 4 cups (1 L) canola or soybean oil
- 1 cup (160 g) thick sweet potato starch (see Note)
- 1½ cups (30 g) fresh Thai basil (see Note)

FOR THE SEASONING:

- ½ teaspoon chili powder, any type
- ½ teaspoon ground white pepper
- ¼ teaspoon fine sea salt

MAKE THE CHICKEN: In a medium bowl, combine the chicken thighs, soy sauce, rice wine, garlic, sugar, salt, white pepper, and five-spice powder, and massage the marinade into the chicken. Cover and refrigerate for 2 hours or overnight.

In a small bowl, combine the all-purpose flour and baking powder (if using), and mix thoroughly. Add it to the chicken marinade, massaging it into the chicken so that everything is thoroughly mixed together.

Heat the oil in a wok over medium-high until it reaches 350°F (175°C) on an instant-read thermometer.

NOTES:

Thick sweet potato starch is coarse—similar to panko bread crumbs but a bit finer. Some brands will specify between thick and thin sweet potato starch. If you can only find thin, lightly spritz the starch with some water so that it clumps up and creates small beads.

Make sure the basil is completely dry; otherwise, oil will splatter everywhere when it's being deep-fried.

(RECIPE CONTINUES)

Place the thick sweet potato starch in a large bowl and, working in batches, coat the chicken in the starch with chopsticks until both sides are fully coated. Shake off the excess starch. Transfer the chicken to a clean plate and repeat with the remaining chicken.

Gently slide the coated chicken into the hot oil in batches and cook until they turn a light golden brown, about 2 to 3 minutes. With a spider strainer, gently remove the chicken from the oil, and drain on a paper towel–lined plate. Skim off and discard any leftover crumbs in the oil with the ladle.

Increase the temperature of the oil to 375°F (190°C) over medium-high heat and slide in the chicken again, working in batches so the wok isn't overcrowded. Fry quickly until golden brown and the thickest part of the meat registers 160°F (70°C), about 1 minute. Transfer the chicken with a spider strainer to a new paper towel–lined plate and drain.

Add the basil to the hot oil and, working quickly, immediately cover the wok with a lid (it will crackle and spray). Quickly fry until the basil crisps up and turns transparent and glassy, about 10 seconds. Turn off the heat and transfer the basil with a spider strainer to a paper towel–lined plate to drain.

SEASON THE CHICKEN: When the chicken and basil are cool enough to handle, transfer them to a large bowl, and add the chili powder, white pepper, and salt. Cover the bowl with a large plate or lightweight cutting board and shake it thoroughly so the chicken is coated completely with the seasoning. Enjoy while hot.

Black Pepper Steak and Spaghetti

鐵板牛排麵
Tiĕ Bǎn Niú Pái Miàn

I was on a really electrifying second date with this dashing guy in Taipei and, after many rounds of beers, drunkenly declared at the end of the night that I wanted bad steak with spaghetti. My date looked at me bewildered, unsure whether to take it as a joke. Low-quality steak smothered with black pepper is a highlight of Taiwanese night markets, served on seasoned cast-iron plates usually etched with tacky cow engravings. This genre of food came to the island in the late 1970s as an aspirational approximation of Western steak houses. It's not very refined at all. In fact, it's offensive to people who really know and love high-quality steak. But I adore it in spite of the stringy cuts of meat because it reminds me of my blind childhood love for the night market, and how I loved watching the black pepper sauce bubble, sizzle, and pop on the jet-black cast-iron plates. I didn't find steak that night, but it all worked out in the end because now I live a couple of blocks away from a cheap Taiwanese steak house. And that man I was on a date with? He's now my husband.

2	strip steaks, about 1 pound (450 g) in total weight		1	tablespoon white sugar
1	teaspoon coarse salt		1¼	teaspoons ground black pepper
1	tablespoon unsalted butter		1	teaspoon Worcestershire sauce
¼	medium yellow onion, peeled and minced		¼	teaspoon fine sea salt, plus more for the spaghetti water
3	garlic cloves, minced		1	tablespoon tapioca starch or cornstarch
2	tablespoons Taiwanese soy paste (store-bought or homemade; page 366)		2	tablespoons plus 2 teaspoons canola or soybean oil, divided
1	tablespoon soy sauce		4	ounces (120 g) dried spaghetti
			2	large eggs

Pat the steaks dry and rub them thoroughly with the coarse salt. Let them rest at room temperature for 1 hour or overnight in the refrigerator.

In a medium saucepan set over medium heat, heat the butter. When the butter is shimmering, add the onion and cook, stirring until soft, about 5 minutes. Mix in the garlic, and stir until aromatic, about 30 seconds. Add the soy paste, soy sauce, sugar, black pepper, Worcestershire sauce, fine sea salt, and 1 cup (240 ml) water, and stir until the sugar melts, about 1 minute. Bring to a boil over medium-high heat, then reduce the temperature to medium-low to briskly simmer.

In a small bowl, mix together the tapioca starch and 1½ tablespoons water to form a slurry. Whisk the slurry into the saucepan, and simmer until

SPECIAL EQUIPMENT:
2 seasoned cast-iron steak plates

(RECIPE CONTINUES)

thickened, about 30 seconds. Add more salt to taste if you'd like. Turn off the heat and set aside.

In a large skillet set over high heat, heat 2 tablespoons of the oil. When the oil is hot, add the steaks. Cook, flipping the steaks occasionally, until the thickest part of the meat registers 130°F (55°C) on an instant-read thermometer, about 4 minutes on each side. If it starts to get charred, reduce the heat to medium. Turn off the heat and transfer the steaks to a clean plate to rest.

Bring a heavily salted medium pot of water to boil over high heat, and add the dried spaghetti, cooking according to package instructions. Drain in a colander and shake dry.

Heat a seasoned cast-iron steak plate over high heat and add 1 teaspoon oil to the side of the plate. Crack an egg on top of the oil. Turn off the heat. Plate the dish by placing one cooked steak and half the spaghetti next to the egg. Spoon as much black pepper sauce as you want all over the dish. Serve immediately. Repeat with the remaining steak plate, using up the remaining 1 teaspoon oil, egg, steak, sauce, and spaghetti. Enjoy immediately.

Every culture has its own take on sausage, and in Taiwan, our version is marked by a heavy dose of sugar, rice wine, white pepper, and five-spice powder. It's very similar to a Cantonese lap cheong in terms of flavor profile, but the main difference is that instead of being cured for many days until it's dehydrated, the Taiwanese rendition is gently air-dried for only a day or two and stays wonderfully plump. It's usually grilled to order and served with a side of raw garlic. Many street vendors also like adding a kiss of maqaw—an indigenous Taiwanese spice reminiscent of lemon pepper—for an extra layer of dimension. The key to sausage making is keeping the meat as cold as possible and being sure you knead it afterward so it's sticky. Don't skip these steps; they're the difference between a dried-out sausage and a juicy one.

Taiwanese Pork Sausage

台式香腸
Tái Shì Xiāng Cháng

煙腸
Ian Tshiân

2 pounds (900 g) pork shoulder

½ pound (225 g) pork back fat

5 garlic cloves, finely minced, plus more whole cloves for serving

¼ cup (50 g) white sugar

2 tablespoons Taiwanese rice wine (michiu) or cooking sake, plus more for brushing

1 tablespoon plus 1 teaspoon fine sea salt

½ teaspoon pink curing salt #1 (optional)

½ teaspoon ground white pepper

½ teaspoon five-spice powder

¼ teaspoon ground cinnamon

Natural hog casing, soaked in warm water for 30 minutes and rinsed thoroughly

Canola or soybean oil, for pan-frying

Cut the pork shoulder and pork back fat into 1-inch (2.5-cm) cubes and transfer to a large bowl. Add the minced garlic, sugar, rice wine, salt, pink curing salt (if using), white pepper, five-spice powder, and cinnamon, and massage into the pork mixture. Transfer everything to a large resealable plastic bag (or two), press the meat so that it's flat and in a single layer, and refrigerate for 4 hours or up to overnight. Put the bowl and paddle of the stand mixer, the meat grinder attachment, and kidney plate in the freezer.

Remove the bag of marinated pork shoulder and pork back fat from the refrigerator to the freezer and chill until partially frozen, about 1 hour. With the meat grinder fitted with the kidney plate or the coarsest grinding plate you have, grind the meat mixture through on medium speed.

Transfer the ground meat to the bowl of a stand mixer outfitted with the chilled paddle attachment and mix at low speed until the meat is super sticky, 1 to 2 minutes. (Alternatively, use pair of chopsticks and stir the meat repeatedly in one direction until very sticky, about 5 minutes.) To test if it's

SPECIAL EQUIPMENT:
stand mixer with meat grinder (preferably with kidney plate); sausage stuffer; cotton twine

NOTE:
Use about ½ teaspoon of oil for each sausage. You can also grill the sausages, which is how it's usually done. The signature red color of the Taiwanese sausage comes from the curing salt. If you're using regular salt, the sausage will be more on the brown side. Don't panic; this is completely normal.

(RECIPE CONTINUES)

sticky enough, press a small patty of meat into your palm. Hold your palm out, facing down on the table. The meat should easily continue to stick to you.

With the sausage stuffer attachment, stuff the sausage into the natural hog casing and twist into 6-inch (15-cm) links, keeping them relatively thin, about 1 inch (2.5 cm) in diameter. With a toothpick, poke holes in the casings to release the air bubbles out of the sausages. Brush or spray rice wine all over the sausages; this helps preserve them.

If you added the pink curing salt, hang the sausages up with cotton twine in a cool, dry room with good ventilation to cure for 1 day (add an extra day if you want a funkier, fermented flavor). If you didn't add pink salt, cook the sausages immediately, or store in the freezer to preserve.

To cook, set a skillet over medium-low heat, and drizzle in oil (see Note). When the oil is hot, add the sausage and cook, turning occasionally, until the thickest part of the sausage registers 160°F (70°C) on a thermometer, 10 to 15 minutes. Turn off the heat, remove from skillet, and let the sausages rest for 5 minutes before enjoying. Enjoy with raw, whole garlic cloves (this sounds odd, but it's traditional to Taiwan and I find it delightful).

These are usually sliced at a steep angle and served with soy paste, or cut in half lengthwise like a hot dog bun and stuffed with a Taiwanese pork sausage. As with many Taiwanese dishes, there's quite a bit of variation to this. When the rice sausages are served à la carte, they're made with thick and rubbery large intestines and flavored with peanuts. When they're served at a night market stuffed with sausage, they're made with paper-thin small-intestine casings. Within Taiwan, northerners like working with precooked rice and a lot more shiitake mushrooms, and southerners will stuff their casings with raw rice and keep the seasoning much simpler. Keeping true to both my heritage and Ivy's, this recipe is inspired by the variants at southern Taiwanese night markets.

Sticky Rice Sausage

糯米腸
Nuò Mǐ Cháng

大腸
Tuā Tn̄g

2	pounds (900 g) long-grain glutinous rice, also known as sticky rice
3	medium dried shiitake mushrooms
3	tablespoons lard or canola or soybean oil, plus more for pan-frying, divided

¼	cup (20 g) fried shallots (store-bought or homemade; page 368)
1	tablespoon fine sea salt
1	teaspoon ground white pepper
	Natural hog casing, soaked in warm water for 30 minutes and rinsed thoroughly

Rinse the glutinous rice under running water. In a large bowl, combine the glutinous rice with enough water to cover. Soak for 4 hours at room temperature or overnight in the refrigerator.

In a small bowl, cover the dried shiitake mushrooms with water, and soak until soft, about 1 hour. If you are in a rush, soak them in boiling water for 30 minutes (though they won't be nearly as flavorful).

Drain the rice in a sieve and set aside. Squeeze out excess water from the shiitake mushrooms, then trim the stems and discard. Mince the caps and set aside.

Heat a wok over medium heat and add 1 tablespoon of the lard. When the lard has melted, add the mushrooms and cook, stirring, until it smells lovely, about 1 minute. Turn off the heat and transfer the cooked shiitakes to a large bowl. Add the rice, shallots, salt, white pepper, and the remaining 2 tablespoons lard, and mix to combine.

Using a good old-fashioned funnel and a stick, stuff the mixture into the natural hog casing by connecting the casing to the funnel and pushing the rice mixture through with a stick or the handle of a long wooden spoon. Shape the sausage into loose links, about 6 inches (15 cm) long and 1 inch

SPECIAL EQUIPMENT:
large funnel, cotton twine

NOTE:
You can also grill the sausages, which is how it's traditionally done.

(RECIPE CONTINUES)

(2 cm) thick, and tie a simple knot with a short cotton string in between each sausage to divide them up. It's very important to keep the filling very loose and almost saggy; the rice will expand as it cooks later, and an overstuffed sausage might explode. With a toothpick, poke holes in the casings to release the air bubbles out of the sausages.

Bring a large pot of water to a slow simmer over low heat. Gently lower the sausage links into the water and cook for 40 minutes. Remove and cool down. The sausage can be eaten as is or pan-fried. Any extras can be frozen for a couple of months.

TO PAN-FRY: Set a skillet over medium-high heat and add lard or oil (about ½ teaspoon for each sausage). When the lard is hot, add the sausage and cook, turning occasionally, until lightly browned, about 2 minutes. Remove from the heat and enjoy immediately.

Little Sausage in Big Sausage

大腸包小腸

Dà Cháng Bāo Xiǎo Cháng

Served like a hot dog, this dish is composed of a pork sausage wrapped in a rice sausage. To do this, first pan-fry the rice sausage until it's slightly browned. Slice it lengthwise down the middle so it's like a hot dog bun, and nestle the pork sausage inside. Season with some sautéed mustard greens and a sprinkle of sugar (page 53), thin slices of pickled cucumbers (page 83), raw garlic slices, and Everyday Garlic Soy Dressing (page 367).

There are two tales about how this dish came to be. One is that there was an old man who planted a bunch of sweet potatoes underneath a bridge, but one day there was a construction project that accidentally excavated all his potatoes. To get rid of them, he decided to fry them up and sell them, and it became a huge hit. The other is that this dish is but a Taiwanese adaptation of Chinese deep-fried sesame balls that instead utilizes the abundance of sweet potatoes on the island. Regardless, it's now a night market staple and a lovely evening snack.

- ¾ pound (340 g) sweet potatoes
- ¼ cup (50 g) white sugar
- ¼ cup plus 1 tablespoon (50 g) sweet potato starch, plus more if needed
- 1½ tablespoons glutinous rice flour, such as Erawan
- 6 cups (1.4 L) canola or soybean oil

Preheat the oven to 400°F (205°C).

Wash and scrub the sweet potatoes and pat them dry thoroughly with a clean kitchen towel. With a fork, poke holes all over. Bake the potatoes on a foil-lined pan for 40 to 50 minutes, until a fork can pierce them with no resistance. When cool enough to handle, peel off the skin. Pass the sweet potatoes through a ricer or mash with a fork. Measure out 1 cup (½ pound; 225 g) of the mashed sweet potato. Reserve any remaining for another use.

Transfer the mashed sweet potato to a large bowl and, while it's still hot, fold in the sugar, sweet potato starch, and glutinous rice flour. Mix and knead until it forms a smooth dough. If it's too crumbly, drizzle in a bit of water. If it's too wet, add 1 teaspoon of sweet potato starch at a time. Because every sweet potato is different, the amount of water and starch really varies. The final consistency should be similar to sculpting clay without any cracks in the dough. Roll into a long cylinder and, with a bench scraper, cut into 23 even pieces, about 15 g each. Roll them into smooth balls.

In a large wok set over medium-high heat, heat the oil until it reaches 300°F (150°C) on an instant-read thermometer. Using a spider strainer and working in batches, tip the sweet potato balls into the hot oil. Cook and stir constantly until they float, 2 to 3 minutes. With the spider strainer, pin the balls very firmly against the bottom of the wok for 3 seconds and release. They will visibly puff up. Maintain the temperature at 300°F (150°C), adjusting the heat as necessary. Do this repeatedly until they're all very puffy, slightly translucent, and crispy, about another 3 minutes. Transfer to a paper towel–lined plate and drain. Enjoy while hot.

Sweet Potato Balls

地瓜球

Dì Guā Qiú

NOTES:

You can steam the sweet potato instead of baking it. Steam until the sweet potato is fork tender, 20 to 30 minutes.

The secret to getting these sweet potato balls to puff up is to pin them down firmly against the bottom of the wok. The pressure buildup will expand the balls and turn them puffy. If you can't tell whether they're puffing up, you aren't pressing hard enough. They should be light as a Ping-Pong ball and almost glassy—a beautiful shade of bright apricot orange.

Vegan Blood Cake

智慧糕
Zhì Huì Gāo

智慧糕
Tî Huī Kué

Blood cake isn't as terrifying as it sounds. While it does include actual pig's blood, the bulk of it is made with glutinous rice, and the blood mostly acts as a coagulant to keep everything together. I opted for the vegan adaptation of this dish because it's really difficult for the average home cook to get access to fresh blood, and because a similar flavor is more or less achievable with just rice. Even here in Taiwan, pork blood is shipped from butchers directly to restaurants and food vendors, and there's no way for the average home cook to buy blood in stores or even at the wet markets. This recipe blitzes black rice into liquid and uses that to bind the whole cake together to give it its signature color. It's then dressed with soy paste and dusted with a generous sprinkle of peanut powder. The name of this vegan dish translates to "wisdom cake," which in the Taiwanese language is a homonym for pig's blood cake (豬血糕 ti hueh kué). The addition of seaweed gives it a clever yet subtle hit of umami.

1	cup (200 g) long-grain glutinous rice, also known as sticky rice
¼	cup (50 g) black rice, also known as forbidden rice
1	sheet dried seaweed, also known as sushi nori (about 3 g in total weight), chopped
¼	teaspoon fine sea salt

⅛	teaspoon ground white pepper
½	cup (75 g) unsalted roasted peanuts (page 368)
2	tablespoons white sugar, plus more to taste
¼	cup (60 ml) Everyday Soy Dressing (page 367)
	Fresh cilantro sprigs, chopped (for garnish)

Rinse the long-grain glutinous rice under running water. Transfer the rice to a medium bowl and add enough water to cover. Rinse the black rice under running water. Transfer to a separate medium bowl and add 1 cup (240 ml) water. Soak the long-grain glutinous rice and the black rice for at least 4 hours at room temperature or overnight in the refrigerator.

Drain the long-grain glutinous rice through a sieve, and transfer to a medium bowl. Drain the black rice through a fine-mesh strainer nestled on top of a medium bowl, reserving ¼ cup plus 3 tablespoons (105 ml) of its soaking liquid.

In a small blender, combine the dried seaweed, salt, white pepper, the reserved black rice soaking liquid, and the black rice. Blend on high speed until it's a smooth and purple creamy liquid, 2 minutes.

In the bowl with the long-grain glutinous rice, pour in the purple liquid, and mix with a silicone spatula until all the kernels are completely covered.

SPECIAL EQUIPMENT:
8 × 4-inch (20 × 10-cm) rectangular glass container or baking pan of a similar size; small blender or immersion blender.

(RECIPE CONTINUES)

Line an 8 × 4-inch (20 × 10-cm) rectangular glass food storage container with enough parchment paper to cover the bottom and the long sides. Pour the rice mixture into the container. Using a spatula or the back of a spoon, smooth out the rice.

Place the container in a steamer and cover. Partially fill a large wok with water (for steaming tips, see page 38). Bring the water to a rapid boil over high heat, and carefully perch the steamer on top. Steam for 30 minutes, replenishing the bottom of the wok with boiling water if needed.

Meanwhile, put the roasted peanuts in a blender, and pulse on high speed for about 30 seconds. The texture should be like fine sand. Transfer to a plate and mix with the sugar. Taste and add more sugar if you'd like.

Lift the rice cake out of the pan and let it cool for about 15 minutes. When it's cool enough to handle but still warm, with a well-oiled knife, cut the cake into 4 rectangular pieces. If you want, you can run a skewer through each piece to mimic how it's served at night markets. Using a silicone brush, coat the pieces with Everyday Soy Dressing all over, and press the rice cake in the ground peanut powder so that it's completely covered. Garnish with the cilantro. Enjoy while warm. The rice cake can be stored in the refrigerator for up to 4 days or in the freezer for up to 3 weeks. Just quickly steam before serving.

For most, the word *tempura* conjures up images of gorgeous platters of deep-fried shrimp and vegetables enveloped in a beautifully light and crisp batter à la Japan. This style of cooking was reportedly introduced to Japan in the 16th century via the Portuguese, who had a habit of deep-frying fish and veggies. However, the Taiwanese interpretation of tempura looks nothing like the afore-mentioned dish, but that's because our version is more similar to what's eaten on the Japanese island of Kyushu. Known as satsuma-age in Japanese, it's a fish paste that's molded with salt, sugar, and starch, and then deep-fried.

In Mandarin, tempura literally translates to "sweet, not spicy"—a nod to the natural sweetness of the fish stick paired with the more-sweet-than-spicy chili sauce typical of Taiwanese cuisine.

Taiwanese Tempura

甜 不 辣
Tián Bù Là

½ pound (225 g) boneless, skinless tilapia fillet

1 ounce (30 g) pork back fat or pork belly

1 teaspoon fine sea salt

1 large egg white

¼ cup (30 g) tapioca starch

1½ tablespoons white sugar

1 tablespoon all-purpose flour

¼ teaspoon ground white pepper

1 garlic clove, chopped

¼ cup (60 ml) ice water

4 cups (1 L) canola or soybean oil

Sweet Chili Sauce (page 369)

Cut the tilapia and pork back fat into 1 inch (2.5 cm) cubes. Put the fish and pork cubes in a plastic bag, flatten it into a single layer, and freeze the fish and pork until partially frozen, about 1 hour.

Transfer the partially frozen tilapia and pork back fat to a food processor and add the salt. Pulse on high speed until it becomes a smooth, sticky paste, about 2 minutes. Add the egg white, tapioca starch, sugar, all-purpose flour, white pepper, and garlic, and blend thoroughly until the starch and flour has disappeared, about 1 minute. Add the ice water and blend again until completely smooth, about another 1 minute. If the sludge gets stuck, use a spoon to loosen up the mixture around the blades and then keep on blending. If you still see visible chunks of meat, keep on blending. The final paste should glisten and have a latex-like sheen.

Put the fish paste in a food storage container and cover. Let it rest in the refrigerator so that the starch can fully absorb the fish, for at least 1 hour or up to overnight.

NOTE:
Ivy spent a lot of time trying to perfect the texture on this one. Initially we thought you could just put regular fish paste designed for fish balls (page 361) directly into hot, sizzling oil, but it didn't retain the signature plumpness of a Taiwanese tempura. So she added a bit of wheat flour and egg white for support, and it made all the difference.

SPECIAL EQUIPMENT:
food processor; wooden spatula with a 3-inch (7.5-cm) blade.

(RECIPE CONTINUES)

In a wok set over medium-high heat, heat the oil until it reaches 300°F (150°C) on an instant-read thermometer. Plaster the flat blade of a large wooden spatula with a ½-inch (1-cm) layer of fish paste. Hold it over the hot oil and use a well-oiled bench scraper or a knife to cut and push off 3-inch (7.5-cm) logs of tempura into the oil. Cook, stirring occasionally so they don't stick, until light golden brown and poofy, 4 to 5 minutes. Remove the tempura with a spider strainer and drain on a paper towel–lined plate. They will begin to deflate and wrinkle. Enjoy while hot with a side of the Sweet Chili Sauce.

節
慶

Special
Occasions

How to Feed the Gods

In Taiwan, the spirits live among us. We're haunted by kitchen guardians, hungry ghosts, and a gaggle of ancestors from both sides of our families. We're graced by earth gods, sea goddesses, retired warlord gods, and gods whose sole job is to oversee the bureaucratic inner workings of a city. Even pieces of household furniture like beds and tables have deities assigned to them. Like mortals, all of these celestial beings have different personalities, wants, and needs. And like us, to appease them, you must feed them.

To feed the gods, you have to first understand that they expect only the best. They want foods that are whole, not cut up haphazardly, and they want a trinity (sān sheng 三牲) of foods that represent the land, sea, and air. The trinity should be only partially cooked, because the Mandarin word for fully cooked (shú 熟) is a homophone for the word *familiar*. That's a bad thing, because you aren't allowed to be familiar with your gods. You have to maintain a respectful distance, and your food should appropriately symbolize that distance.

To prepare and serve the trinity: Get a large slab of pork belly (land) and boil it, take a full chicken (air) with its head and feet still attached and poach it, and acquire a whole fish (sea) and quickly deep-fry it. Lay that all on the altar at the temple. The pork goes in the middle, the chicken on the left, and the fish on the right (though this configuration might differ by family). Light some incense and say your prayers; the gods are done eating when the incense stick has completely burned through. Some of the more pious practitioners might throw some divinity blocks into the air and see how they land. How the blocks are positioned will indicate whether the gods have finished their meals.

Food is never wasted. When the gods are done eating, it's time to actually eat the trinity and fully cook the ingredients. Dice the pork belly, put it in a slow-cooker, and make a long and hearty braise. Deep-fry the fish again and slather it with a sweet-and-sour sauce with colorful, julienned vegetables. Chop the chicken into large chunks and toss it into a soup with rice wine and sesame oil. The essence of your ingredients has already been eaten up by the gods; now it's time for the physical food to provide sustenance to actual blood, flesh, and bone. In a way, it goes full circle. The best of the land, air, and sea is offered to the gods, and in turn comes back to nourish you.

Gua Bao

刈包 or 割包
Kuah Pau

Taiwan is overflowing with deities, and toward the end of the lunar calendar year, the gods will take a break and return to their celestial homes to reunite with the Jade Emperor for an annual vacation. It's during this time of year when people start bribing the gods with delicious food in hopes that they'll put in a good word for their families during the celestial retreat. And out of this ritual, the gua bao was born.

A snack that originated in northern Taiwan, the gua bao is designed to look like a wallet and is an omen for more money. Slices of braised pork are nestled within soft, plump pockets of dough, then garnished with crushed sweet peanuts and sharp mustard greens. The sprinkle of golden peanuts represents money, and the white bun is supposed to be a purse. In Taiwanese Hokkien, it's also sometimes called "tiger bites pig"(hóo kā ti 虎咬豬), with the bun symbolizing the mouth of a tiger and the pork slab in the middle the pig.

FOR THE FILLING:

1 pound (450 g) skin-on pork belly

1 tablespoon canola or soybean oil

2 cups (470 ml) water

¼ cup plus 2 tablespoons (90 ml) soy sauce

1 tablespoon Taiwanese rice wine (michiu) or cooking sake

1 tablespoon white sugar

1 tablespoon fried shallots (store-bought or homemade; page 368)

1 dried tangerine or mandarin orange peel, about the size of a quarter

1 small cassia or cinnamon stick, about 2 inches (5 cm) long

FOR THE BUNS:

2 teaspoons white sugar

½ cup plus 2 tablespoons (150 g) lukewarm water

1 teaspoon active dry yeast

1¾ cups (220 g) all-purpose flour, plus more for dusting

¼ cup (30 g) cake flour

¼ teaspoon fine sea salt

1 teaspoon canola or soybean oil, plus more for brushing

FOR GARNISH:

¼ pound (115 g) pickled mustard greens (store-bought or homemade; page 347)

1 tablespoon canola or soybean oil

2 garlic cloves, minced

2 teaspoons white sugar

¼ teaspoon fine sea salt

¼ cup (45 g) Sweet Peanut Powder (page 369)

Fresh cilantro sprigs, chopped

SPECIAL EQUIPMENT:
stand mixer (optional)

(RECIPE CONTINUES)

MAKE THE PORK FILLING: Cut the pork belly into 2-inch (5-cm) rectangles, about ½ inch (1 cm) thick. In a large pot set over medium-high heat, add the oil. When the oil is hot, add the pork, and cook until both sides are lightly browned, 4 to 5 minutes. Add the water, soy sauce, rice wine, sugar, fried shallots, tangerine peel, and cassia stick. Bring the liquid to a rolling boil, then reduce the heat to low. Cover and simmer, leaving the lid slightly ajar,

until the pork is melt-in-your-mouth tender, 1 to 1½ hours. Stir occasionally so the pork doesn't stick to the bottom of the pot.

MAKE THE BUNS: In a medium bowl, combine the sugar and lukewarm water, and stir until the sugar is dissolved. Sprinkle the active dry yeast on top, and wait until the top gets frothy, 2 to 3 minutes.

In a large bowl or the bowl of a stand mixer, combine the all-purpose flour, cake flour, and salt. Slowly drizzle in the frothy yeast water and mix to form a lumpy dough. Add the oil, then bring the dough together with your hands and knead until smooth, about 10 minutes. (Alternatively, mix in a stand mixer on low speed with the dough hook attachment until smooth, about 2 minutes.)

With a pastry brush, grease a large bowl with a thin layer of oil, and put the dough inside. Cover with plastic wrap, and let it rest at room temperature until it has doubled in size, 1 to 2 hours. (This will depend on how hot your kitchen is. The hotter it is, the shorter the resting time.)

Punch the air out of the dough and transfer it to a lightly floured surface. Divide the dough into 6 equal pieces, about 67 g each. Knead each piece by pushing the dough down with the heel of your palm, bringing the edges in, and rotating the dough counterclockwise until it forms an extremely smooth and shiny ball, about 2 minutes each. Cover and let rest for 10 minutes.

Cut out 6 squares of parchment paper, about 3 × 3 inches (7.5 × 7.5 cm) each.

With a rolling pin, flatten each dough ball into an oval, about 5.5 inches (14 cm) long and 3 inches (7.5 cm) wide. With a pastry brush, apply a thin layer of oil onto the dough, and fold it in half. Place the bun on a

parchment paper square and repeat with the remaining dough balls. Arrange the buns in a tiered bamboo steamer, leaving 1 inch (2.5 cm) of space in between each bun.

Cover the steamer and let rest until the buns have inflated again to about 1½ times in size, 30 to 40 minutes. If you press on it gently, it should spring back slowly.

MEANWHILE, PREPARE THE GARNISHES: Briefly rinse the pickled mustard greens under running water. In a small bowl, cover the greens with water, and soak for 10 minutes. Drain, squeeze out the excess water, and pat dry with paper towels. Mince finely.

Heat a wok over medium heat, and swirl in the oil. When hot, add in the garlic and cook until it smells lovely, about 30 seconds. Add the pickled mustard greens, sugar, and salt, and cook, stirring constantly, until the sugar has melted and the greens are slightly dried out, 4 to 5 minutes. Remove and set aside on a small plate.

Partially fill a large wok with water (for steaming tips, see page 38) and bring to a rolling boil over medium-high heat. Place the bamboo steamers with the buns inside on top of the wok, and steam for 15 to 18 minutes. (If you're using one steamer, cook for 15 minutes. If you're using two steamers, cook for 18 minutes.) Turn the heat off, but leave the steamer on the wok with the lid on for an additional 3 minutes so the buns don't collapse.

To assemble, open a bun and place a slice of pork belly inside. Add a spoonful of peanut powder, some pickled mustard greens, and cilantro to taste. Enjoy immediately. The steamed buns can be stored in the freezer for up to 2 months. Steam for 5 minutes over high heat before serving.

Kueh: A Fading Culinary Art

Stepping into husband and wife Huang Teng-Wei 黃騰威 and Chou Pei-Yi's 周佩儀 cooking studio Siang Kháu Lū 雙口呂 is like taking a step back in time to an era that I've only heard about in whispers from elders, so distant and elusive it might as well have been made up. It was a time well before the industrialization of Taiwan, when most families lived in the countryside and resided in gorgeous U-shaped brick courtyard compounds known as sān hé yuàn 三合院.

The center—or heart—of the compound was almost always a family altar, with photos of the ancestors plastered in the middle of the room, and the wings that forked out from there were where different branches of the extended family resided. Multiple generations would live under one roof, and the matriarch would do most of the cooking in a single giant wok fitted perfectly into the round indent of a wood-fired brick stove. It's here where Teng-Wei and Pei-Yi have made a sanctuary for themselves, and it's here where they teach students from all over Taiwan the art of kueh.

The word *kueh* refers to a type of pastry that's often—but not always—made of rice. With a wide range from southern China and all throughout Southeast Asia, kueh used to be a cornerstone in agrarian Taiwan, where the rice harvest was celebrated and not eaten as just an empty carb, like it is today.

To think of rice as just a pile of cooked kernels in a bowl is disrespectful to the astounding versatility of the grain. Much like wheat flour, rice can be processed and reinvented, and in the old days, it would be soaked overnight and then fed by one person through the mouth of a small stone mill, while another turned the wheel with the torque of their body. Out of the mouth of the mill would splutter fresh rice milk, which could be steamed into a pudding or a cake or filtered through a tightly woven muslin cloth to make rice flour.

These rituals gave birth to a cornucopia of sweet and savory pastries known as kueh—like bright white rice dumplings stuffed with daikon and pork, or pink tortoise-shaped discs filled with sweet adzuki beans. Different types of rice gave off different textures, and everyone back then knew the differences: Long-grain rice was used to make puddings, short-grain and glutinous rice for the dumplings. Savory kuehs would be offered to the ancestors. Sweet kuehs—because of how expensive sugar was—would be given to the gods.

But unlike Western pastries, which have dedicated storefronts and culinary schools, kueh is a dying culinary art, in part because it was never seen as anything out of the ordinary. "In the old days, you would never gift someone a kueh," Teng-Wei explains to me. "It meant that someone in the recipient's family was incapacitated and unable to make kueh themselves." Just a handful of generations ago, most housewives knew how to make kueh. But as more women joined the workforce, it became a skill that was no longer prioritized or valued.

Teng-Wei and Pei-Yi take me on a stroll through their local wet market in Taoyuan, where we meet some grannies who sell the confectionery. Many of them are hunched over with age, and most are the last of their line who can make kueh. Teng-Wei and Pei-Yi tell me they're trying their best to learn as much as they can from these matriarchs before it's too late.

The seed for their cooking school was planted many years ago when they went to Europe and some friends offhandedly asked them what foods best represented Taiwan. Without thinking, they quickly listed off internationally known Taiwanese dishes like beef noodle soup and soup dumplings. But after careful consideration, they felt their answers were a bit cliché. "These are all dishes that came after 1949 with the Chinese immigrants," Teng-Wei says. Eventually, they settled on kueh because of its longer history. Rice, they feel, embodies the true spirit of Taiwanese cuisine better, and they've made it their mission to bring awareness of the grain's multiplicity through hands-on courses and lectures. Most of the recipes and techniques taught in their courses are sourced from Pei-Yi's own grandmother.

"The effort it takes to make kueh is the same as making cake, but the price is a fifth or a sixth of that," says Teng-Wei. He notes that the glitzy neighborhoods of Taipei are populated with brightly lit bakeries and patisseries, many of them French-inspired. There's a die-hard admiration for European confectionaries on

the island. But the only places where you can really find traditional Taiwanese pastries like kueh are at select wet markets, sold for a few coins apiece. It's a strange dichotomy, considering that the former is internationally accessible and the latter is relatively unique to this part of the world. Both take immense precision and skill to make.

It's their hope—and mine—that with time, education, and written recipes such as the ones provided in this book, kueh will once again rise to prominence.

KUEH DISHES IN THIS BOOK:

A proper red tortoise kueh should glisten the moment it's lifted out of the steamer. The outside has an almost latex-like sheen to it, and the inside is a wonderful, almost fudge-like mixture of crushed sweet adzuki bean paste. "The tortoise represents longevity," Huang Teng-Wei tells me as he shows off his collection of antique hand-carved tortoise molds. This recipe is from Teng-Wei's wife, Chou Pei-Yi, who learned how to make it from her grandmother. Traditionally, the red tortoise kueh is brought to the temple to be given as an offering to the gods, and then taken home to be shared and enjoyed by the family. Teng-Wei and Pei-Yi make all their kueh doughs from a very specific blend of raw rice kernels, which are first soaked overnight and then blended and filtered through a muslin cloth. I've simplified their recipe and converted it to rice flour to make it easier for the average home cook, but for instructions on how to make the kueh dough from raw rice, see page 273.

- ¾ cup (150 g) adzuki beans, also known as red beans
- 2 cups (260 g) glutinous rice flour, such as Erawan
- ¼ cup (30 g) Thai rice flour, such as Erawan
- 2 tablespoons unsalted butter, softened
- ¼ cup plus 2 tablespoons (75 g) coarse raw sugar, such as demerara
- ⅛ to ¼ teaspoon red food dye or ½ teaspoon red yeast rice powder
- Canola or soybean oil

Rinse the adzuki beans under running water. In a medium bowl, soak the adzuki beans in enough water to cover for 4 hours at room temperature or overnight in the refrigerator.

In a large bowl, combine the glutinous rice flour and Thai rice flour, then stir in ¾ cup plus 2 tablespoons (210 ml) water to form a shaggy dough. Cover and let rest for 1 hour or up to overnight in the refrigerator. Resting the dough and letting the rice flour hydrate will make the kueh smoother.

Drain the adzuki beans in a fine-mesh strainer, and shake dry. In a medium pot set over high heat, combine the adzuki beans and 2 cups (470 ml) water. Bring the water to a rolling boil, then reduce the heat to medium-low. Cover and cook at a brisk simmer, stirring occasionally, until the red beans can be easily smashed with the back of a spoon, about 1 hour. By now most of the water should have been absorbed. If it hasn't, strain the beans through a fine-mesh sieve. In the same pot set over low heat, combine the boiled adzuki beans, butter, and sugar. Stir constantly with a silicone spatula and press down on the mixture until the butter and sugar melt. It will turn from a mashed potato texture to a very dense paste, 15 to 20 minutes. The paste

Red Tortoise Kueh

紅龜粿
Âng Ku Kué

SPECIAL EQUIPMENT:
2 × 3-inch (6 × 7.5-cm) red tortoise kueh mold, also known as an ang ku kueh mold (plastic or wood)

NOTES:
Pei steams the kueh over shell ginger leaves, which can easily be foraged from all around Taiwan. You can probably find them in the wild if you live in a tropical state like Florida or Hawaii (please pick responsibly!). Banana leaves are another great alternative. If you're using a leaf instead of parchment paper, brush it with oil before you put the kueh on.

Tortoise kueh molds can be difficult to procure, though they can occasionally be found online and are sometimes mislabeled as "tortoise moon cake molds." If you can't find them, the best alternative is to use a large oval-shaped wooden ma'amoul mold.

(RECIPE CONTINUES)

should be rather chunky, and you will still be able to see the skin of the red bean kernels ("Grandma prefers it really smooth, but I like it like this," says Pei). Remove from the heat and let cool down to room temperature.

Fill a small pot halfway with water and bring to a gentle simmer over medium heat.

Take the rice dough out of the refrigerator and transfer it to a clean work surface. Measure out 3 rounded tablespoons of dough, about 50 g each. Roll the dough into a circle and flatten with your palms to form a flat disc. Plop the disc into the simmering water, and cook until it floats, about 2 minutes. If it doesn't float, gently pry open the dough with chopsticks. It's done when the center is translucent all the way through. If you still see chalky white chunks in the middle, keep on simmering.

Ladle the disc out of the water and put it on top of the rest of the rice dough on the table. Add ⅛ teaspoon red food dye. When it's cool enough to handle—but still very warm—knead everything with your hands to form a very smooth dough, about 5 minutes. It might be quite wet at first and stick to the table; lift it off the bench with a bench scraper, and put some muscle into it. It will turn a very pale pastel pink (it will become more vibrant after you steam it) and will become more cohesive as you knead it. If you want more color, add a little bit more dye. The dough should be smooth and pliable like modeling clay. If it cracks around the edges, it's too dry. Adjust by adding ½ teaspoon water at a time.

Divide into 10 equal balls, about 50 g each. When the red bean filling is cool enough to handle, separate into 10 equal piles, about 37 g each. Flatten a pink rice ball with your palm and, using a rolling pin, roll it into a 4-inch (10-cm) disc. Lift the dough up with a bench scraper, and put the filling inside. Bring together the edges of the dough and cup your hands together around it to seal and smooth out any creases. Shape into a round circle. Cover with plastic wrap and repeat with the remaining rice dough and filling.

Brush your tortoise kueh mold with oil, and gently press a dough ball against it. If you're not using a mold, shape it into a flat oval disc, about ¼ inch (6 mm) thick.

Partially fill a large wok with water and bring to a rolling boil over high heat (for steaming tips, see page 38).

Remove the kueh from the mold and place it on a piece of parchment paper. Cut out an outline of it, leaving a ½-inch (1-cm) border around the edges. Repeat with the remaining kueh.

Arrange the kuehs on parchment paper in a tiered bamboo steamer basket, leaving about two fingers' worth of space in between them. Cover and lower the bamboo steamer basket into the wok. Reduce the heat to medium, and steam for 30 minutes, replenishing the bottom of the wok with boiling water if needed. Lift up the lid of the steamer every 5 minutes to release the steam buildup, or steam with the lid slightly ajar (you can jam a wooden spoon or long chopstick underneath the lid to prop it up). This prevents the kueh from melting and completely turning into a goo. Turn off the heat, remove the basket from the wok, and cool—uncovered—before enjoying, about 5 minutes. These don't keep particularly well; it's best to eat them fresh. To store, place in a plastic bag and freeze. To reheat, steam over medium heat for 10 minutes.

How to Make the Red Tortoise Kueh Dough with Raw Rice Kernels

2   cups (400 g) short-grain glutinous rice, also known as sweet rice

3   tablespoons (40 g) short-grain rice, also known as sushi rice

⅛   to ¼ teaspoon red food dye

SPECIAL EQUIPMENT:
high-speed blender or food processor; tightly woven muslin cloth bag; scale

Rinse the short-grain glutinous rice and short-grain rice under running water. Transfer to a large bowl, and soak with enough water to cover at room temperature for at least 4 hours or overnight in the refrigerator.

Drain the rice in a sieve. Transfer the rice to a blender and add 4 cups (1 L) water. Blend on high speed until smooth and milky, about 1 minute. To test if it's smooth enough, dip your index finger into the liquid and rub it against your thumb. The rice powder should be fine; if it's still gritty like coarse sand, it isn't blended well enough.

Line a colander set over the sink with a muslin cloth bag. Pour the rice milk over the bag, and tie it closed. Put a very heavy object on top and drain until the water is completely gone and you're left with a chalky dough, about 1 hour.

Fill a small pot halfway with water and bring to a gentle boil over medium heat.

Remove the dough from the bag and weigh it on a scale. The exact amount will vary depending on how porous your muslin cloth is and how long you drained it for. Because there are so many variables here, I've generously overestimated the quantity of rice needed to make sure there's definitely more than enough dough to make this dish.

Take out 10 percent of the dough weight. For example, if you have 700 g dough, measure out 70 g. If you have 600 g, measure out 60 g. Roll it into a circle, and flatten it with your palms to form a flat disc. Plop the disc into the simmering water, and cook until it floats, about 2 minutes. If it doesn't float, gently pry open the dough with chopsticks. It's done when the center is translucent all the way through. If you still see chalky white chunks in the middle, keep on simmering.

Ladle the disc out of the water and put it on top of the rest of the rice dough on the table. Add ⅛ teaspoon red food dye. When it's cool enough to handle—but still very warm—knead everything with your hands to form a smooth dough. It will turn a very pale pastel pink (it will become more vibrant after you steam it). If you want more color, add up to ⅛ teaspoon more dye. Measure out 500 g of dough and divide it into 10 balls, measuring 50 g each. Continue as directed on page 270.

The cons of using raw rice kernels to make kueh dough are that it requires more work, extra equipment, and a bit of math. But the trade-off is that you'll enjoy the natural nutty fragrance of the rice, something that's often lost or stripped out in store-bought rice flour. The key to this is a very tightly woven muslin cloth. If you use a cheesecloth with a loose weave, the rice flour will literally fall through the cracks. But because every cloth is literally cut differently, I've overestimated the amount of rice that's actually needed for the kueh recipes in order to make sure you definitely have enough dough.

Daikon Kueh

菜包
Cài Bāo

菜包粿
Tshài Pau Kué

NOTE:
Pei steams the kueh over pomelo leaves, but you can use any large citrus leaves. Banana leaves are another great alternative. If you're using a leaf instead of parchment paper, brush it with oil before you put the kueh on.

(RECIPE CONTINUES)

It sounds like a bit of a stretch if you've never seen them, but these adorable bite-size kueh are meant to be shaped like olden-day pig cages. Traditionally woven out of bamboo, the cages were used to transport pigs from place to place and eventually became symbols of agrarian life on the island. This kueh is a nod to the humble roots of Taiwanese cuisine, and the recipe is from Pei-Yi's grandmother, who uses a 50-50 blend of glutinous and short-grain rice to make the dough. It's stuffed with a pile of shredded daikon with ground pork, celery for crunch, and white pepper for flavor. Pei-Yi's family—who are from Taoyuan in northern Taiwan—will make a batch of these during late autumn when it's daikon season and use them as an altar offering for their ancestors. This dish has different significance depending on family roots. In southern Taiwan, it's made especially for the winter solstice, while Hakka families make it for the Lunar New Year. The adapted recipe below uses rice flour, but for instructions on how to make the kueh dough from raw rice, see page 278.

1½ cups (195 g) glutinous rice flour, such as Erawan	2 tablespoons canola or soybean oil
½ cup (65 g) Thai rice flour, such as Erawan	2 ounces (60 g) ground pork
2 medium dried shiitake mushrooms (6 g)	¾ teaspoon fine sea salt
1 tablespoon small dried shrimp	½ teaspoon ground white pepper
2½ pounds (1.1 kg) daikon, peeled and shredded with a box grater on the coarsest side	3 tablespoons (20 g) minced celery

In a large bowl, combine the glutinous rice flour and Thai rice flour, and stir in ¾ cup plus 1 tablespoon (195 ml) water to form a crumbly dough. Bring it together with your hands to form a solid dough. Cover and let rest for 1 hour at room temperature or up to overnight in the refrigerator. Resting the dough and letting the rice flour hydrate will make the kueh smoother.

In a small bowl, cover the dried shiitake mushrooms with water and soak until soft, about 1 hour. If you are in a rush, soak them in boiling water for 30 minutes (though they won't be nearly as flavorful). In a small bowl, cover the shrimp with water and soak for 10 minutes.

Fill a medium pot halfway with water and bring to a rolling boil over high heat. Add the shredded daikon and quickly blanch, about 30 seconds. Drain in a colander and transfer the daikon into a cheesecloth. Manually squeeze out the water with your hands until it weighs around 310 g. Don't overdo it; we don't want the daikon to be too dry.

Drain the small dried shrimp in a fine-mesh sieve, discarding the soaking water. Remove the dried mushrooms from the bowl and squeeze out excess water, then trim the shiitake stems and discard. Finely mince the shiitake caps and small dried shrimp.

Heat a wok over medium heat, and swirl in the oil. When the oil is shimmering, add the shiitake mushrooms and small shrimp, and cook, stirring until fragrant, about 1 minute. Add the pork, and cook, stirring, until the edges of the meat are white, about 30 seconds. Add the grated daikon, salt, and white pepper, and cook, mixing constantly, until the daikon is slightly dried out, about 5 minutes. Turn off the heat. Add the celery and give it one last stir to combine. This mixture should weigh around 330 g now (though it's fine as long as it's in the 300 g to 350 g range). Remove from heat and set aside.

Fill a small pot halfway with water and bring it to a gentle simmer over medium heat.

Transfer the rice dough it to a clean work surface. Measure out 3 tablespoons of dough, about 45 g. Roll it into a circle, and flatten with your palms to form a flat thin disc. Plop the disc into the simmering water and cook until it's completely translucent and floats, about 2 minutes. If it doesn't float, gently pry open the dough with chopsticks. It's done when the center is translucent all the way through. If you still see chalky white chunks in the middle, keep on simmering.

Ladle the disc out of the water and put it on top of the rest of the rice dough on the table. When it's cool enough to handle—but still very warm—knead everything together with your hands to form a very smooth dough, about 5 minutes. It might be quite wet at first and stick to the table; lift it off with a bench scraper, and put some muscle into it. The dough will become more cohesive as you knead it. If the dough still cracks around the edges or is too dry, add ½ teaspoon water

at a time. The dough should be smooth and pliable like modeling clay. Divide the dough into 10 equal balls, about 45 g each. Divide the filling into 10 equal piles, about 33 g each.

With a rolling pin, flatten a dough ball into a 4-inch (11-cm) disc. Lift it up with a bench scraper and put the filling in the middle. Bring the sides together and pinch together any gaps. Cup your hands together around the dough to seal and smooth out any creases. Mold into an egg shape and, with your thumb and index finger, pinch a ridge going lengthwise down the egg. Cover with plastic wrap and repeat with the remaining rice dough and filling.

Partially fill a large wok with water and bring to a rolling boil over high heat (for steaming tips, see page 38).

Place the kueh on a piece of parchment paper, and cut out an outline of it, leaving a ½-inch (1-cm) border around the edges. Repeat for the remaining kueh.

Arrange the kuehs on parchment paper in a tiered bamboo steamer basket, leaving about two fingers' worth of space in between them. Cover and lower the bamboo steamer basket into the wok. Reduce the heat to medium, and steam for 30 minutes, replenishing the bottom of the wok with boiling water if needed. Lift up the lid of the steamer every 5 minutes to release the steam buildup, or steam with the lid slightly ajar (you can overlay a wooden spoon or long chopstick underneath the lid to prop it up). This prevents the kueh from melting and completely turning into a goo. Turn off the heat, remove the basket from the wok, and cool—uncovered—for 5 minutes before enjoying. Eat them fresh; these don't keep particularly well and will get hard if they're left out too long. To store, place in a plastic bag and freeze. To reheat, steam over medium heat for 10 minutes.

How to Make the Daikon Kueh Dough with Raw Rice Kernels

1 cup (200 g) short-grain glutinous rice, also known as sweet rice

1 cup (200 g) short-grain rice, also known as sushi rice

SPECIAL EQUIPMENT:
high-speed blender or food processor; tightly woven muslin cloth bag; scale

Rinse the short-grain glutinous rice and short-grain rice under running water. Transfer the rice to a large bowl, and soak with enough water to cover at room temperature for at least 4 hours or overnight in the refrigerator.

Drain the rice in a sieve. Transfer the rice to a blender and add 3 cups (710 ml) water. Blend on medium-high speed until smooth and milky, about 1 minute. To test if it's smooth enough, dip your index finger into the liquid and rub it against your thumb. The rice powder should be fine; if it's still gritty like coarse sand, it isn't blended well enough.

Line a colander set over the sink with a muslin cloth bag. Pour the rice milk over the bag, and tie it closed. Put a very heavy object on top and drain until the water is completely gone and you're left with a chalky dough, about 1 hour.

Fill a small pot halfway with water and bring to a gentle boil over medium heat.

Remove the dough from the bag and weigh it on a scale. The exact amount will vary depending on how porous your muslin cloth is and how long you drained it for.

Take out 10 percent of the dough weight. For example, if you have 510 g dough, measure out 51 g. Roll it into a circle, and flatten with your palms to form a flat disc. Plop the disc into the simmering water, and cook until it floats, about 5 minutes. If it doesn't float, gently pry open the dough with chopsticks. It's done when the center is translucent all the way through. If you still see chalky white chunks in the middle, keep on simmering.

Ladle the disc out of the water and put it on top of the rest of the rice dough on the table. When it's cool enough to handle—but still very warm—knead everything with your hands to form a very smooth dough. If the dough is still too dry and cracks around the edges, add up to ½ teaspoon water at a time. Measure out 450 g of dough and divide into 10 balls, measuring 45 g each.

Continue as directed on page 276.

The traditional way to stuff kueh is to shape each rice dough into a smooth ball and dig a hole in the middle with your thumbs. Gently push against the sides of the hole with your thumb to form a crater and put the filling inside. Rotate the dough clockwise while pushing in the filling with your thumbs. Pinch together any gaps and cup your hands together to seal and smooth out any creases. Go ahead and give this a go if you're comfortable with it, though it's a bit difficult for beginners to grasp. The benefit, though, is that you'll end up with a much tighter kueh without as many air pockets.

In Taiwan, the art of making zongzi is a social affair linked to the Dragon Boat Festival in the summer. Ladies will gather around in a big group at someone's house and tie bundles of sticky rice and pork inside long bamboo fronds. Compacted in neat pyramid shapes, zongzi is designed to be a social token, given as a gift to friends and extended family. So when I moved to Taiwan full-time in 2020, my maternal grandmother—who I called wàipó 外婆—started sending over large bundles of zongzi to me and my husband and, as an act of love, instructed us to eat them all.

Born on April 1, 1947, in the southern Taiwanese city of Chiayi, my grandmother grew up in a family that specialized in processing rice. She moved to Tainan in her teens to apprentice as a barber and fell in love with a dashing customer who soon became her husband. They had my mother—their firstborn—at the age of 18, and my aunt a couple of years afterward. Eventually they divorced, and my grandmother was kept at arm's length from her daughters. "When your mom was at school, I'd wait outside to give her candy," she said with sadness. "But they wouldn't let me see her for long."

While essentially estranged, my mother and grandmother kept in touch sporadically over the years, enough for her to send over zongzi when I moved to Taiwan, and enough for me to feel comfortable about asking her for her recipe, which is made in the southern Taiwanese way. Now, southern Taiwanese zongzi is markedly different from its northern Taiwanese counterparts in a couple of ways: Northerners use the brownish-beige husk of the bamboo as a wrapper; southerners use the dehydrated green leaves from the bamboo. Northerners will sometimes stuff dried squid in their zongzi; in the south, we'll add a sprinkle of peanuts instead. They steam their zongzi in the north; in the south, we boil it.

My grandmother patiently showed me all the following steps at her home, and while she didn't say much, I could tell she was glad to have connected. "Thanks for teaching me this," I said as I left her house.

"Of course; you're my granddaughter," she said, smiling, and sent me off with a giant bag of fresh longans and more bundles of zongzi.

Unfortunately, shortly after these photographs were taken, my grandmother passed away; a cancer spread from her liver and quickly took over before I could say goodbye in person. As of this writing, I still have a single parcel of zongzi that she made for me sitting in my freezer, and I have no intention of ever defrosting it.

Zongzi

粽子
Zòng Zi

肉粽
Bah Tsàng

SPECIAL EQUIPMENT:
cotton twine

(RECIPE CONTINUES)

1 pound (450 g) long-grain glutinous rice, also known as sticky rice

¼ pound (115 g) raw peanuts

10 small dried shiitake mushrooms

¼ cup (30 g) small dried shrimp

10 salted duck egg yolks

1 teaspoon Taiwanese rice wine (michiu) or cooking sake

¼ cup plus 1 tablespoon (75 ml) soy sauce

1½ tablespoons white sugar

1 teaspoon fine sea salt

¼ teaspoon five-spice powder

½ pound (225 g) skin-on pork belly

½ cup lard (120 g) or canola or soybean oil, divided

6 large shallots (150 g), thinly sliced

20 dried bamboo leaves

Everyday Garlic Soy Dressing (page 367) and/or Sweet Chili Sauce (page 369)

Rinse the long-grain glutinous rice under running water. Transfer to a large bowl and add enough water to cover. In a medium bowl, combine the raw peanuts with enough water to cover. Soak both the rice and the peanuts at room temperature for at least 4 hours or overnight in the refrigerator.

In a medium bowl, cover the dried shiitake mushrooms with water, and soak until soft, about 1 hour. If you are in a rush, soak them in boiling water for 30 minutes (though they won't be nearly as flavorful). In a separate medium bowl, cover the dried shrimp with water, and soak until soft, about 10 minutes. Drain the long-grain glutinous rice in a fine-mesh sieve and set aside. Drain the dried shrimp in a fine-mesh sieve. Remove the shiitake mushrooms from the bowl and squeeze out any excess water. Trim off the shiitake stems and discard.

Preheat the oven to 250°F (120°C).

Drain the peanuts in a fine-mesh sieve and transfer them to a medium pot. Add enough water to cover by 1 inch (2.5 cm), and briskly simmer over medium-high heat for 10 minutes.

In a medium bowl, combine the salted duck egg yolks and rice wine, and mix it around gently until the rice wine coats the yolks. Bake the egg yolks on a parchment paper–lined baking sheet for 3 minutes. Remove and set aside to cool.

In a small bowl, make a sauce by combining the soy sauce, sugar, salt, and five-spice powder, and mix thoroughly to combine. When the peanuts are done cooking, drain them in a fine-mesh sieve.

Cut the pork belly crosswise into 10 even rectangular chunks, each about 1 inch (2.5 cm) wide.

In a wok set over medium heat, heat 1 tablespoon of the lard. When the oil is shimmering, toss in the pork belly, and cook until the edges are opaque and they are partially cooked through, 2 to 3 minutes. Add in 1 tablespoon of the sauce and cook, stirring constantly, until the pork belly is completely cooked through, 2 to 3 minutes.

In a wok set over medium-low heat, heat ¼ cup (60 ml) of the lard. When the lard has melted completely, add the shallots and cook, stirring constantly, until slightly crisp around the edges but still soft, 6 to 7 minutes. Add the soaked shrimp and shiitake mushrooms and add in 1 tablespoon of the sauce. Cook, stirring to combine, for about 1 minute. Transfer everything to a plate, pluck out the shiitake mushrooms, and set them aside in a small bowl.

Heat a wok over medium-high heat, and swirl in the remaining 3 tablespoons of the lard. When it's hot, add the long-grain glutinous rice, peanuts, and the remaining sauce and cook, stirring, until the rice is completely coated with the sauce, about 3 minutes. Remove from the heat, and transfer to a clean bowl.

Fill a large stockpot with water and bring to a boil over high heat. Add half of the bamboo leaves, and blanch about 20 seconds. Remove the leaves from the pot and set in a colander. Repeat with the remaining bamboo leaves. Wash all the leaves thoroughly under running water and set aside.

Cut the cotton twine into 5 very long pieces. Each piece should be about 5 feet (150 cm) long. Hold them together and fold in half. Take the folded end and tie a knot about 2 inches (5 cm) from the top. Hang it on a hook. You will have 10 strings in total.

Take 2 bamboo leaves and overlay them on top of each other, with the smooth side of the leaf facing toward you and the protruding midrib of the leaf facing out. The pointy ends of the leaves should be opposite of one another. Hold the leaves horizontally and bring the right edge of the bamboo leaf up and around the body of the leaf to form a cone.

Put a scoop of the long-grain glutinous rice and peanut mixture, about 42 g, inside the cone. Then add 1 salted duck egg yolk, 1 pork belly slice, and 1 tablespoon of the fried shallot and shrimp mix. Cover with another scoop of glutinous rice, another 42 g. Add 1 shiitake mushroom on top of the rice ("It looks prettier this way," my grandma said). Fold the top leaf over the glutinous rice, then fold the protruding piece over to the side to form a pyramid.

With the string bundle secured on a hook, take a string and wrap it tightly against the grain on the zongzi, and tie a knot to secure. Repeat for the remaining zongzi.

Put the zongzi in a large stockpot and add enough water to cover them by 2 inches (5 cm). Set the heat to high and bring the water to a rolling boil. Reduce the heat to low, cover, and simmer for 2 hours. Remove from the water and unwrap. Enjoy while hot with the Everyday Garlic Soy Dressing or Sweet Chili Sauce. To store, freeze the zongzi. To reheat, steam over high heat for 40 minutes.

With the exception of summer, which is so blazing hot it practically knocks you over, seasonal shifts in Taiwan are very subtle. My marker for when fall transitions to winter is when I start to see fat piles of ivory daikon roots at the wet markets. The daikon season reaches a natural crescendo during the Lunar New Year in the thick of winter, when they're most commonly grated and folded into steamed rice cakes dotted with minced shiitake mushrooms and savory dried shrimp. The Taiwanese word for daikon (tshài thâu 菜頭) is a homophone for good luck (tshái thâu 彩頭), and, therefore, cakes made from the root are a natural part of the festivities. While daikon cakes are quite popular throughout southern China and Southeast Asia as well, the Taiwanese variation is marked by the use of ground pork instead of chopped-up dry-cured sweet sausages, and the batter is made with a pure long-grain rice flour instead of a blend of rice flour and miscellaneous starches. This dish is more popular in northern Taiwan because the cool, temperate winters of the north are more conducive to nurturing daikon compared to the south. In the south, this dish is actually made sans daikon.

Daikon Cake

蘿蔔糕
Luó Bo Gāo

菜頭粿
Tshài Thâu Kué

1 pound (450 g) daikon, peeled and shredded with a box grater on the coarsest side

2 teaspoons fine sea salt, divided

2 medium dried shiitake mushrooms

4 ounces (120 g) ground pork

1 tablespoon soy sauce

1 teaspoon Taiwanese rice wine (michiu) or cooking sake

1 tablespoon small dried shrimp

2 cups (260 g) Thai rice flour, such as Erawan

1 teaspoon toasted sesame oil

½ teaspoon ground white pepper

2 tablespoons plus ½ teaspoon canola or soybean oil, plus more for brushing, divided

2 tablespoons fried shallots (store-bought or homemade; page 368)

Everyday Garlic Soy Dressing (page 367)

In a large bowl, combine the shredded daikon with 1 teaspoon of the salt. Mix to combine, and let rest for 1 hour at room temperature. It will naturally start to release water.

In a small bowl, cover the dried shiitake mushrooms with water and soak until soft, about 1 hour. If you are in a rush, soak them in boiling water for 30 minutes (though they won't be nearly as flavorful).

In a medium bowl, combine the ground pork, soy sauce, and rice wine. Mix and marinate for 15 minutes.

SPECIAL EQUIPMENT:
8 or 9-inch- (20 to 23-cm-) round springform pan

NOTE:
During the Lunar New Year, this dish is eaten right after it's steamed. The next day, the leftovers are cut up into bite-size slabs and gently pan-fried.

(RECIPE CONTINUES)

SPECIAL OCCASIONS

285

In a separate small bowl, cover the dried shrimp with water, and soak until soft, about 10 minutes. Drain in a fine-mesh sieve, and finely mince the dried shrimp. Set aside. Remove the mushrooms from the bowl and squeeze out any excess water. Trim off the shiitake stems and discard. Finely mince the shiitake caps.

In a sieve, drain the daikon and shake to dry.

In a large bowl, make the rice milk by combining the rice flour, sesame oil, white pepper, the remaining 1 teaspoon salt, and 3 cups water (710 ml). Mix very thoroughly.

Brush canola oil on the inside of an 8-inch springform pan and set aside for later.

In a wok set over medium-high heat, add 2 tablespoons of the canola oil. When hot, add the dried shrimp and shiitake mushrooms, and cook, stirring often, until fragrant, about 1 minute. Add the marinated pork, and cook, stirring, until the pork is cooked through, about 1 minute. Add the fried shallots and shredded daikon, and mix to combine, about 5 seconds.

Reduce the heat to medium-low. Give the rice milk one final stir, then pour it into the wok, stirring it constantly so that the ingredients are evenly distributed and the batter turns thick and heavy, like a very dense cake batter, about 3 minutes.

Turn off the heat, and immediately transfer the batter to the springform pan. Drizzle the remaining ½ teaspoon oil on top, and use a rubber spatula to flatten it into a smooth cake.

Partially fill a large wok with water and bring to a rolling boil over high heat (for steaming tips, see page 38). Nestle the springform pan inside a large 12-inch (30-cm) bamboo steamer and put it on the wok (alternatively, put the pan directly on top of a large steamer rack centered in a wok). Cover the steamer with a large lid, and steam for 1 hour. Replenish the bottom of the wok with boiling water if needed.

Let the dish cool down a bit before serving so that it can completely solidify. Enjoy as is with a side of the Everyday Garlic Soy Dressing or cut into bite-size pieces and pan-fry in a little bit of oil until the edges are crispy. The daikon cake can be stored in the refrigerator for 2 to 3 days.

How to Make the Rice Milk with Raw Rice

1¼ cup (250 g) basmati rice

1 teaspoon fine sea salt

1 teaspoon toasted sesame oil

½ teaspoon ground white pepper

SPECIAL EQUIPMENT:
high-speed blender or food processor

Rinse the basmati rice under running water. Transfer to a medium bowl and add enough water to cover at room temperature for at least 4 hours or overnight in the refrigerator.

Drain the rice in a fine-mesh sieve. Transfer the rice to a blender, and add the salt, sesame oil, white pepper, and 2¾ cups (650 ml) water. Blend on high speed until smooth and milky, about 1 minute. To test if it's smooth enough, dip your index finger into the liquid and rub it against your thumb. The rice powder should be fine; if it's still gritty like coarse sand, it isn't blended well enough. Continue as directed in the left-hand column.

On the first full moon after her second pregnancy, my mother—despite being more than 6,000 miles away from Taiwan—knew exactly what she had to do. She called up a local Taiwanese restaurant in Los Angeles and ordered platters of oil rice for all her friends. And with plates of rice packed with slivers of shiitake and dried shrimp, they celebrated the birth of my younger brother.

While this dish can be found on Taiwanese dining tables all year round, it's notably given as a gift to others after the arrival of a new baby boy. It's a privilege reserved exclusively for male offspring, and the finished rice is often paired with a braised chicken thigh and two hard-boiled eggs dyed red, a celebratory color. The add-ons are a tongue-in-cheek play on the chicken and the egg paradox, and a good omen for future children. Contrary to its name, this dish isn't oily at all. The small amount of oil that's used in the recipe merely coats the rice, which gives it a nice, even glisten. The dish is also a regular fixture at wedding banquets, where it's steamed together with a bright red mangrove crab.

Oil Rice

油飯
Yóu Fàn

油飯
Iû Pn̄g

2	cups (400 g) long-grain glutinous rice, also known as sticky rice
8	medium dried shiitake mushrooms
1	tablespoon small dried shrimp
7	ounces (200 g) pork tenderloin, cut into matchsticks
1½	tablespoons plus ¼ cup (80 ml) soy sauce, divided
1	tablespoon white sugar
2	teaspoons Taiwanese rice wine (michiu) or cooking sake
1	teaspoon black vinegar
¼	cup (60 ml) lard or canola or soybean oil
3	large shallots, thinly sliced
3	garlic cloves, minced
1	large carrot (100 g), peeled and cut into matchsticks
1	cup (150 g) sliced bamboo shoots, canned or fresh, cut into matchsticks (see Note; optional)

Fresh cilantro sprigs (for garnish)

¼ cup (60ml) Haishan Sauce (page 370; optional)

Cook the long-grain glutinous rice according to instructions on page 360. Transfer the rice to a large heatproof mixing bowl, and cover to keep warm.

In a medium bowl, cover the dried shiitake mushrooms with water, and soak until soft, about 1 hour. If you are in a rush, soak them in boiling water for 30 minutes (though they won't be nearly as flavorful). In a separate small bowl, cover the dried shrimp with water, and soak until soft, about 10 minutes.

Remove the mushrooms from the bowl and squeeze out the excess liquid, reserving ¼ cup (60 ml) of the soaking liquid for later use. Trim off the

NOTE:
Bamboo shoot quality really varies, especially outside Taiwan. Taste it before you add it in; if it's bitter or stringy, blanch it in boiling water first. When Ivy shops for bamboo, she looks for tender shoots with fat bottoms and smooth edges.

(RECIPE CONTINUES)

shiitake stems and discard. Thinly slice the mushroom caps. Drain the small shrimp in a fine-mesh sieve and set aside for later.

In a small bowl, combine the pork tenderloin and 1½ tablespoons soy sauce, and marinate for 15 minutes.

In a small bowl, make the sauce by combining the remaining ¼ cup (60ml) soy sauce, the sugar, rice wine, black vinegar, and the reserved ¼ cup (60 ml) shiitake mushroom soaking water. Stir and set aside for later.

Warm up the lard in a wok over medium heat. Add the shallots, and cook, stirring, until soft, about 1 minute. Be careful not to burn them; they will turn the whole dish bitter otherwise. Toss in the sliced shiitakes, shrimp, and garlic, and gently stir-fry until the fragrance comes out, about 30 seconds. Add in the sliced pork, and cook until the edges become opaque, about 1 minute. Toss in the carrots and bamboo shoots (if using), then pour in the sauce. Cook until the carrots and bamboo shoots are slightly softened, 2 to 3 minutes.

Turn off the heat and pour everything from the wok into the large mixing bowl with the sticky rice inside. Mix with a spatula so that the sauce and the vegetables are evenly distributed throughout (the sauce is poured into the sticky rice versus the other way around in order to prevent the rice from crisping up in the hot wok). Transfer the rice to a serving plate and top it off with bright sprigs of cilantro. A fat scoop of the Haishan Sauce over the rice is another great way to tie this dish together, though it's completely optional.

PHOTOGRAPHY NOTE:
The rice is served in what's called a "water plate." Lent to us by the Taiwan Dish and Bowl Museum, it's a traditional, festive banquet basin specifically paired with either this dish or a thick soup.

Braised Pork Trotters with Vermicelli

紅燒豬腳麵線

Hóng Shāo Zhū Jiǎo Miàn Xiàn

豬跤麵線

Ti Kha Mī Suànn

Pig's trotters are an incredibly auspicious ingredient, embraced especially for the Lunar New Year, for birthdays, for when a new business opens, or for when folks are just in need of a change of luck. It's said that a pig's feet are strong enough to kick all the bad things away. Commonly served over a bed of long, thin wheat noodles—which represent longevity—this is a comforting dish that melts off the bone if you braise it for the proper amount of time.

2	pounds (900 g) pig's trotters, chopped into 3-inch (7.5-cm) pieces
1	tablespoon canola or soybean oil
1	tablespoon coarse raw sugar, such as demerara
¼	cup plus 1 tablespoon (75 ml) soy sauce
2	tablespoons Taiwanese soy paste (store-bought or homemade; page 366)
2	tablespoons Taiwanese rice wine (michiu) or cooking sake
2	scallions, tied into a knot
1	1-inch piece fresh ginger (10 g), unpeeled and sliced
1	whole star anise
1	small cassia or cinnamon stick, about 2 inches (5 cm) long
1	dried tangerine or mandarin orange peel, about the size of a quarter
1	teaspoon fine sea salt
4	small bok choy
¾	pound (340 g) Japanese somen noodles or any dried wheat thin noodle, at least 1 mm thin

In large pot set over high heat, combine the pig's trotters with enough water to cover. Bring to a boil, reduce the heat to medium, and briskly simmer for about 5 minutes. Drain in a colander placed over the sink. Rinse the pork trotters under cool running water to get rid of excess scum.

In a large pot, add the oil and sugar. Reduce the heat to medium-low and cook, stirring constantly, until the sugar is caramelized and turns amber brown, about 2 minutes. Add the pork trotters, soy sauce, soy paste, rice wine, scallions, ginger, star anise, cassia stick, tangerine peel, salt, and 4 cups (1 L) water. Increase the heat to high and bring everything to a boil. Cover, with the lid slightly ajar, reduce the heat to low, and simmer until the trotters are fork-tender, about 1½ to 2 hours. Pluck out the solid spices and aromatics with chopsticks or tongs.

Bring a medium pot of water to boil over high heat and add the bok choy. Quickly cook for 30 seconds and remove with a spider strainer. Add the somen noodles and cook according to package instructions. Turn off the heat and drain the noodles in a colander.

To serve, divide the noodles and bok choy into serving bowls, and ladle the pork trotters and some soup over. Enjoy while hot.

Taiwan Pork

Once a year during the Lunar New Year, a select number of pig farmers in northern Taiwan will load up their trucks with astronomically fat swine. The pigs, so bloated they can't move and sometimes weighing up to 1,700 pounds (800 kg), are enclosed in giant steel cages and hoisted up toward the sky in massive cranes to be weighed. The heaviest pig is killed with a dagger and sacrificed to the gods. Its body is adorned with tassels and painted in ornate patterns of black and white; its mouth is stuffed with a whole pineapple. The swollen carcass is paraded through the streets as people cheer and take photographs.

This is the Holy Pig Festival, a centuries-old tradition in Taiwan in which prized pigs are offered to the local deities for protection and good luck. While it's quite controversial these days and fading in prominence at the urging of animal rights activists, the extremity to which the pig is reared and then celebrated is a testament to the sheer significance of pork to Taiwanese culture and cuisine.

Wild boars have existed in Taiwan since the end of the last ice age, but the domestic pig was introduced in the 19th century by Chinese settlers and was originally a black-haired breed from southern China. In time, they were interbred with imported swine from the United States and Europe, and today there are both white and black pigs in Taiwan. As in many places around the world, white pigs are more common because they're easier to breed. But the black pigs, notable for their high fat content, are still valued in society because they're now considered heirloom breeds. Many older home cooks swear by Taiwanese black pig; they say that its flavor is more pronounced, and that the meat is much more tender.

Regardless of what type of pig you're looking for, to find quality pork in Taiwan, you must solicit the local wet markets. Pigs are slaughtered fresh in the early morning at two a.m. in central slaughterhouses concentrated in the south of the island, transported to vendors all around the country, and then expertly portioned out by master butchers before the sun rises. There's always a scramble for the best cuts, and usually by the early afternoon the entire pig has been bought. This daily ritual is a testament to the Taiwanese reverence for pork.

One of my good friends, Amy Yu, is best friends with her grandmother, and I was always really intrigued about their dynamic until I met her grandmother in person for lunch one day and saw firsthand why. Grandma is friggin' adorable. A lively lady who plays mah-jongg well into middle of the night with her friends and who likes to regale complete strangers with tales about her ballroom dancing escapades in her youth, she's a whimsical and proud lady who continues to feed her family on the daily, despite being confined to a wheelchair most of the time. When I went over for lunch, she whipped up a quick sesame oil chicken soup with so much alcohol it was shocking. "I use all alcohol. No water," she said, giggling. In preparation for my visit, grandma had ordered a whole lean, free-range chicken, had it chopped into pieces, threw it in a pot, and poured in two large bottles of pure Taiwanese rice wine. A couple of minutes in, the pot caught on fire, which took everyone—including Amy's grandma—by surprise. "Grandma doesn't drink, though sometimes she gets drunk on this," joked Amy.

In Taiwan, sesame oil chicken soup is a classic postpartum dish, part of a ritual known as "sitting the month" in which women who have just given birth are confined at home and fed a diet of therapeutic dishes to help with the recovery process. Rice wine and black sesame oil are considering warming ingredients, thought to help boost the qi and increase blood flow. This recipe is an adaption of Amy's grandma's, but made with considerably less rice wine. Because of alcohol regulations around the world, many rice wines for export are actually salted, and a pure salted rice wine concoction would taste strange and overwhelming. This recipe is a good compromise and retains a delicious medicinal punch. And no worries—if you follow the directions below, all the alcohol will be completely burned off, and you definitely won't get drunk on this soup.

Sesame Oil Chicken Soup

麻 油 雞 湯
Má Yóu Jī Tāng

麻 油 雞 湯
Muâ lû Ke Thng

NOTE:
Different types of michiu have different alcohol percentages. Amy's grandma is partial to the red label michiu, which has 19.5 percent alcohol and is relatively mild. It's also the most widely available type of michiu in Taiwan. You're totally welcome to use a michiu with a higher percentage, but note that the water-to-alcohol ratio has to be adjusted. If you have a michiu with more than 30 percent alcohol, start with just ½ cup (120 ml) and add more to taste.

- 1 tablespoon canola or soybean oil
- 1 4-inch piece fresh ginger (40 g), unpeeled and cut into ¹⁄₁₆-inch (1.5-mm) slices
- 2 tablespoons plus ¼ cup (60 g) black sesame oil, divided
- 2 pounds (900 g) skin-on, bone-in chicken thighs, chopped into 2-inch- (5-cm-) thick pieces
- 1 cup (240 ml) Taiwanese rice wine (michiu), preferably red label with 19.5 percent alcohol (see Note)
- 2½ cups (600 ml) water
- ½ teaspoon fine sea salt (optional)
- 2 teaspoons dried goji berries (for garnish; optional)

(RECIPE CONTINUES)

SPECIAL OCCASIONS

In a wok set over medium-high heat, heat the oil. When it begins to shimmer, add the ginger and cook, stirring, until the edges of the ginger begin to curl, about 2 minutes.

Remove the ginger from the wok and set it aside. Swirl in 2 tablespoons of the black sesame oil. When it's hot and shimmering, add the chicken. Sear until the chicken is well-browned on all sides, about 4 minutes.

Return the ginger into the wok, add the rice wine, and bring to a boil. Continue cooking, stirring occasionally, 3 to 4 minutes. Add in the water and bring to a boil again. Reduce the heat to low, and simmer until the chicken is tender, skimming off any scum that has accumulated on top, 15 to 20 minutes. Add the remaining ¼ cup (60 ml) black sesame oil. Taste and add salt if needed. Give it a stir and cook for another 2 minutes. Garnish with the goji berries if you'd like. Enjoy while hot.

When it comes to food offerings for the gods, fish represents the best of the sea. But to make sure the fish doesn't spoil in the humidity as it sits on the altar, many people will usually coat it with starch and deep-fry it first. Once the gods have eaten, the fish is then taken home and fried for a second time until it's gorgeous, crispy, and golden brown. But because a plain deep-fried fish isn't the prettiest thing, it's then smothered with a festive sweet-and-sour sauce and served with bright vegetables. The translation for this dish is "five willow branches," because the five types of thinly julienned vegetables that are draped over the fish are said to look like willow branches. This is a common Lunar New Year dish, and is usually offered to the gods on the eve of the festivities. Any white-fleshed fish will do for this, but a red fish like snapper is prized because the color red is good luck.

Fish with Five Vegetables

五柳枝
Wǔ Liǔ Zhī

五柳居
Ngóo Liú Ki

FOR THE SAUCE:

- ¾ cup (180 ml) water
- 1½ tablespoons soy sauce
- 2 tablespoons white sugar
- 1½ tablespoons rice vinegar
- 1½ teaspoons black vinegar
- 1 teaspoon Taiwanese rice wine (michiu) or cooking sake
- ½ teaspoon fine sea salt
- ⅛ teaspoon ground white pepper

FOR THE FISH:

- 1 medium dried shiitake mushroom
- 1 whole sea bass or snapper, about 1 pound (450 g) in total weight
- 1 teaspoon Taiwanese rice wine (michiu) or cooking sake
- 1 teaspoon fine sea salt
- ¼ teaspoon ground white pepper
- 1 large egg, yolk only
- ½ cup (80 g) thick sweet potato starch plus ½ tablespoon for the slurry (see Notes)
- 3 cups (710 ml) canola or soybean oil
- ¼ cup (25 g) thinly sliced yellow onion
- ¼ cup (25 g) thinly sliced carrots, cut into matchsticks
- ¼ cup (25 g) sliced bamboo shoots, canned or fresh, cut into matchsticks (see Notes)
- ¼ cup (25 g) thinly sliced green bell pepper
- 1 teaspoon toasted sesame oil

Fresh cilantro sprigs, chopped (for garnish)

MAKE THE SAUCE: In a small bowl, combine the water, soy sauce, sugar, rice vinegar, black vinegar, rice wine, salt, and white pepper. Stir to combine until the sugar is dissolved. Set aside for later.

MAKE THE FISH: In a small bowl, cover the dried shiitake mushroom with water, and soak until soft, about 1 hour. If you are in a rush, soak it in boiling water for 30 minutes (though it won't be nearly as flavorful). Remove the shiitake mushroom from the bowl, squeeze out excess water, then trim the stem and discard. Thinly slice the shiitake mushroom cap and set aside.

NOTES:
Thick sweet potato starch is coarse—similar to panko bread crumbs but a bit finer. Some brands will specify between thick and thin sweet potato starch. If you can only find thin, lightly spritz the starch with some water so that it clumps up and creates small beads.

Bamboo shoot quality really varies, especially outside Taiwan. Taste it before you add it in; if it's bitter or stringy, quickly blanch it first. When Ivy shops for bamboo, she looks for tender shoots with fat bottoms and smooth edges.

(RECIPE CONTINUES)

Slice two diagonal slashes crosswise on both sides of the fish, deep enough so that they reach the center bone. Arrange the fish on a plate, and add the rice wine, salt, and the white pepper. Rub the seasoning onto the fish and into the slashes so that it's well coated. Let it rest for 20 minutes at room temperature. Pat the fish completely dry with paper towels.

In a small bowl, break the egg yolk, and use a pastry brush to brush it all over the fish on both sides.

Put ½ cup (80 g) of the sweet potato starch on a plate and press the fish into the starch until both sides are fully coated.

In a wok set over medium-high heat, heat the oil until it reaches 320°F (160°C) on an instant-read thermometer. Slide in the fish and cook, flipping twice, until it's crispy with a golden brown crust, 5 to 7 minutes. To check if the dish is done, pierce the thickest part of the fish with a chopstick. If it slides right though, it's done. Turn off the heat. Remove the fish from the wok and transfer it to a paper–towel lined plate to drain.

Safely discard the oil, reserving 1 tablespoon of the oil in the wok. Make sure there are no large chunks of starch in the oil; if there are, lift the chunks up with a mesh spoon and discard.

Heat the wok over medium heat and add the sliced mushroom and sliced onion. Cook, stirring until it smells lovely, about 1 minute. Add the carrots, bamboo shoots, and green bell peppers, and cook, stirring often, until the vegetables are slightly soft, about 30 seconds. Pour the sauce into the wok, bring it to boil over high heat, then reduce the heat to medium to a briskly simmer. In a small bowl, whisk the remaining ½ tablespoon sweet potato starch with 1 tablespoon water to form a slurry. Immediately pour the slurry slowly into the wok, stirring it so that it's incorporated completely. The sauce will thicken and glisten after about 30 seconds. Turn off the heat.

Arrange the fried fish on a rimmed serving plate and pour the sauce with vegetables over the fish. Garnish with the sesame oil and fresh cilantro sprigs. Enjoy while hot.

Around the Hot Pot Circle

My mother was raised by her grandparents, who lived above a doctor's clinic they owned in the heart of Tainan, where the hours stretched from nine in the morning to late into the evening. When the mercury dropped in the winter and they'd seen the last patients of the day, it was finally time to decompress. My great-grandparents would whisk my mom and her younger sister out for late-night hot pot. The family were regulars at How-Chou Shacha Sauce Hot Pot 小豪洲沙茶爐, one of Taiwan's first hot pot chains—and more than 50 years later, it's still very much around and bustling today. The format is thus: A propane burner sits in the middle of every table, and on top of it, a bubbly cauldron of broth made of a comforting brew of pork bones and dried flatfish.

While hot pot exists all over Asia, the cornerstone of the Taiwanese-style hot pot experience is a condiment known as shacha, which is used for dipping and seasoning the cooked ingredients. It's a gritty, dark brown sauce made with a concentrated punch of dried shrimp, flatfish, shallots, and garlic brought over by Teochew immigrants who came to Taiwan from Chaozhou after World War II. Shacha was their approximation of Southeast Asia's satay sauce. The Teochew diaspora had spent a lot of time in the Malay Archipelago in previous generations; hence the affinity for satay. But with time, their version evolved to become virtually unrecognizable from its original form, more salty than sweet and devoid of peanuts. When it was introduced to Taiwan, it slowly became an important part of our culinary fabric and became firmly associated with hot pot.

Gathered around in a circle, my family's compounded stress would gradually melt away as they ordered baskets of jadeite greens, bouncy milkfish balls, crinkly sheets of bean curd, and thin, marbled slices of beef. The more fibrous veggies were tossed into the steaming pot first, like corn, taro, and whole, thick chunks of Napa cabbage. Then came the fish balls and

the tofu, which could simmer indefinitely and still hold up. The meats were next. My mom liked to dip a piece of raw meat into a whole, trembling raw egg yolk and then swish it around in the broth with her chopsticks until it turned opaque. Then she'd dip the cooked meat in a sauce composed of a bit of rice vinegar, a heaping of scallions, and a dollop of shacha.

There's an unspoken rhythm to the hot pot experience, a ritual designed to be both communal and drawn out. And while the tradition of gathering around a fire is universal, there's actually a long, sentimental history to it in Taiwan. During the Lunar New Year, families in the countryside used to light a charcoal fire ring in the family courtyard and step over it for good luck, a Chinese folk tradition that symbolized crossing into the new year. At the height of the Japanese colonial era, intellectuals and members of the elite class hosted private hot pot parties among themselves and indulged in sukiyaki—a cast-iron pot with simmering slices of beef, a leafy bouquet of garland chrysanthemums, enoki mushrooms, and cubes of tofu, all packed densely in a broth of soy sauce, sugar, and mirin. And then after World War II, the Teochew diaspora brought over the shacha hot pot my mother grew up eating,

which forms the backbone of most of the hot pot experiences in Taiwan today.

As more women joined the workforce in the mid-20th century and spent less time in the kitchen, hot pot became even more integrated into the cuisine. For the Lunar New Year, instead of whipping up elaborate multi-dish feasts with mandatory platters of intricately poached chicken, braised pork, and beautifully seasoned fish, all people had to do was bring out the hot pot burner and put out a bevy of ingredients that could be cooked then and there. Then, in the 1950s, immigrants from China introduced their own regional styles of hot pot, like lamb hot pot with pickled mustard cabbage à la the northern provinces and tongue-tingling spicy and oily hot pot from Sichuan.

Today, the hot pot scene in Taiwan is both diverse and abundant, and it's a ceremony that can be found in homes around the island and in restaurants. It's a perennial favorite—a way to bring friends and family together for long stretches of time and decompress without ever having to get out of their seats.

Shacha Hot Pot

沙茶火鍋
Shā Chá Huǒ Guō

沙茶火鍋
Sa Te Hué Ko

NOTES:

Dried flounder (biǎn yú 扁魚) is also sometimes labeled as brill fish, dà dì yú 大地魚, or ròu yú 肉魚. Chinese medicine stores might also have it in stock, sometimes in powdered form. If you can only get your hands on the powder, substitute it 1:1 by weight and add it directly to the broth.

At hot pot restaurants, there's usually a sauce bar where people can make whatever dipping sauce they'd like. Take the instructions above as a suggestion, but feel free creative with it.

FOR THE BROTH:

2   pounds (900 g) chopped pork bones, cut into 2-inch (5-cm) pieces

2   pounds (900 g) chicken bones or bone-in thighs

¾   pound (340 g) Taiwanese flat cabbage or green cabbage, cut into 2-inch (5-cm) segments, divided

1   yellow onion, peeled and halved

1   medium apple, unpeeled, cored, and halved

1   1-inch piece fresh ginger (10 g), unpeeled and sliced

3   scallions, tied into knots

2   tablespoons Taiwanese rice wine (michiu) or cooking sake

2   tablespoons preserved cabbage, also known as Tianjin preserved vegetable

1   tablespoon small dried shrimp

2   tablespoons canola or soybean oil

½   ounce (15 g) dried flounder, sometimes known as dried stockfish, cut into 1-inch (2.5-cm) squares (see Notes)

Fine sea salt (optional)

Favorite ingredients for serving (see Sidebar)

FOR THE DIPPING SAUCE (PER SERVING):

2   tablespoons shacha sauce, such as Bullhead Barbecue Sauce (for homemade, page 371)

1   teaspoon rice vinegar

1   scallion, green parts only, finely minced

Minced garlic, to taste

Minced bird eye's chili, to taste

MAKE THE BROTH: In a large pot, add the pork bones, chicken bones, and enough water to cover. Bring to a boil, then reduce the heat to medium and briskly simmer for 5 minutes. Drain in a colander set in the sink, and rinse quickly under running water to get rid of the excess scum.

In a large stockpot, bring 16 cups (4 L) of water to a rolling boil over high heat. Add the pork and chicken bones, ½ pound (225 g) of the cabbage, the onion, apple, ginger, scallions, and rice wine. Bring to a boil again, then reduce the heat to low and slowly simmer, uncovered, about 3 hours. Strain the broth through a fine-mesh sieve into a large pot. You should have 8 to 9 cups (2 L) of liquid left.

Bring the broth to a rapid simmer over medium-high heat and add the preserved cabbage, dried shrimp, and the remaining ¼ pound (115 g) cabbage.

In a wok set over medium-low heat, drizzle in the oil. When the oil is hot and shimmering, toss in the dried flounder pieces, and fry until they turn a golden brown and begin to crisp up like bacon, about 4 minutes. This part is really important; if they're not crisp, they will completely disintegrate, and the dish will be ruined by tiny fish bones. Remove the fried flounder from

the wok and transfer into the broth. The broth is usually unsalted, but feel free to add a pinch of salt to taste.

Serve the broth on top of a portable burner table-side. To cook, keep the broth at a brisk simmer and add in your ingredients of choice.

MAKE THE DIPPING SAUCE: In a small bowl, combine the shacha sauce, rice vinegar, scallion, garlic, and bird's eye chili, and mix.

Some of My Favorite Hot Pot Ingredients

Thinly sliced beef

Thinly sliced pork

Calamari rings

Enoki mushrooms

Chrysanthemum greens

Napa cabbage

Bok choy

Tofu skin

Frozen tofu

Clams

Shrimp

Fish balls

Imitation crab

Corn, cut into 2-inch (5-cm) discs

Mung bean vermicelli

Tang Yuan

湯圓
Tāng Yuán

圓仔
Înn Á

Ching-Hao 慶豪 and Hui-Yun 慧芸 are Ivy's friends—a married couple who left their comfy salaried jobs in Taipei to pursue rice farming in the countryside of Hualien. They've been growing rice for more than a decade using natural farming methods on a plot of rented, verdant land at the foot of a mountain range, and when we visit them, we're greeted by a large, smiling golden retriever and a pile of fresh rice powder the couple blended and strained for us the night before. "We had so much rice and realized there are a lot of products you can make with it," says Ching-Hao. "In our culture, if there are friends over, you treat them to rice. You can grind it to powder or sculpt it into different forms. For offerings to the gods, we can make it into rice wine." They gave Ivy and me this recipe for tang yuan, which they make out of raw rice kernels that they grow themselves. Tang yuan is a dish tied to the Lantern Festival—a celebration of the winter that falls on the last day of the 15-day-long Lunar New Year festivities. While the dessert can be shaped into spheres the size of golf balls and stuffed with peanut or black sesame paste, the classic way to prepare tang yuan here on the island is to roll out the rice dough into these miniature balls and serve it plain in a lovely brown-sugar soup with ginger. The pink and white colors symbolize fortune and happiness. For ease of access, this recipe uses rice flour, but if you want to challenge yourself, I've included instructions for how to make this dish with raw rice kernels.

1	cup (130 g) glutinous rice flour, such as Erawan, plus more for dusting
	Red food dye
¼	cup plus 2 tablespoons (60 g) dark brown sugar
1	½-inch piece fresh ginger (10 g), unpeeled and sliced

In a medium bowl, combine the glutinous rice flour and ¼ cup plus 3 tablespoons (105 ml) water. Stir to form a shaggy dough, then bring it together with your hands. Transfer to a clean work surface and knead very thoroughly until it turns into a smooth, shiny ball, about 5 minutes. Cover with plastic wrap, and let it rest for 1 hour at room temperature or up to overnight in the refrigerator so that the rice flour fully hydrates.

Fill a small pot halfway with water and bring to a gentle simmer over medium heat.

Take the rice dough out of the refrigerator and transfer it to a clean work surface. Measure out 1 rounded tablespoon of dough, about 20 g. Roll it into a circle and flatten with your palms to form a flat disc. Plop the disc into the simmering water, and cook until it floats, about 2 minutes. Turn off the heat. If it doesn't float, gently pry open the dough with chopsticks. It's done when

(RECIPE CONTINUES)

the center is translucent all the way through. If you still see chalky white chunks in the middle, keep on simmering.

Ladle the disc out of the water and put it on top of the rest of the rice dough on the table. When it's cool enough to handle—but still very warm—knead everything with your hands to form a very smooth dough, about 5 minutes. The dough should be smooth and pliable like modeling clay. If it sticks on the table, lift it up with a bench scraper and continue kneading. If it cracks around the edges, it's too dry. Adjust by adding ½ teaspoon water at a time. Divide the dough in half. Take one of the dough halves and add a drop of red food dye. Knead until it turns pastel pink. If it's too light, add a few drops more.

Shape the doughs into 2 separate long cylinders, about ½ inch (1 cm) thick. With a bench scraper, cut out 72 pieces, about 3 g a piece. With your hands, roll each chunk into a smooth ball.

Lightly dust a rimmed baking sheet with glutinous rice flour and put the balls on top. Shake the baking sheet until the balls are lightly covered with rice flour.

In a medium pot, combine the dark brown sugar, ginger, and 2 cups (470 ml) water, and bring to a boil over high heat, stirring often so that the sugar dissolves. Reduce the heat to low, cover, and slowly simmer for 5 minutes. Turn off the heat and set aside for later.

In a medium pot, bring 4 cups (1 L) of water to rolling boil over high heat. Add the tang yuan balls, and cook until all of them float, 2 to 3 minutes. Lift the balls up with a spider strainer and transfer them into 4 small serving bowls. With a ladle, spoon the brown sugar water over the tang yuan. Enjoy while warm.

How to Make the Tang Yuan Dough with Raw Rice Kernels

¾ cup (150 g) short-grain glutinous rice, also known as sweet rice

SPECIAL EQUIPMENT:
high-speed blender or food processor; tightly woven muslin cloth bag; scale

Rinse the short-grain glutinous rice under running water. Transfer the rice to a large bowl, and soak with enough water to cover at room temperature for at least 4 hours or overnight in the refrigerator.

Drain the rice in a sieve, and transfer to a blender. Add 2 cups (470 ml) water. Blend on medium-high speed until smooth and milky, about 1 minute. To test if it's smooth enough, dip your index finger into the liquid and rub it against your thumb. The rice powder should be fine; if it's still gritty like coarse sand, it isn't blended well enough.

Line a colander set over the sink with a muslin cloth bag. Pour the rice milk over the bag, and tie it closed. Put a very heavy object on top and drain until the water is completely gone and you're left with a chalky dough, about 1 hour.

Fill a small pot halfway with water and bring to a gentle boil over medium heat.

Remove the dough from the bag and weigh it on a scale. The exact amount will vary depending on how porous your muslin cloth is and how long you drained it for.

Take out 10 percent of the dough weight. For example, if you have 290 g dough, measure out 29 g. Roll it into a circle, and flatten with your palms to form a flat disc. Plop the smooth disc into the simmering water, and cook until it floats, about 2 minutes. If it doesn't float, gently pry open the dough with chopsticks. It's done when the center is translucent all the way through. If you still see chalky white chunks in the middle, keep on simmering.

Ladle the disc out of the water and put it on top of the rice dough on the table. When it's cool enough to handle—but still very warm—knead everything with your hands to form a smooth dough, about 5 minutes. Shape and cook immediately according to instructions on the previous page.

While mooncakes originated in China, they radiated all throughout East and Southeast Asia with time and the diaspora. A celebration of the harvest moon, mooncakes are consumed exclusively during the Mid-Autumn Moon Festival in the fall, and in Taiwan, the early Chinese immigrants who brought over the tradition of the lunar pastry were forced to make do with whatever was available. "The earliest mooncakes were very simple. They would stuff them with sugar, sweet potatoes, or beans," says Chang Tsun-Chen 張尊禎, a writer and researcher who has authored several books on traditional Taiwanese pastries. "When the economy got better, you started to see fillings like pork." Today there are dozens of glitzy mooncake styles in Taiwan—some stuffed with pineapple jam and others with taro or a salted egg yolk. This luxurious mung bean and pork rendition is perhaps the most classic and unique to the island. Designed to be relatively shelf-stable, the ground pork is sautéed until it's quite dry, wrapped in a sweet mung bean shell, and then enclosed in a flaky layered, lard-infused bun. The mooncakes are also meant to puff up, which is achieved by gently pressing on the pastries with the heel of your palm right before you bake them. As they cook, they'll start to slowly expand in the oven, which is a delightful and charming feature special to this pastry. For a visual guide on how to combine the doughs, see page 234.

Mung Bean Pork Mooncake

綠豆椪
Luʼü Dòu Pèng

綠豆膨
Lik Tāu Phòng

FOR THE MUNG BEAN FILLING:

- 1 cup (215 g) split mung beans, also known as moong dal or yellow split peas
- ½ cup (100 g) white sugar
- 2 tablespoons (30 g) lard or unsalted butter, softened

FOR THE PORK FILLING:

- 1 teaspoon (5 g) lard or unsalted butter, softened
- 7 ounces (200 g) ground pork
- 2 tablespoons soy sauce
- 1 tablespoon Taiwanese rice wine (michiu) or cooking sake
- 2 teaspoons white sugar
- ¼ cup (20 g) fried shallots (store-bought or homemade; page 368)
- 2 tablespoons toasted white sesame seeds (page 368)
- ⅛ teaspoon ground white pepper
- ⅛ teaspoon five-spice powder (optional)

FOR THE WATER DOUGH:

- 2 cups (250 g) all-purpose flour
- ¼ cup plus 1 tablespoon (75 g) lard or unsalted butter, softened
- 2 tablespoons white sugar
- ⅛ teaspoon fine sea salt
- ½ cup (120 ml) water

FOR THE OIL PASTE:

- 1¼ cups (160 g) cake flour
- ¼ cup plus 1 tablespoon (75 g) lard or unsalted butter, softened

Red food dye, for decoration

SPECIAL EQUIPMENT:
food processor;
stand mixer (optional)

(RECIPE CONTINUES)

MAKE THE MUNG BEAN FILLING: In a medium bowl, cover the spilt mung beans with water. Soak for 4 hours at room temperature or up to overnight in the refrigerator.

Partially fill a large wok with water (for steaming tips, see page 38) and place a steamer rack in the middle. Bring the water to a rolling boil over high heat. Drain the soaked spilt mung beans through a fine-mesh sieve and transfer them to a heatproof bowl for steaming. Pour ¾ cup (180 ml) water over the mung beans. Put the bowl on top of the steamer rack and cover. Steam until the split mung beans are soft and can be smashed easily with the back of a spoon, about 35 minutes.

When cool enough to handle, transfer the steamed spilt mung beans with any remaining reserved water in its steaming bowl to a food processor. Add the sugar, and pulse on medium speed until it turns into a paste, about 3 to 5 times. Do not over process; it will become rubbery and inedible. It should look crumbly and soft, like wet sand.

Heat the lard in a wok set over low heat, add the sweet mung bean paste, and stir with a silicone spatula until the lard has melted into the paste and the paste begins to resemble the texture of mashed potatoes, about 2 minutes. Turn off the heat, and transfer to a plate. The paste will start to firm up as it cools down. When it's cool enough to handle, shape into 15 balls, about 43 g each. Cover with plastic wrap so it doesn't dry out and set aside at room temperature.

MAKE THE PORK FILLING: In a wok set over medium heat, heat the lard. When it's hot and shimmering, add the ground pork and cook, stirring, until the edges are opaque, about 1 minute. Reduce the heat to low, and add the soy sauce, rice wine, and sugar. Cook, stirring continuously, until the sauce has completely been absorbed and the ground pork is slightly dried out, 8 to 10 minutes. Stir in the fried shallots, sesame seeds, white

pepper, and five-spice powder (if using). Turn off the heat and let it cool down.

MAKE THE WATER DOUGH: In a large bowl or the bowl of a stand mixer, mix the all-purpose flour, lard, sugar, and salt. Stream in the water and mix to form a shaggy dough. Knead with your hands until it's smooth and cohesive, about 5 minutes. (Alternatively, knead in a stand mixer with the dough hook attachment on low speed until smooth, about 2 minutes.) Divide into 15 even pieces, about 30 g each, and roll them into individual balls. Cover with plastic wrap and let rest for at least 20 minutes.

MAKE THE OIL PASTE: In a medium bowl, mix the cake flour and lard, and combine with your hands until it forms a cohesive mass. Divide into 15 pieces, about 15 g each. Cover with plastic wrap and let it rest.

Take a ball of mung bean paste and gently create an indent in the middle with your thumb. Stuff 1 scant tablespoon (about 13 g) of the pork filling inside the indent, and seal it up into a smooth ball. Repeat with the remaining mung bean paste and pork filling. If the mung bean paste is too crumbly and dry and does not hold together, mix a bit of water into it. Keep the balls covered with plastic wrap.

Take a water dough ball and flatten it with your palm into a 3-inch (7.5-cm) disc. Place an oil paste ball at the center of the disc and wrap the disc around the oil paste, pinching it closed and rolling it in your hands so it's smooth, larger ball. Cover with plastic wrap and repeat with all the remaining water dough and oil paste balls. Let them rest for 10 minutes.

Preheat the oven to 375°F (190°C).

Take a dough ball and, with a rolling pin, flatten it into an elongated oval, about 6 inches (15 cm) long. From the narrow, bottom tip of the oval, roll it away from you like it's a burrito to form a cigar. Rotate the cigar on the table 90 degrees so that it's vertical. Flatten it up and down with a rolling pin again into another long oval, also about 6 inches (15 cm) long. Once again, roll it away from you like it's a burrito. Stand it up on the table like an erect pillar so that one of the swirled ends points up to the ceiling. Flatten it with your palm into a disc. It will look a bit like a swirly snail shell. Cover with plastic wrap and repeat with the remaining dough balls. Let rest for another 10 minutes.

With a rolling pin, flatten one of the snail shell–shaped discs into a round disc, about 4.5 inches (11 cm) wide. Place a mung bean and pork ball in the middle, and gently envelope the dough around and over it. Pinch the dough together to seal. Repeat with the remaining dough and filling.

Arrange the mooncakes on a parchment paper–lined baking tray with the pinched side of the dough facing down, leaving at least 1 inch (2.5 cm) of space between each mooncake. Push down on the center of the mooncakes with the heel of your palm so that they look like a fat hockey puck with a subtle indent in the middle.

Dip the tip of a chopstick into the red food dye, and lightly dab 3 or 5 dots in the center of each mooncake.

Bake the mooncakes on the lower rack of the oven for 8 minutes. Then put a sheet of aluminum foil over the mooncakes to prevent them from browning, and bake for another 14 to 17 minutes, until they poof up. The cakes should come out ivory white. Enjoy while hot if you'd like, though because this pastry is often given as a gift, it's usually eaten at room temperature. To store, put them in an airtight container. They will last 3 days at room temperature, a week in the refrigerator, or a couple of months in the freezer.

甜點飲料

Sweets &
Drinks

Dessert with a Side of Beans and Starch

Sometimes when I'm in need of a laugh, I think of the story of my friend Amy, who told me she was hit with a large dose of culture shock when she traveled abroad to Australia for the first time and saw rows of canned baked beans in the supermarkets. She was horrified at the sight, and then further traumatized when her Australian roommate made a dish called toasties, composed of melted cheese and baked beans sandwiched between two pieces of toast. "Beans are desserts in Taiwan!" she exclaimed as she told me the story.

Unlike Western desserts, which are punctuated by a generous amount of butter, cream, and milk, Taiwanese sweets embrace native products like beans, root vegetables, and starch. Ingredients like taro and sweet potato are steamed, mashed with sugar and starch, molded into colorful balls, and served cold over a perky pile of shaved ice or warm in a bath of brown sugar water. And because dairy ingredients like whole milk and cream aren't traditional to our culture, fruit, nuts, and pulses like pineapples, peanuts, red adzuki beans, and pinto beans are our default ice cream flavors of choice, blitzed and combined with nondairy milk powder and starch to make ice cream. Lard, instead of butter, is the fattening agent of choice, and starch forms the basis of a lot of our classic desserts,

and was traditionally used not just as a thickener but as folk medicine to help cool the body down during the hot summers.

For a country whose cuisine veers toward the sweeter side of things, we ironically don't actually have much of a dessert culture here. Most home-cooked meals are finished with a large platter of fruit. Our iconic sweets, like mochi, ice cream rolls, and shaved ice, are usually bought and eaten outside the house, sold by street vendors and quickly scarfed down as impromptu treats. And our more rustic baked pastries, like pineapple cakes, sun cakes, and mooncakes, are designed to be gifts or offered to the gods and ancestors. They're packaged in the prettiest boxes and given to acquaintances and friends only when the occasion calls for it. Ovens are quite rare, and so very few of our desserts are actually made at home.

There's also a general disdain for sweets that are cloyingly sugary (paradoxical, I know, considering how sweet many of our savory dishes are). Perhaps this is a cultural quirk unique to Taiwan, because no matter what the dish is, be it brown sugar–infused boba milk tea or ice cream, the greatest compliment a vendor can get from a customer is "This tastes great. Because it's not too sweet."

A lard-infused dessert stuffed with maltose sugar, this pastry is basically just fat on sugar, which is what makes it so delightful. Iterations of this cake have been around Taiwan since the first Chinese immigrants, and some sources say that it used to be an engagement present that matchmakers would give out to betrothed couples. The pastry allegedly got its name in 1959, coined by a baker named Wei Ching-Hai 魏清海 in Taichung, who was the first to sell it on a commercial scale. Some dispute Wei's claim to the sun cake altogether and say there was an earlier bakery in Taichung with a sunflower mural inside that sold the pastry. Others say the red dot in the middle is reminiscent of the Japanese flag and makes it look like a sun. Regardless of its origins, the sun cake is now a national treasure and uniquely Taiwanese. Like many other Taiwanese pastries, it's made by layering together two types of lard-infused doughs, which is what gives it its flaky texture. For a visual guide on how to combine the two doughs, see page 234.

Sun Cake

太陽餅
Tài Yáng Bǐng

太陽餅
Thài lông Piánn

FOR THE WATER DOUGH:

- 2 cups (250 g) all-purpose flour
- ½ cup plus 1 tablespoon (135 ml) water
- ½ cup (60 g) lard or unsalted butter, softened
- 1½ tablespoons (25 g) white sugar
- ¼ teaspoon fine sea salt

FOR THE OIL DOUGH:

- 1½ cups plus 1 tablespoon (195 g) cake flour
- ¼ cup plus 2 tablespoons (90 g) lard or unsalted butter, softened

FOR THE FILLING:

- ½ cup (60 g) cake flour
- 1½ tablespoons tapioca starch
- ½ cup plus 2 tablespoons (90 g) confectioners' sugar
- ¼ teaspoon fine sea salt
- 3 tablespoons (40 g) maltose, also known as malt sugar
- 2 tablespoons (30 g) lard or unsalted butter, softened
- 1 tablespoon (20 g) condensed milk
- 2 teaspoons water

Red food dye, for decoration

MAKE THE WATER DOUGH: In a large bowl or a bowl of stand mixer, combine the all-purpose flour, water, lard, sugar, and salt. Mix to form a shaggy dough, then knead with your hands until it's smooth and cohesive, about 5 minutes. (Alternatively, knead in a stand mixer with the dough hook attachment on low speed for 2 minutes.) Divide into 12 even pieces, about 38 g each, and roll each piece into a ball. Cover with plastic wrap and set aside.

MAKE THE OIL DOUGH: In a medium bowl, combine the cake flour and lard, and mix with your hands until it forms a cohesive mass. Divide into 12 even balls, about 23 g each.

SPECIAL EQUIPMENT: stand mixer (optional)

(RECIPE CONTINUES)

Take a water dough ball and flatten it with your palm into a 3½-inch (9-cm) disc. Place an oil paste ball at the center of the disc, and wrap the disc around the oil paste, pinching it closed and rolling it in your hands so it's smooth, larger ball. Cover with plastic wrap and repeat with all the remaining water dough and oil paste balls. Let rest for 10 minutes.

Take a ball and, with a rolling pin, flatten it up and down into an elongated oval, about 6 inches (15 cm) long. From the narrow, bottom tip of the oval, roll it away from you like it's a burrito to form a cigar. Rotate the cigar 90 degrees in a counterclockwise direction so that it's vertical. Flatten it up and down with a rolling pin again into another long oval, also about 6 inches (15 cm) long. Once again, roll it away from you like it's a burrito. Stand it up on the table like an erect pillar so that one of the swirled ends points up to the ceiling. Flatten it with your palm into a disc. It will look a bit like a swirly snail shell. Cover with plastic wrap and repeat with the remaining dough balls. Let rest for another 10 minutes.

MAKE THE FILLING: In a large bowl, combine the cake flour, tapioca starch, confectioners' sugar, and salt. Wet a stainless steel spoon with water and pry the maltose out of the jar with the spoon. Put the maltose into the bowl with the flour mixture and, with your hands, pull it apart with your fingers so that it gets thin and stringy like a spiderweb. Add the lard, condensed milk, water, and bring everything together with your hands until it's a solid mass. Knead until smooth, and divide into 12 even balls, about 21 g each.

Preheat the oven to 375°F (190°C).

With a rolling pin, flatten one of the snail shell–shaped discs into a round disc about 3½ inches (9 cm) wide. Place a filling ball in the middle, and gently envelope the dough around and over it. Pinch the dough together to seal. Repeat with the remaining dough and filling.

Flatten the dough with your palms, flip it over, and use a rolling pin to gently roll it into a flat disc, about 4 inches (10 cm) wide and ½ inch (1 cm) thick. Flip it over. Dip the tip of a chopstick into the red food dye, and lightly dab 1 dot in the center of each sun cake. Repeat for the remaining dough and filling.

Arrange the sun cakes on a parchment paper–lined baking tray, leaving at least 1 inch (2.5 cm) of space in between each. Bake on the lower rack of the oven for 20 minutes, until the top is a very light golden brown.

Enjoy while hot if you'd like, though because this pastry is often given as a gift, it's usually eaten at room temperature. Store in an airtight container. The sun cakes will last 3 days at room temperature, a week in the refrigerator, or a couple of months in the freezer.

Tapioca Pearl Milk Tea

粉圓奶茶

Fěn Yuán Nǎi Chá

SPECIAL EQUIPMENT:
clean compost sieve, pizza pan with holes, or a colander with distinct large holes (the holes should be 3 mm wide); spray bottle filled with water

NOTE:
Do not refrigerate the pearls. Homemade pearls stiffen up in cold temperatures.

(RECIPE CONTINUES)

Chiu Si-Chuan 邱四川 still has the 40-year-old bicycle that his father used to sell his homemade pearls out of, an antique workhorse with a removable compartment that contained freshly cooked pearls covered in sugar syrup. The bike is now no longer functional but has been refurbished as a prop in front of Chiu's shop, A Chuan 阿川古早味粉圓冰, where he and his son are continuing the family tradition of handmade tapioca pearls.

Now, most people who know a thing or two about the food of Taiwan have heard of boba milk tea—large, chewy, brown sugar–infused tapioca balls served in milk tea. It's said the beverage was invented on a whim one day when someone decided to put the tapioca pearls in milk tea. Popularized in the 1980s, some say Chun Shui Tang Teahouse in Taichung was the progenitor of the drink. Others are confident that title belongs to Hanlin Tea Room in Tainan. But these miniature tapioca pearls you see here, known as fěn yuán 粉圓, actually predate the boba. The two are anatomically more or less the same, but fen yuan is significantly smaller and more on the translucent side.

The narrative around this ingredient usually stops there, but in actuality, starch-based pearls have been used for centuries in Taiwan as a folk remedy to prevent heat stroke. Chiu says his elders used to chew on sweet potato starch balls when they worked in the field underneath the scorching sun. While these pearls are often called tapioca pearls, the truth is that they're almost always made with a mixture of starches. An ingredient native to South America, tapioca was only widely introduced to Taiwan in the 20th century during the Japanese colonial era, but its starch was quickly embraced because of its soft and gelatinous texture. Tapioca pairs beautifully with sweet potato starch, which tends to be more firm. "Traditional fen yuan only used sweet potato," Chiu tells me.

And unlike machine-made pearls that are chock-full of preservatives, fresh pearls have a shelf life of only a few days. This recipe is based on the technique that Chiu and his son showed me. They usually serve it in plain sugar water or in shaved ice—which is traditional—but I've taken the liberty of adjusting the recipe so that it works in milk tea.

FOR THE MILK TEA:

½ cup (14 g) loose-leaf black tea

Nondairy coffee creamer, or any type of milk to taste

Coarse raw sugar, such as demerara, to taste

FOR THE PEARLS:

1 cup (120 g) tapioca starch

¼ cup (40 g) sweet potato starch

1 tablespoon dark brown sugar

½ cup (120 ml) Warm Sugar Syrup (recipe follows)

Ice cubes (optional)

MAKE THE MILK TEA: In a pot set over high heat, warm up 7 cups (1.6 L) water. When the water just begins to boil (or reaches 215°F (100°C) on an instant-read thermometer), add the loose-leaf black tea. Turn off the heat, cover, and wait until the water is a lovely amber red, about 5 to 6 minutes. Strain the tea through a fine-mesh sieve into a heatproof pitcher. Add the coffee creamer and sugar, to taste. Mix thoroughly, and chill in the refrigerator.

MAKE THE PEARLS: In a large, wide stainless steel mixing bowl, combine the tapioca starch, sweet potato starch, and dark brown sugar. Stir thoroughly so that the starches and sugar are completely mixed together (this part is important, or else the pearls won't form).

Slowly drizzle ¼ plus 2 tablespoons (90 g) water into the bowl with the starch and, with your palm and fingers outstretched, rub the starch in a sweeping circular direction against the side and bottom of the bowl with your palm until little pearls begin to form, 5 to 10 minutes (they will look like Dippin' Dots). If some of the starch begins to stick to the sides and bottom of the bowl, just gently push it off. Continue to spritz water on the starch with a spray bottle as you go. If it gets too wet, add more tapioca starch.

Pour the formed starch pearls over a compost sieve set over a large baking tray, and shake. The finished pearls will stay on top of the sieve, and the rest of the starch will fall into the baking tray. Pick out any abnormally large pearls and crumble them back into the mixing bowl. Transfer the finished pearls to a large bowl.

Transfer the excess starch back into the large mixing bowl and repeat the process. Rub in a circular direction to form little pearls, spraying water as you go. Sift them through the sieve. Repeat the process over and over again until most the starch has been processed into pearls. This can take up to 30 minutes. The pearls won't

be completely uniform in shape, but they should all relatively be the same size.

When all the pearls have been formed, bring a large pot of water to a boil over medium-high heat. Pour the pearls in and cook, stirring occasionally, until the outer shells of the pearls begin to turn translucent, 5 minutes. Turn off the heat, cover the pot, and steep for an additional 10 minutes.

Remove the pearls from the pot with a spider strainer and plop them directly into the Warm Sugar Syrup, adding more syrup if you need. Let the pearls infuse for at least 5 minutes.

TO SERVE: Divide the pearls into large serving cups. Add ice cubes into the cups if you'd like. Pour in the milk tea. Enjoy immediately.

Warm Sugar Syrup

1   cup (200 g) coarse raw sugar, such as demerara

In a wok set over low heat, combine the sugar and 1 tablespoon water. Cook, stirring occasionally, until the sugar has completely melted and has caramelized, 6 to 7 minutes. Lift the wok off the heat and slowly pour in 1 cup (240 ml) water (careful; it will start to splutter). Put the wok back onto the heat and bring the liquid to a brisk boil over medium heat. Reduce to a low simmer, and continue to cook, stirring often, until the liquid has reduced and the syrup can coat the back of a spoon, 5 to 10 minutes. Turn off the heat and cover to keep warm.

The Art of Tea

There was a brief spring in my early twenties when my social life in Taipei revolved primarily around tea, and my friends and I would wander around looking for cool spaces to get what we called "tea drunk"—a term used among tea aficionados about the subtle, calming high that the beverage imparts to the psyche. Sometimes we'd perch underneath a quiet pagoda in the hills on the outskirts of the city, and I'd have a portable tea set and a camping stove in my backpack with enough tiny teacups for everyone. We'd each bring bottles of water and our own stash of loose-leaf teas and would rotate among ourselves, taking turns brewing for one another and basking in the mild, subtropical weather. Every brew my friends and I made was a meditation on the leaf, and by virtue of our location, we mostly focused on the teas of Taiwan—usually either floral oolongs grown at high elevations with bright cotton candy–like notes or darker, earthier, low-elevation oolongs with hints of cinnamon or dark chocolate. We would share tales about how we procured our teas, or whatever tidbits of information we knew about the stash we were sharing. Our gatherings were magical, lasting hours, and our conversations about terroir and the seasonality of tea were sometimes spontaneously illuminated by the glitter of fireflies as the velvety dusk transitioned into night.

All teas are made with the same plant: *Camellia sinensis*. But how the plant is processed is what makes all the difference. There are six major categories of tea: white, green, yellow, oolong, black, and dark. And of the six, Taiwan is best known for oolongs—partially oxidized teas that are usually rolled and compacted into tight pill bug–like balls.

There are indigenous subspecies of *Camellia sinensis* on the island, but as an industry, Taiwan's tea scene started out as a cash crop for export to China during the 19th century, propped up by imported varieties that trickled in from the Fujian province. The harvested leaves were sent directly back to the Chinese mainland for processing and export, and it wasn't until a Scottish entrepreneur by the name of John Dodd and a Chinese businessman named Li Chungsheng 李春生 teamed up and began processing the tea themselves and shipping it directly out from Taiwanese ports to New York that local tea—marketed as Formosan Oolong—became an internationally known product.

When Japan took over Taiwan in the early 20th century, oolong production dropped precipitously. Japan instead jump-started a burgeoning black tea market and established a tea research institute known today as the Tea Research and Extension Station to breed new black tea varieties. But then the Chinese Civil War and World War II broke out, with the Chinese Nationalist Party eventually taking over Taiwan from Japan. Demand for Taiwanese oolong in Taiwan rose again, and it remains the darling of the island today.

For years, tea in Taiwan was either too expensive for the average family to afford, reserved for the elite, or associated with illicit triad gatherings, where tea set configurations were used to convey secret messages to the members. But then in the 1970s—at the height of Taiwan's economic prosperity—the term chá yì 茶藝,

translated as "the art of tea," began to seep into society. The terminology started out in art galleries around the island, where people would pour tea for prospective customers looking to buy art. In previous generations, tea used to be just a communal beverage, doled out like quick shots at a bar on a Friday night. But it slowly evolved to become a more refined ceremony, inspired by a brewing style that originated in the Fujian province of China called gong fū tea 功夫茶. The multi-step ritual involved brewing loose-leaf tea in a small teapot, and Taiwanese tea practitioners began to infuse the steps with the polished aesthetic of Japanese tea ceremonies.

How it works: The leaves are awakened with the perfect temperature of hot, bubbling water, then steeped and poured out into individual small cups. This step is repeated over and over again until all the flavor is extracted from the tea. It's conducted in a hushed environment, and one must keep one's back straight and operate with deep respect for the terroir, color, taste, and aroma of the leaves. Now, some argue that these ceremonies aren't new or Japanese-influenced at all but just updated and codified versions of dynastic Chinese brewing rituals. But whatever its lineage, the movement undoubtedly inspired a fervent community of practitioners and courses in Taiwan, and eventually made its way across the strait to China, where there are now certification courses and competitions for tea art masters.

"It's a direct connection to nature," says tea teacher and scholar David Tsay 蔡奕哲 of the process, as he demonstrates a tea ceremony that dates back to the 18th century. For years, David has been my go-to source for single-origin tea leaves and all inquiries relating to *Camellia sinensis* both in Taiwan and in China. "The most important criterion is that you do this in a clean space and draw out the flavor of the tea," he says. To drink the tea, he grabs the tiny drinking cup with three fingers and shoots the beverage into his mouth without moving his head at all. "It's three dragons congregating over one point," he says, referring to the configuration of fingers around the cup. "You keep your body and your back straight at all times. The art of tea is a type of self-cultivation." He solemnly passes individual cups to each of us at the table.

"How do we respond to you?" Ryan, the photographer for this cookbook, asks politely as he reaches for a cup.

"We silently just acknowledge each other's presence through eye contact," David replies, giving Ryan a nod.

That period of my life when I was obsessed with tea eventually passed, not out of waning fondness for the leaf but because all my closest tea friends eventually moved away from Taiwan. For me, the experience of tea is very much a shared experience, and I no longer have that lovely cohort who inspired me to dive deeply into it. I still regularly drink the same types of single-origin, high-quality Taiwanese tea I did back then, but alone and from a large, warm mug that I constantly top off throughout the day. Of course, drinking out of a large mug isn't the same as slowing down and appreciating the turbidity, aroma, and color of the brew in a tiny porcelain teacup. Because I chug tea like water, I often miss its whole profile and all the quick changes in its subtleties. But occasionally—rarely—I'll get a whiff of those notes of cotton candy or caramel, depending on what I'm steeping, and it brings me back to those slow, velvety evenings with good company.

There's a photogenic little seaside town northeast of Taipei called Jiufen, perched on the cliffs with adorable narrow, meandering alleyways. Illuminated by a string of crimson paper lanterns, Jiufen is strikingly reminiscent of the whimsical cartoon universe depicted in Hayao Miyazaki's *Spirited Away* (though Miyazaki himself has denied the association and inspiration). This dish is a distinguished specialty of the area. Taro and sweet potato are steamed and rolled into chewy little chunks with a mix of sweet potato starch and glutinous rice flour and served either hot in a brown sugar soup or cold over shaved ice. This recipe is for the latter, and makes for a delightful summer snack.

A very important note: There are many different types of taros and sweet potatoes out there, and because their starch and moisture content vary wildly depending on season and variety, you'll have to use your senses for this recipe. Use these instructions as a base, then adjust the water and starch content as needed. The dough should be smooth and pliable, like modeling clay. The taro dough will naturally be a little bit chalkier, and that's okay; taro is just like that. And while the finished sweet potato balls will come out a stunning orange, the taro balls might come out looking dull and gray. That's normal and is just the natural color of taro. It looks vibrant purple only in stores and on social media because of food dyes, taro extract, or really good filters.

Here in Taiwan, I'm partial to betel nut taro and a waxy sweet potato with a reddish interior known as Tainong #66. Most grocery stores don't label these details, so just work with what you have.

FOR THE SUGAR WATER:

2   cups (480 ml) water

¼   cup plus 2 tablespoons (90 g) coarse raw sugar, such as demerara

FOR THE REST OF THE DISH:

½   pound (225 g) peeled taro

½   pound (225 g) peeled sweet potato

1   tablespoon white sugar

½   cup plus 2 tablespoons (100 g) sweet potato starch, plus more for sprinkling, divided

3   tablespoons glutinous rice flour, such as Erawan, divided

20   to 30 large ice cubes, plus more if you'd like

Warm Sugar Syrup (page 318)

PREPARE THE SUGAR WATER: In a medium pot set over medium heat, combine the water and raw sugar. Cook until the sugar has completely dissolved, stirring often, about 1 minute. Set the pot aside to cool down to room temperature.

MAKE THE REST OF THE DISH: Partially fill a large wok with water and bring to a rolling boil over high heat (for steaming tips, see page 38).

MAKES AROUND 140 TO 160 BALLS

Sweet Potato and Taro Ball Shaved Ice

芋圓地瓜
圓刨冰
Yù Yuán Dì Guā Yuán Bào Bīng

芋圓蕃薯
圓礤冰
Ōo Înn Han Tsû Înn Tshuah Ping

SPECIAL EQUIPMENT:
blender or ice shaver

(RECIPE CONTINUES)

SWEETS AND DRINKS

323

Cut the taro into 1-inch (2.5-cm) cubes, and cut the sweet potato into ½-inch (1-cm) slices. Arrange separately on shallow, heatproof plates. Put the plates in a tiered steamer basket, cover, and place the basket in the wok. Steam until the taro and sweet potato chunks are fork-tender, 20 to 30 minutes.

Put the steamed taro and sweet potato into separate bowls, and mash them with a fork. In the taro bowl, add the white sugar, ¼ cup plus 1 tablespoon (50 g) sweet potato starch, and 1½ tablespoons glutinous rice flour. In the sweet potato bowl, add the remaining ¼ cup plus 1 tablespoon (50 g) sweet potato starch and 1½ tablespoons glutinous rice flour. Mix and knead both mixtures into 2 very smooth doughs. If it's too crumbly and falls apart easily, add 1 teaspoon of hot water at a time to hold it together. If either of the doughs are too wet, add 1 teaspoon of sweet potato starch at a time. Don't be afraid to adjust the texture accordingly; different taro and sweet potato varieties all have different levels of moisture. The texture should be like modeling clay, though the taro dough will be slightly denser and chunkier than the sweet potato. Divide each dough into 4 pieces (there will be 8 in total). Roll each individual piece into long cylinders about ½ inch (1 cm) thick and, with a bench scraper, cut into ½-inch- (1-cm-) thick chunks, about 5 g each.

Lightly dust a rimmed baking sheet with sweet potato starch and put the finished taro and sweet potato chunks on top. Shake the baking sheet so that the taro and sweet potato chunks are gently covered with starch. Cover with plastic wrap, and let it rest at room temperature for 30 minutes.

Prepare a large ice water bath to the side. Fill a large pot with 8 cups (2 L) water, and bring to a rolling boil over high heat. Add the taro and sweet potato chunks, and cook, stirring occasionally, until they all float

PHOTOGRAPHY NOTE:
This table, adorned with Mandarin phonetic symbols and the English alphabet, was a popular furniture item for children in the 1980s and '90s.

and expand, 1 to 2 minutes. Pour 1 cup (240 ml) water into the pot, and continue to cook, stirring, until they all float up again, about 1 minute. Turn off the heat. Remove the balls with a spider strainer and transfer them to the ice bath to cool down, about 30 seconds. Remove the balls with a spider strainer and transfer them immediately to the pot with the dissolved sugar water. The sugar water should just barely cover the balls. Soak at room temperature for at least 30 minutes and up to 3 hours.

Put half of the ice in a blender. Pulse on medium speed until all the ice cubes have been shaved, about 20 seconds. Repeat with the remaining ice cubes (or use an ice shaver if you have one!).

Divide the ice into serving bowls. Plop some taro and sweet potato balls on top, and dress them with a drizzle of Warm Sugar Syrup. The cooked balls can be stored in the refrigerator for 3 days. Uncooked balls can be stored in the freezer for 2 months.

QQ

飪飪
Khiū Khiū

One of the most prized textures in Taiwanese cuisine is an elusive concept known as Q. The term comes from the Taiwanese Hokkien language, a fact corroborated by Taiwanese-Japanese dictionaries dating back to the Japanese colonial era. Unique to our island nation but now used widely across the Chinese-speaking world, Q is an adjective that is often mistranslated as "al dente." But Q doesn't just mean al dente; Q is when you can forcefully bounce a meatball on a table and have it hit you in the head. It describes a food that's both elastic and chewy, like warm tapioca pearls soaked in brown sugar or springy, alkaline noodles. It's more reminiscent of a gummy bear than a perfectly cooked strand of spaghetti. It's so sought-after that some street vendors will actually advertise their goods with a giant Q sign, oftentimes even doubled into QQ for emphasis.

When Ivy was a kid, her mother would steam a big tray of mochi and leave it on the table to cool. But before her mom had time to mold the mochi into individual balls, Ivy and her siblings would hungrily dig in and swirl the warm, soft rice dough around the tip of their chopsticks and dip the dough into sweet peanut or black sesame powder.

½   tablespoon (10 g) maltose, also known as malt sugar

1¾ cups (260 g) glutinous rice flour, such as Erawan

1   tablespoon canola or soybean oil, plus more for kneading

¼   cup Sweet Peanut Powder (page 369)

¼   cup Sweet Black Sesame Powder (recipe follows)

Wet a stainless steel spoon with water and pry the maltose out of the jar with the spoon. In a large bowl, combine the maltose with the glutinous rice flour, and repeatedly pull the maltose apart with your fingers so that it gets thin and stringy, like a spiderweb. Add the oil and ¾ cup plus 2 tablespoon (210 ml) water and knead with your hands to form a smooth dough, about 5 minutes. Cover and let rest for 1 hour at room temperature or up to overnight in the refrigerator so that the rice flour can properly hydrate.

Partially fill a large wok with water and bring to a rolling boil over high heat (for steaming tips, see page 38). Brush a shallow, heatproof plate with oil and put the rice dough inside. Nestle the plate in a steamer basket, cover, and place in the wok. Reduce the heat to medium, and steam for 25 minutes. Lift up the lid every 5 minutes to release the steam buildup, or steam with the lid slightly ajar (you can jam a wooden spoon or long chopstick underneath the lid to prop it up). Turn off the heat, and let it rest with the lid still on for 5 minutes.

Remove the plate from the heat. Cover the plate tightly with plastic wrap, and let it rest until it's cool enough to handle. Transfer the dough to a lightly oiled work surface, and knead repeatedly until smooth, 2 to 4 minutes.

Pour the peanut powder and the sesame powder on separate plates.

Oil your hands and pinch the mochi into 17 pieces, about 30 g each. Shape into smooth spheres. To serve, press the mochi into the peanut powder or the black sesame powder and coat so that it's completely covered. Repeat for the remaining mochi. The maltose will keep the mochi soft for a couple of hours at room temperature, so it's best to enjoy this dish within that time period.

Taiwanese Mochi

麻糍

Muâ Tsî

NOTE:
While sticky pounded rice is a common dessert throughout Asia, the secret to Taiwanese mochi is the use of maltose, also known as malt sugar. The maltose is what keeps the mochi soft and chewy and prevents it from getting too hard after it has cooled down.

(RECIPE CONTINUES)

Sweet Black Sesame Powder

¼ cup (20 g) toasted black sesame seeds (page 368)

2 tablespoons white sugar

SPECIAL EQUIPMENT:
small blender

Put the toasted black sesame seeds in a small blender, and pulse on high speed for about 30 seconds. The texture should be like fine sand. Transfer the powder to a bowl, and combine with the sugar, mixing so that the sugar is evenly distributed throughout. If you prefer, add more sugar to taste.

NOTE:
Alternatively, mix 2 tablespoons black sesame powder and with 2 tablespoons white sugar

---

MAKES 15

How to Make the Mochi Dough with Raw Rice Kernels

1½ cups (300 g) short-grain glutinous rice, also known as sweet rice

½ tablespoon (10 g) maltose, also known as malt sugar

1 tablespoon canola or soybean oil, plus more for brushing

SPECIAL EQUIPMENT:
high-speed blender or food processor; tightly woven muslin cloth

Rinse the short-grain glutinous rice under running water. Transfer to a medium bowl and combine with enough water to cover. Soak for 4 hours at room temperature or up to overnight at room temperature.

Drain the rice in a sieve. Transfer the rice into a blender and add 2 cups (470 ml) water. Blend on high speed until smooth, like milk, about 1 minute. To test if it's smooth enough, dip your index finger into the liquid and rub it against your thumb. The rice powder should be fine; if it's still gritty like coarse sand, it isn't blended well enough.

Pour the rice milk into a tightly woven muslin bag, and tie it closed. Place the bag in a fine-mesh sieve strainer nestled on top of a large bowl. Place a really heavy object on top of the bag in order to filter out the liquid and extract just the rice powder, about 1 hour.

Open the muslin bag and transfer the rice powder to a medium bowl. The liquid can be discarded.

Wet a stainless steel spoon with water and pry the maltose out of the jar with the spoon. Combine the maltose with the rice powder, and repeatedly pull the maltose apart with your fingers so that it gets thin and stringy, like a spiderweb. Add the oil and mix with your hands to form a dough. The dough should hold together into a solid mass. If it does not hold up, add up to 1 teaspoon water at a time to combine. Knead the dough until it's very smooth, about 2 minutes. Steam, cook, and shape immediately according to the instructions on the previous page. This will make around 15 mochi, about 30 g each.

Peanut Ice Cream Roll

花生捲
冰淇淋

Huā Shēng Juǎn Bīng Qí Lín

Based in Yilan—a rainy coastal city known for its steamy hot springs—Huang Chiu-Chung's 黃秋璟 family has been making peanut ice cream rolls for more than half a century. "To my knowledge, the ice cream roll is not only special to Taiwan but special to Yilan," Huang, who owns Lianfa Taro Ice Cream Shop 聯發芋冰老店, says. Composed of three scoops of differently flavored ice cream seasoned with caramelized peanut powder and cilantro, this dessert is a fun summer snack, and the marriage of peanut and cilantro is a quintessentially Taiwanese combination. Vendors will usually have a large handmade block of peanut brittle on their station that they shave off and sprinkle over the ice cream à la minute. While technically you could just sprinkle pulverized peanuts and white sugar (Sweet Peanut Powder, page 369) on it instead, Ivy insisted that we go the extra mile and make the actual peanut brittle from scratch, because the caramelization of the sugar really does add a lovely but subtle complexity to the ice cream roll.

1 ounce (30g) Peanut Brittle (page 334)

2 Spring Roll Wrappers (page 119)

3 small scoops of Taiwanese Ice Cream of choice (recipes follow)

Fresh cilantro sprigs

In a blender, blend the peanut brittle until it turns into a fine powder. Remove and set aside.

Place 1 spring roll wrapper on a clean work surface and overlay a second wrapper on top of it, leaving a 1½-inch (4-cm) gap on the top.

Spread the powdered peanut brittle in an even row on the bottom half of the wrapper, then put the scoops of ice cream on top in a row. Sprinkle with cilantro.

To wrap, fold the left and right sides inward toward the filling. Keeping the sides folded, crease the bottom of the spring roll up and over the filling, and tightly roll it away from you like it's a burrito. Enjoy immediately.

NOTE:
Taiwanese ice cream scoops are significantly smaller than American ones.

Taiwanese Ice Cream

Fair warning: Taiwanese ice creams are more texturally akin to sorbets. "Taiwanese ice cream is fruitier," Huang says. "The texture is different." Dairy products aren't traditional to the island, so old-school ice creams were made with nondairy milk powder and starch instead. But because milk powder isn't the most easily accessible ingredient, Ivy and I have substituted it with condensed milk.

SPECIAL EQUIPMENT:
high-speed blender or food processor; ice cream maker

Taro Ice Cream

¼	pound (115 g) peeled taro, cut into 1-inch (2.5-cm) cubes
¼	cup (50 g) white sugar
2	tablespoons (40 g) condensed milk
1	tablespoon (20 g) maltose, also known as malt sugar
1½	teaspoons tapioca starch or cornstarch

Partially fill a large wok with water and bring to a rolling boil over high heat (for steaming tips, see page 38). Arrange the taro on a shallow, heatproof plate. Put the plate in the steamer basket or on top of a steamer rack. Lower the steamer into the wok, cover, and steam until the taro is fork-tender, 15 to 20 minutes.

When cool enough to handle, in a blender, combine the steamed taro and 2 cups (470 ml) water, and blend on high speed until smooth and creamy, about 1 minute. Pour the taro mixture into a medium saucepan, and add the sugar, condensed milk, and maltose. Bring to a boil over medium-high heat, stirring until the sugar and maltose are completely dissolved, about 2 minutes. Reduce the heat to medium so it's at a brisk simmer.

In a small bowl, make a slurry by combining the tapioca starch and 1 tablespoon water. Pour it into the saucepan, and stir until the liquid is thick and creamy, about 1 minute.

If the mixture is lumpy, strain it through a fine-mesh sieve into a bowl. Cool to room temperature. Cover and chill in the refrigerator for 4 hours or up to overnight. Churn in an ice cream machine according to the machine's directions. Store the ice cream in the freezer until frozen, about 3 hours.

Pineapple Ice Cream

½ pound (225 g) peeled pineapple, cut into 1-inch (2.5-cm) cubes

¼ cup (50 g) white sugar

1½ tablespoons (30 g) maltose, also known as malt sugar

1 tablespoon (20 g) condensed milk

1 tablespoon tapioca starch or cornstarch

In a blender, combine the pineapple and 1 cup (240 ml) water, and blend on high speed until smooth, about 1 minute.

Pour the pineapple juice into a medium saucepan, and add the sugar, maltose, and condensed milk. Bring to a boil over medium-high heat, stirring until the sugar and maltose are completely dissolved, about 2 minutes. Reduce the heat to medium so it's at a brisk simmer.

In a small bowl, make a slurry by combining the tapioca starch and 2 tablespoons water. Pour it into the saucepan, and stir until the liquid is thick and creamy, about 1 minute. Cool to room temperature. Cover and chill in the refrigerator for 4 hours or up to overnight. Churn in an ice cream machine according to the machine's directions. Store the ice cream in the freezer until frozen, about 3 hours.

Peanut Ice Cream

¼ pound (115 g) unsalted roasted peanuts, skin off (page 368)

¼ cup (50 g) white sugar

2 tablespoons (40 g) condensed milk

1 tablespoon (20 g) maltose, also known as malt sugar

1¼ teaspoons tapioca starch or cornstarch

In a blender, combine peanuts and 2 cups (470 ml) water, and blend on high speed until smooth, about 1 minute.

Pour the peanut liquid into a medium saucepan, and add the sugar, condensed milk, and maltose. Bring to a boil over medium-high heat, stirring until the sugar and maltose are completely dissolved, about 2 minutes. Reduce the heat to medium so it's at a brisk simmer.

In a small bowl, make a slurry by combining the tapioca starch and 1 tablespoon water. Pour it into the saucepan, and stir until the liquid is thick and creamy, about 1 minute. Cool to room temperature. Cover and chill in the refrigerator for 4 hours or up to overnight. Churn in an ice cream machine according to the machine's directions. Store the ice cream in the freezer until frozen, about 3 hours.

Peanut Brittle

花生糖 Huā Shēng Táng
土豆糖 Thôo Tāu Thn̂g

½ cup (180 g) maltose, also known as malt sugar

¾ cup (150 g) coarse raw sugar, such as demerara

½ teaspoon fine sea salt

1 pound (450 g) raw peanuts

¼ cup (60 ml) canola or soybean oil

SPECIAL EQUIPMENT:
small rectangular baking pan with sides, about 9×6 inches (15×22 cm)

Dip a stainless steel spoon in water and pry out the maltose from the jar. In a wok, combine the maltose, sugar, salt, and ¼ cup plus 2 tablespoons (90 g) water. Set over medium heat and cook, stirring occasionally, until the sugar and maltose have completely dissolved, 4 to 5 minutes.

Add the peanuts and oil and reduce the heat to medium-low. Cook, stirring constantly, until the water completely evaporates and the sugar caramelizes and gets really thick and stringy, 15 to 30 minutes. You might also hear an occasional popping sound from the peanuts, and the sugar will start to bubble. To test if it's ready, take a peanut and plop it in a bowl of cold water. Taste it. If it's crunchy, it's done. If it falls flat and still tastes raw, keep on stirring.

Line a rectangular baking pan with enough parchment paper to cover the sides.

Turn off the heat and remove some peanuts with a spider strainer, letting the oil drip back into the wok. Transfer the peanuts to the parchment paper–lined baking pan and repeat until all of the peanuts have been moved into the pan. The oil in the wok can be discarded or saved for another use (it's basically sweet peanut oil at this point).

Let the tray cool down to room temperature until the peanut brittle is warm and comfortable to the touch, 5 to 10 minutes. Immediately flip it upside down over a cutting board and cut into bite-size pieces. This will only work if the brittle is still relatively warm; if it has cooled down too much, it will be difficult to cut. Peanut brittle can be kept in an airtight jar at room temperature for up to a month.

This is the most well-known pastry on the island, and appropriately so because it's one of the few sweets in Taiwan that truly embraces the nation's tropical abundance. Describing it as a cake is a bit of a misnomer, though. The pineapple jam is actually enclosed in a shortbread pastry crust, which makes it more of a tart than a cake. In Taiwanese Hokkien, pineapple is ông lâi 王梨, which sounds exactly like the Taiwanese phrase for incoming fortune (ông lâi 旺來). Over the years, the pineapple cake has become the auspicious pastry of choice to give to friends, family, and business acquaintances.

Now, despite its name, not all pineapple cakes are filled with pineapple. Because a single pineapple plant takes up to two years to reach maturity, the fruit was considered a luxury ingredient back in the day. Old-school versions of this cake were actually made with winter melon, a cheap rotational crop grown over fallow rice fields. Only a hint of pineapple for flavor and luck was used.

Even today, pineapple cakes made with 100 percent pineapple are quite rare, because pineapples are rather low in pectin—a thickener needed to get the jam to the right consistency. Many commercial bakeries use artificial pectin, but this recipe, which is used by Ivy in her cooking classes, utilizes the natural pectin in an apple as a thickener and to complement the pineapple. It's a lovely innovation, because the filling still retains the dominant flavor of pineapple without compromising texture.

FOR THE FILLING:

- 1½ pounds (680 g) peeled pineapple, chopped into cubes (about half a large pineapple)
- 1 large peeled and cored apple (215 g), chopped into cubes
- ¼ cup (50 g) coarse raw sugar, such as demerara, plus more if needed
- 1 tablespoon lemon juice, plus more if needed

FOR THE CRUST:

- ½ cup plus 1 tablespoon (130 g) unsalted butter, softened
- 3 tablespoons (45 g) white sugar
- 1 large egg (50 g)
- 2 cups (240 g) cake flour, plus more for dusting
- 3 tablespoons (20 g) almond flour

MAKE THE FILLING: Put the pineapple and apple in a food processor. Pulse until it's a rough, chunky puree, about 10 seconds.

In a medium saucepan set over low heat, add the pureed pineapple, apple, sugar, and lemon juice. Bring to a slow simmer, stirring constantly, until all the liquid has evaporated and it turns dark amber yellow, about 2 hours. Taste as you go. Every pineapple tastes a bit different, so add up to ¼ cup (50 g) more sugar if it tastes too tart and 1 tablespoon more lemon juice if

Pineapple Cake

鳳梨酥
Fèng Lí Sū

王梨酥
Ông Lâi Soo

SPECIAL EQUIPMENT:
food processor; stand mixer or hand mixer; 15 stainless steel square pineapple cake molds, about 1.8 × 1.8 inches (4.8 × 4.8 cm)

NOTE:
A rectangular pineapple tart mold would work as well. You can also use cookie cutters or mooncake molds. If you can't find a mold, just make rustic, free-form tarts.

(RECIPE CONTINUES)

it's too sweet. It will turn from a mushy puree to a sticky, thick, dark paste. The final weight of the filling should be around 330 g.

With a silicone spatula, transfer the pineapple jam to a parchment paper–lined sheet pan, and spread it out so it's in a single layer. Let it cool to room temperature.

MAKE THE CRUST: Place the butter in a bowl of a stand mixer and, with the whisk attachment, mix on high speed until the butter is a pale ivory and looks fluffy, about 30 seconds (if you don't have a stand mixer, use a hand mixer). Add the sugar in batches, and continue mixing until the sugar is gone and the mixture is light and airy, like whipped cream, about 3 minutes. Scrape down the sides of the mixer with a silicone spatula to make sure everything is incorporated.

Crack the egg into a small bowl and mix until the white and the yolk have blended together. Add the egg mixture into the bowl with the butter and sugar and mix on medium speed until it's completely incorporated and everything looks a bit like mayonnaise, about 1 minute.

In a medium bowl, mix the cake flour and almond flour together so that they're fully incorporated. In batches, add the cake and almond flour mixture to the stand mixer bowl, and combine with the rest of the ingredients using a silicone spatula. Use the blade of a silicone spatula, and cut the dough in the bowl repeatedly so that the flour is mixed in. Be gentle; over kneading the dough will make the final cake chewy and tough. Use your hands, and gently pinch the dough together so that all the flour is finally mixed in. Gently divide into 15 pieces, about 31 g each, and roll to form smooth balls, compacting the mixture together with your hands so that it comes together. If the dough is too crumbly and falls apart, add 1 teaspoon water at a time. Cover with plastic wrap so they don't dry out.

Roll the pineapple jam into 15 balls, about 22 g per piece. They should come together very easily. If for some reason your filling isn't solid enough, roll the dough into balls, and freeze for 1 hour.

Preheat the oven to 350°F (175°C).

Flatten the dough ball into a 3-inch (7.5-cm) disc with your palm. Put the pineapple filling in the middle, and gently envelope the dough around and over it. Pinch the dough together to seal. Roll the filled dough ball in between your palms to form a smooth ball. Repeat with the remaining dough and filling. Keep the balls under plastic wrap so they don't dry out.

Place a wrapped dough ball into a square mold, and gently press the cake with your palm to flatten. Keep the molds on. Repeat with the remaining balls.

Arrange the pineapple cakes on a sheet pan and bake on the middle rack for 14 to 16 minutes, until the edges are golden brown. Quickly remove the baking tray from the oven and, with tongs, flip the pineapple cakes over (do not remove the molds yet). Bake for another 5 to 6 minutes, until both sides of the cake are a light golden brown.

Remove the cakes from the oven and let cool at room temperature. Gently push the cakes out of their molds. These can be enjoyed immediately while warm or at room temperature. They will last 2 weeks at room temperature or 2 months in the refrigerator. To reheat, bake at 300°F (150°C) for 7 minutes.

Summer Beverages

These drinks are all special to Taiwan and especially popular during the summer months because they're said to help cool the body down:

GRASS JELLY 仙草 (*Platostoma palustre*): A low-growing herb in the mint family with light smoky undertones, the grass jelly plant is typically harvested only once a year in the spring. It's dried, left to oxidize in the sun, and then boiled in water for at least eight hours until it morphs into a jet-black tea. At this point, it's either cooled down and sold as a summer beverage or turned into a jelly by adding a bit of arrowroot starch. In jelly form, it's usually served with sugar water or in cold milk.

AIYU 愛玉 (*Ficus pumila* var. *awkeotsang*): Aiyu is a refreshing, transparent citrine-hued jelly made from the seeds of a climbing fig native to Taiwan. In the wild, the fig vines grow by snaking up taller neighboring trees, and in the old days, the only way to get them down was to climb up the trees and harvest the prized fruit. To make the jelly, cut open the fruit, dry the seeds, put them in cheesecloth, and rub with water. The outsides of the seeds are extremely high in pectin, so when they react with water, a natural jelly will begin to form. No additives or extra binders are needed. The ratio of water to seeds really depends on where you get your aiyu, and some seeds yield a thicker jelly than others. It's usually cut up and served in cold, sweet lemon water. Today, most aiyu figs are cultivated on farms, and skilled climbers are no longer needed.

WINTER MELON TEA 冬瓜茶 (*Benincasa hispida*): Also sometimes known as a wax gourd, winter melon is boiled down and mixed with a lot of sugar to form a classic summer tea. It tastes like a cross between a very sweet watermelon and a cucumber. This tea can easily be found in a lot of specialty Asian grocery stores around the world, though it's usually already condensed with sugar and sold in a solid block form. Simply melt the block down in hot water and enjoy either hot or cold.

My mom always told me to drink papaya milk for big boobs, and I always thought that was her being facetious until I realized that every Taiwanese woman I know was told the same thing by their mother. It's an old wives' tale, of course, presumably made up because papayas look like giant (albeit saggy) boobs. This beverage is always made to order because it needs to be consumed immediately or else it will spoil. Within ten minutes, the enzymes in the papaya will react with the milk and turn the whole drink bitter.

1   pound (450 g) ripe papaya

2   cups (470 ml) whole milk, chilled

White sugar (optional)

Papaya Milk

木瓜牛奶
Mù Guā Niú Nǎi

木瓜牛奶
Bȯk Kue Gû Ni

Cut the papaya in half lengthwise and scoop out the seeds. Use a vegetable peeler to remove the skin, and then cut the papaya into chunks. Put the papaya chunks in an airtight container and chill in the refrigerator for at least 3 hours or overnight.

In a blender, combine the cold papaya and milk and blend on high speed until smooth, about 30 seconds. Add sugar to taste, if desired. Drink immediately.

Peanut Rice Milk

米漿
Mǐ Jiāng

米奶
Bǐ Ni

A very thick, resplendent beverage that can be served warm or cold, peanut rice milk is a classic early morning drink made with roasted peanuts, toasted sesame seeds, and a handful of rice. Traditionally, the texture is akin to that of a creamy milkshake, but you're welcome to dilute it as much as you want.

½ cup (100 g) short-grain rice, also known as sushi rice

1 cup (130 g) unsalted roasted peanuts, skin off (page 368)

1 tablespoon toasted white sesame seeds (page 368)

¼ cup plus 2 tablespoons (75 g) coarse raw sugar, such as demerara

¼ cup plus 2 tablespoons (75 g) dark brown sugar

¼ teaspoon fine sea salt

Rinse the short-grain rice under running water. Transfer the rice to a large bowl, and soak with enough water to cover at room temperature for at least 4 hours or overnight in the refrigerator.

Drain the rice in a sieve. In a blender, combine the rice, peanuts, sesame seeds, raw sugar, brown sugar, salt, and 3 cups (710 ml) water. Blend on high speed until it turns into a smooth beige-colored rice milk, about 1 minute.

In a large pot set over medium-low, combine the rice milk and 5 cups (1.2 L) water. Cook, stirring constantly with a balloon whisk so it doesn't burn, until it starts to thicken and bubble and easily coats the back of a spoon, 5 to 6 minutes.

This beverage can be enjoyed either hot or cold. To chill, cover the pot and let it cool down to room temperature before refrigerating. If the lid is off, a film will begin to form on the top of the milk.

SPECIAL EQUIPMENT:
high-speed blender

MADE IN TAIWAN

Soy milk is the lifeblood of Taiwanese breakfasts and the first thing that's made every day. If it isn't made and consumed on the same day, it loses its robustness. A fresh, hot cup is imperative. A kiss of sugar at the end is a nice touch, though I prefer mine unadulterated, with all its beany flavors intact.

Soy Milk

豆漿
Dòu Jiāng

豆奶
Tāu Ni

1 cup (180 g) soybeans	White sugar (optional)

In a medium bowl, soak the soybeans with enough water to cover it by 1½ inches (4 cm) for at least 8 hours or overnight in the refrigerator. Drain and rinse thoroughly under running water.

In a blender, combine the soybeans with 6 cups (1.4 L) water. Blend on high speed until it's smooth and silky, about 1 minute.

Strain the liquid through a cheesecloth into a large pot. The pulp inside the cheesecloth can be discarded or reserved for another use.

Bring the soy milk liquid to a boil over medium heat, stirring constantly so that the sediment at the bottom doesn't clump up and burn. When it boils, the liquid will begin to foam up quickly and threaten to overflow. If it does this, immediately remove the pot from the heat and wait until the foam subsides. Simmer over low heat, stirring occasionally, about 10 minutes. Enjoy while hot. Add sugar to taste. Fresh soy milk only keeps for 3 to 5 days in the refrigerator.

SPECIAL EQUIPMENT:
high-speed blender, cheesecloth

醃漬菜

Pickles

Bathing in Pickles

I can smell the pickles before we see them, and when we hop out of the car and head in the direction of the aroma, I spot a small stream of green pickle brine trickling down the open sewage system parallel to the road. We follow the brine to its source, a leaking hole in the base of a giant concrete pit. Inside are the pickles and on top are bags upon bags of salt, the weight that holds them down. Soon enough, all around us is cacophony. Large flatbeds of mustard greens are being offloaded via a crane into the heart of these empty concrete pits reinforced with wooden planks. Dozens of workers are in each pit, wearing knee-high rubber boots and floppy sun hats, joshing around while throwing salt on top of each new layer of greens. From ground level, it looks like they're bathing in pickles and rejoicing in confetti made of salt.

This is Dapi, the epicenter of pickles in Taiwan. It's here where 80 percent of the nation's lacto-fermented pickled mustard greens are made every winter. The vegetables are grown in the adjacent fields, harvested, and then left to wither for a couple of days. They're picked up, transported to these massive pits—each of which holds up to 20 to 30 tons of mustard greens—sprinkled with coarse salt, and then weighed down for a couple of months. Time softens the petals of the mustard greens and turns them tangy and sour. In a month or so, they're excavated out and shipped to wet markets around the country in large blue barrels. This is the life cycle of a pickled mustard green before it ends up in kitchens around the country to be chopped up and used as an accoutrement in a hearty bowl of beef noodle soup or braised pork belly draped over rice.

It's incredible what salt and a lot of time can do to an ingredient. My biggest takeaway from the experience? Always, always wash store-bought pickled mustard greens before you use them.

Pickle Queen

Hsu Chiang-Mien 許江麵 is a pickle queen, a soft-spoken matriarch who got into fermentation when she married a man from Dapi and noticed all her neighbors were adept in the art of pickling. So she got to work, observing and learning, and picked up the craft with such an intense fervor that in her younger years, she'd stay up all night, scrubbing salt on mustard greens in the family courtyard. "It's her hobby," her daughter Hsu Hsueh-Ling 許雪鈴 says, recalling how in childhood she would help her mom make pickles late into the evening after she finished her homework. Introverted as she is, Chiang-Mien is fiercely proud of her work. When she heard a photographer for this book was coming over to shoot her at work, she dressed to the nines and put on a face full of makeup. I was connected to her through Ivy, and though Ivy has met her only a few times throughout the years, Chiang-Mien will, without fail, send Ivy her latest batch of pickles every time pickle season rolls around. Ivy says she has been getting pickles from her for seven years and counting. The following recipes for Pickled Mustard Greens, Preserved Radish, and Cucumber Soy Sauce Pickles are inspired by her instructions.

Sometimes known as long-life vegetables, mustard greens are consumed heavily during the Lunar New Year as an omen for longevity. In northern Taiwan, some folks swear that the leaves must be eaten whole. "My grandma says if you cut it, you're cutting down your life expectancy," one of my friends tells me. To extend their shelf life, leftover greens are pickled in a process similar to that of sauerkraut. The general rule of thumb is to use 3 percent of the vegetable's weight in salt. These greens can be thrown into hot pot or a hearty stew, or chopped and stir-fried on low heat with a bit of sugar as a nice side.

2 pounds (900 g) thick-stemmed Chinese mustard greens, thoroughly washed	2 tablespoons fine sea salt

If you have the space for it, hang the Chinese mustard greens upside down on a clothesline with a cotton string to dry under the sun until the leaves are slightly withered, 1 to 2 days. If you don't have the space, you can be lazy like me and just leave them out on the kitchen counter to wilt at room temperature, and that's completely fine.

Trim off the base of the mustard greens and separate the leaves. Arrange the leaves on a large sheet pan and rub the salt all over. Pack the salt-rubbed leaves tightly into a clean sterile jar. They will begin to sweat and release water. Put a pickling weight on top, making sure the leaves are completely submerged in their own juices. Seal and keep the jar in a cool, dark place until the greens turn an olive green hue, about 2 weeks. Open and close the jar every day to release any built-up gas bubbles. Transfer to the refrigerator and enjoy within 1 to 2 months.

Pickled Mustard Greens

酸菜
Suān Cài

鹹菜
Kiâm Tshài

SPECIAL EQUIPMENT:
large disinfected pickle jar
and pickling weight
(see Note on the following page)

How to Sterilize Your Jars

Wash the jars, submerge them in a large pot of water, and boil for 10 minutes. Do the same thing with the lids. Cool down completely before using.

Preserved Pickled Mustard Greens

梅乾菜 **Méi Gān Cài**

Once you've successfully made your pickled mustard greens, you can dry them. This works best if you have access to a sunny outdoor space. Squeeze them dry over the sink and run them through a salad spinner. On a wire rack set over a large sheet pan (or, better yet, a large mesh bamboo tray, if you have one), arrange them in a single layer and sun-dry until they're completely leathery and dry, 2 to 3 days. Bring them indoors during the evening and let them rest at room temperature. Chop into ½-inch (1-cm) segments and stuff them into a clean glass jar. Age at room temperature until fragrant, 1 to 3 months. These can keep indefinitely.

Quick Daikon and Carrot Pickle

蘿蔔泡菜

Luó Bo Pào Cài

菜頭泡菜

Tshài Thâu Phàu Tshài

This is my go-to solution for whenever I find myself with an excess of daikon or carrots. It takes less than a minute to put together and pairs especially well with a plate of Pork Liver Stir-Fry (page 163).

1   cup (240 ml) filtered water

½   cup (120 ml) rice vinegar

¼   pound (115 g) peeled daikon, cut into matchsticks

¼   pound (115 g) peeled carrots, cut into matchsticks

¼   cup (50 g) white sugar

½   teaspoon fine sea salt

In a large food storage container, combine the water, rice vinegar, daikon, carrots, sugar, and salt. Cover and shake to combine. Refrigerate for at least 2 hours before enjoying.

NOTE:
If the daikon is too sharp and a bit spicy, marinate it with ¼ teaspoon salt first. Let sit for 20 minutes. Liquid from the daikon will naturally leech out. Drain, rinse, and continue as directed above.

Taiwanese Pickled Cabbage

台式泡菜

Tái Shì Pào Cài

A very common pickle that can be found both in homes and at restaurants, this is a speedy side dish that can be kept in your refrigerator for up to a week.

½   pound (225 g) Taiwanese flat cabbage or green cabbage, cored and ripped into 2-inch (5-cm) chunks

1   ounce (30 g) carrot, peeled and cut into matchsticks

1   teaspoon fine sea salt

1   cup (240 ml) filtered water

1   red jalapeño or any medium fresh red chili, deseeded and sliced diagonally

2   garlic cloves, sliced (optional)

½   cup (120 ml) rice vinegar

¼   cup plus 2 tablespoons (75 g) white sugar

In a large bowl, combine the cabbage, carrot, and salt. Massage the salt into the vegetables. Let rest at room temperature for 1 hour. The cabbage will begin to release water.

Drain the vegetables in a colander and briefly rinse the cabbage and carrot under running water. Shake dry, and transfer to a large glass food storage container with a tight-fitting lid. Add the filtered water, jalapeño, garlic, rice vinegar, and sugar. Cover the container and shake until the sugar is dissolved. Chill in the refrigerator for at least 2 hours before serving.

Making preserved daikon radish from scratch is a little bit more involved than all the other ferments in this chapter, but you'll be fine as long as you have access to a dry outdoor space with full sun. Basically, thick strips of unpeeled daikon are rubbed with salt and then left to cure and dehydrate in sunlight. When they're done, they're caramel brown and leathery. To use, simply rinse them in water, chop into pieces, and add to any stir-fry or soup for a salty kick.

| 2 | pounds (900 g) small or medium daikon, unpeeled and scrubbed clean | 2½ tablespoons coarse salt, divided |

Trim the top and bottom off of the daikon and cut in half lengthwise. Place cut side down on a cutting board and cut lengthwise again into ¼-inch (1-cm) strips. If the daikon strips are more than 1 foot (30 cm) long, cut them in half. Arrange the daikon in a single layer on a baking sheet and add 2 tablespoons of the salt. Massage the salt into the daikon, arrange in a single layer, cover with parchment paper, and then put a heavy weight on top. Leave in a dark, dry place for 1 day. The daikon will begin to sweat and release water.

Drain the daikon in a colander and squeeze out as much water as you can.

Arrange the daikon in a single layer on a clean baking sheet and rub with the remaining ½ tablespoon salt. Cover with parchment paper, and then put a heavy weight on top. Leave in a dark, dry place for 1 day.

Drain in a colander again and squeeze out as much water as you can. Arrange the daikon strips in a single layer on a wire rack set over a large sheet pan (or, better yet, a large mesh bamboo tray, if you have one), and place outside in direct sunlight until yellow and leathery, 2 to 4 days. Bring the daikon back inside during the evening and let it rest at room temperature.

To store, pack tightly in a sterilized jar and refrigerate. Age in the refrigerator until it turns yellow and has a distinct mushroom-like fragrance, about 1 month. Wash under running water and soak in room-temperature water before use, about 10 minutes.

Preserved Radish

菜脯
Cài Pú

菜脯
Tshài Póo

Don't have access to sunny outdoor space? Use a dehydrator or an oven. First, squeeze out as much water as possible from the pickle or spin it dry in a salad spinner. Arrange in a single layer on a sheet pan and dehydrate, or bake in the oven on the lowest temperature possible for 1 to 2 hours until dry.

Cucumber Soy Sauce Pickles

醬脆瓜
Jiàng Cuì Guā

醬瓜
Tsiònn Kue

Typically eaten as an accoutrement to morning congee, this is a very special pickle that's more savory than acidic. It's made by quickly boiling the cucumbers in a brine, cooling them down, boiling them again, and cooling them down again until the skin of the cucumbers shrinks and gets pruny. The process is tedious, but it's necessary for the cucumbers to retain a crunch. I've had many grocery store variants of this throughout my life, and they're usually too concentrated and slightly bitter. This homemade version, inspired by instructions from pickle queen Hsu Chiang-Mien, is light yet savory, and by far the best I've ever had.

2	pounds (900 g) small Japanese cucumbers or any seedless cucumber, trimmed
¾	cup (180 ml) soy sauce
¾	cup (180 ml) water
½	cup plus 1 tablespoon (125 g) coarse raw sugar, such as demerara
¼	cup plus 2 tablespoons (90 ml) rice vinegar
1	tablespoon Taiwanese rice wine (michiu) or cooking sake
1	teaspoon fine sea salt

Trim the edges off the cucumbers and cut into 1-inch (2.5-cm) rounds. In a large pot set over medium-high heat, combine the soy sauce, water, sugar, rice vinegar, rice wine, and salt and bring to a near boil, stirring often so that the sugar dissolves. Add the cucumbers and simmer briskly for about 1 minute. Turn off the heat, remove the cucumbers with a spider strainer, and transfer to large sheet pan to cool down in a single layer (ideally in a well-ventilated place with airflow or, if you can, point a fan at the cucumbers), about 5 minutes.

Bring the soy sauce mixture to a near boil again over medium-high heat and add the cucumbers. Simmer briskly for about 1 minute (the cucumbers will be a bit on the brown side now), remove, and transfer to the sheet pan. Repeat this process one last time: Bring the soy sauce mixture to a near boil again and add the cucumbers. Simmer briskly for about 1 minute, remove, and transfer to the sheet pan.

Wait until the cucumbers and the soy sauce mixture cool down to room temperature, about 1 hour.

Transfer the cucumbers to a sterilized glass jar and pour the soy sauce mixture over. Let rest in the refrigerator until the cucumbers are wrinkly and tan, about 1 week. Enjoy chilled. The cucumbers will last in the refrigerator for up to 2 months.

備料醬汁

Basics &
Sauces

Taiwanese Bodega

"How do you make this?" I ask the auntie who staffs my local kám á tiàm 咁仔店, pointing to an open plastic bag of diced, preserved radish next to her on the table. A kám á tiàm is the Taiwanese equivalent of a bodega—a small, traditional corner store that usually lacks air-conditioning or proper doors but is filled from floor to ceiling with all the shelf-stable goods an average Taiwanese grandma would need to whip up a meal. It's usually just two to three aisles of pantry items like soy sauce, MSG, all the different types of rice, starches, rice wine, and a small but fortifying collection of pickles, staffed and managed by an owner as old as its aging clientele. Upon hearing my question, the auntie—an older woman with blue-faded tattooed eyebrows and a bad perm—begins crudely spitting out the mouthful of sunflower seeds she's been chewing on. She looks visibly confused. "Did you make this yourself?" I ask, rephrasing the question.

"No. We buy it. It's too inconvenient to make. Not worth the effort." She shrugs.

Inconvenience is why many of these core recipes have faded from the average Taiwanese kitchen. Most people don't bother simply because these products are so easy to procure. In the old days, when many lived in the countryside, people went through the effort of preserving their own winter vegetables and making stock from leftover bones out of sheer necessity. But today in Taiwan, many of these items can be purchased anywhere and everywhere. Shelf-stable flavor enhancers like dashi powder or bouillon cubes have replaced the need for constant bubbling cauldrons of stock, and lard has largely fallen out of vogue among home cooks because people think it's unhealthy. As time-consuming as some of these recipes may be, they're not actually all that difficult, and I find making many of the items in this section a meditative experience of what life was like for my ancestors in the countryside.

A couple of weeks after my interaction with the auntie, she begins to recognize me and starts to get curious. Most young women my age in Taipei work office jobs during the day. "Are you actually cooking with all of this?" she asks me one afternoon as she rings up my purchases: some garlic, shallots, a large jug of soy sauce, and a bag of sticky rice.

"Yeah, I'm writing a cookbook," I say, handing her money.

Auntie looks me up and down, expressionless. "You don't look like someone who knows how to cook," she deadpans.

This is a really minimalistic stock that can be used in lieu of water in nearly any savory recipe. Unless otherwise indicated, most recipes in this book are centered around pork bone stock, but there are many times when I've had only a leftover chicken carcass at hand, and I promise it does the trick just fine. This same recipe can also be used with beef bones, which comes in handy for a dish like Beef Noodle Soup (page 128). You can totally use low-sodium chicken stock in a recipe that calls for pork stock, or mix the chicken bones with the pork bones to form a flavor-packed brew. Just keep the beef bones reserved for beef-centric recipes, because their flavor tends to overpower everything else.

4   pounds (2 kg) chopped pork bones with meat on them, cut into 2-inch (5-cm) pieces

1   yellow onion, peeled and cut in half

2   tablespoons Taiwanese rice wine (michiu) or cooking sake

1   1-inch piece fresh ginger (10 g), unpeeled and sliced

2   scallions, tied in a knot

In a large pot set over high heat, add the pork bones and enough water to cover. Bring to a boil, then reduce the heat to medium and briskly simmer for 5 minutes. Turn off the heat. Drain in a colander set in the sink, and rinse quickly under running water to get rid of the excess scum.

In a large pot, bring 12 cups (2.8 L) water to a rolling boil over high heat. Add the pork bones, onion, rice wine, ginger, and scallions. Bring to a boil again, then reduce the heat to the lowest setting. Slowly simmer, uncovered, about 3 hours. Strain the broth through a fine-mesh sieve into a large pot. You should have 8 to 9 cups (2 L) of liquid left.

Bone Broth

大骨高湯
Dà Gǔ Gāo Tāng

大骨湯
Tuā Kut Thng

Pork Lard

豬 油
Zhū Yóu

豬 油
Ti lû

In Taiwan, we use the phrase "ancient early taste" (gǔ zǎo wèi 古早味) to describe foods of yesteryear—dishes that remind us of grandma's house and the street foods of our childhood. And in the course of writing this book, I discovered that lard is the secret ingredient that's responsible for conjuring up that nostalgic flavor. The use of lard makes a noticeably delicious difference in dishes as simple as Fried Rice (page 210) and as intricate as Mung Bean Pork Mooncakes (page 307). Don't be shy with it.

2   pounds (900 g) pork back fat,
    cut into 1-inch (2.5-cm) cubes

¾   cup (175 ml) water

In a wok, combine the pork back fat and water. Set over medium-high heat and cook, stirring often with a spatula so the fat doesn't stick to the wok and burn. The murky water will begin to evaporate, the fat will start rendering, and a pool of clear oil will begin to form. At this point, lower the heat to medium-low and begin scooping out the oil with a ladle, filtering it through a fine-mesh sieve and into a large heatproof bowl.

Keep on stirring the fat in the wok so it doesn't burn, and continue to scoop out the oil. You're done when there's no more oil and only a collection of golden brown, crispy pork rinds in the wok (which can be reserved for another use), about 40 minutes.

When the oil is cool enough to handle, transfer it into a clean ceramic or heatproof jar. When it cools down to room temperature, pop it into the refrigerator. The oil will begin to solidify and turn creamy and ivory white. Lard will last for about 6 months in the refrigerator.

PHOTOGRAPHY NOTE:
This is my late grandmother's ceramic lard jar, which I inherited after she passed away during the writing of this book.

Stovetop White Rice

白米 *Bái Mǐ*

白米 *Pe̍h Bí*

Like many kids who grew up with a rice cooker, I had no idea how to make rice on a stove until I went to college and was left without the creature comforts of home. Through the influence of Japan, most Taiwanese families have a singing Zojirushi rice cooker. The machine has a computer chip that detects variables like temperature and time and adjusts its settings accordingly to ensure consistently perfect rice every time. For those like me who also grew up with a rice cooker, consider this practice in case of emergencies.

2 cups (400 g) short-grain rice, also known as sushi rice

Wash the rice by rinsing it in several changes of water until the water is clear. Drain well in a fine-mesh sieve. In a large pot, combine the rice and 2 cups (470 ml) water. Bring the water to a rolling boil over medium-high heat, uncovered and without stirring. When it begins to boil, stir the rice with a wooden spatula, then cover the pot. Reduce the heat to low and simmer for 20 minutes. At the end of the 20 minutes, you will see visible steam holes in the rice, and all the water should have evaporated.

Turn off the heat and let the rice rest for 10 minutes before serving.

Glutinous Rice

糯米 *Nuò Mǐ*

糯米 *Tsu̍t Bí*

2 cups (400 g) long-grain glutinous rice, also known as sticky rice

SPECIAL EQUIPMENT:
cheesecloth

Wash the rice by rinsing it in several changes of water until the water is clear. In a large bowl, cover the sticky rice with water, and soak it for at least 4 hours at room temperature or overnight in the refrigerator.

Drain the rice well in a fine-mesh sieve and spread it evenly inside a bamboo steamer basket lined with a wet cheesecloth. Poke evenly spaced holes into the rice mound with your finger; this will help the rice cook uniformly. Fold the flaps of the cheesecloth over the rice and cover.

Partially fill a large wok with water and bring to a rolling boil over high heat (for steaming tips, see page 38).

Cover and lower the bamboo steamer basket into the wok. Steam for 30 minutes, replenishing the bottom of the wok with boiling water if needed. The cooked rice will be al dente and shiny.

All around the world, meatballs have traditionally been a way to make use of scraps and leftovers. In Taiwan in particular, catches of unsold fish and miscellaneous shellfish are pulverized together with starch to form a batter, shaped into balls, and cooked in barely simmering water to form the foundation of a beautiful meal.

½ pound (225 g) boneless skinless tilapia fillet

2 ounces (60 g) pork back fat

1 teaspoon fine sea salt

¼ cup (40 g) sweet potato starch

1 large egg, white only

1 tablespoon white sugar

¼ teaspoon ground white pepper

1 garlic clove

¼ cup (60 ml) ice water

Cut the tilapia and pork back fat into 1-inch (2.5-cm) cubes. Transfer everything to a large resealable plastic bag (or two), press the meat into a flat, single layer, and freeze until partially frozen, about 2 hours.

In a food processor, combine the partially frozen tilapia, pork back fat, and salt and pulse on high speed until it forms a slimy, shiny paste, about 1 minute. Add the sweet potato starch, egg white, sugar, white pepper, and garlic and pulse again on high speed until the seasoning is completely incorporated into the fish paste, about another minute. Finally, add the ice water and mix for another minute. The paste will be white, glistening, and smooth. Transfer the paste to a food storage container and let it rest in the refrigerator for 1 hour before using; this allows the starch to absorb the paste.

TO MAKE THE FISH PASTE INTO FISH BALLS: Bring a medium pot of water to a simmer over medium heat until tiny bubbles begin to break on the surface of the water. Turn off the heat.

Shape the fish paste into 20 even meatballs, about 20 g each, plopping them into the water as you vm. You can do this with a wet spoon, with wet hands, or by picking up a large handful of the pink sludge with one hand and pushing it through the space between your index finger and thumbs (strange, but really effective!).

When all the fish balls are in, increase the heat to high and bring the liquid to a rolling boil. Reduce the heat down to medium and briskly simmer until the balls are completely cooked through and begin to float, 5 to 7 minutes. To test, cut one in half. It should be an even color throughout. Drain in a colander and eat while warm.

Fish Paste and Fish Balls

魚漿魚丸
Yú Jiāng Yú Wán

魚漿魚丸
Hî Tsiunn Hî Uân

NOTES:

The fish paste can be stored for up to 2 days in the refrigerator or 3 months in the freezer. Fish balls can be stored in the freezer for up to 3 months.

If you're making fish paste for hot pot, the paste can be cooked directly in the hot pot.

A sleek and bouncy noodle akin to ramen, oil noodles can be served cold, in a soup, or in a stir-fry. The alkalinity of the dough is what gives the noodles their signature bounce and flexibility, and they're incredible versatile ingredients that get their name from being lightly tossed in oil after they're cooked to prevent them from sticking. This is a rather low-hydration dough, but it will smooth itself out once you run it through the pasta machine. If you don't feel like making these from scratch, fresh ramen noodles are the best and closest alternative, and they can be found in the refrigerated section in many Asian specialty stores.

Oil Noodles

油 麵
Yóu Miàn

大 麵
Tuā Mī

- 2 cups (250 g) all-purpose flour
- 1 teaspoon food-grade lye water, also known as kansui (see Sidebar)
- ½ teaspoon fine sea salt
- ¼ cup plus 2 tablespoons (90 g) water
- Canola or soybean oil, for coating

In a large bowl or the bowl of a stand mixer, combine the all-purpose flour, lye water, and salt. Slowly drizzle in the water and mix to form a crumbly dough. Bring the dough together with your hands and knead until it's smooth, about 5 minutes. (If using a stand mixer, knead with the dough hook attachment on the lowest speed for 2 minutes.) It's a rather dry dough, but it will smooth itself out once you put it through the pasta machine. Cover the dough with plastic wrap, and let it rest at room temperature for 30 minutes.

Set up a pasta machine with the rollers set at the widest setting. Unwrap the dough and cut it in half. Flatten one piece of the dough and feed it through the machine. Fold it into thirds like a letter and run it through again. Repeat until the dough is completely smooth and glistening, passing it through the next few settings 2 to 3 times until it's ⅟₁₆ inch (2 mm) thick. Cut the noodles into thin spaghetti shapes and set aside. Repeat with the second piece of dough.

Bring a large pot of water to a boil over high heat and add the fresh noodles. Cook until al dente, about 3 minutes. Drain in a colander, drizzle oil over the noodles to coat, and toss to combine. Use immediately.

TO MAKE LYE WATER FROM SCRATCH:
In an oven set at 250°F (120°C), bake 1 teaspoon baking soda on a foil-lined pan for 1 hour. Combine in a small bowl with 1 tablespoon water.

SPECIAL EQUIPMENT:
stand mixer (optional); pasta machine

Pork Floss

豬肉鬆
Zhū Ròu Sōng

豬肉酥
Ti Bah Soo

Before the advent of refrigeration, making pork floss was just a way to elongate the shelf life of meat. It's dehydrated pork flavored with soy sauce, sugar, and five-spice powder, shredded so finely that it's reminiscent of a clump of hair. These days, pork floss can be purchased at most Asian specialty stores, which is what I recommend doing, because making it at home can be quite time-consuming. However, the steps are well worth it if you have a craving and don't have access to a store that sells it, or just want to take on a fun challenge.

1	pound (450 g) pork tenderloin
1	scallion, tied in a knot
1	½-inch piece fresh ginger (5 g), unpeeled and sliced
2	tablespoons white sugar
1	tablespoon soy sauce

1	tablespoon Taiwanese rice wine (michiu) or cooking sake
½	teaspoon fine sea salt
⅛	teaspoon ground white pepper
⅛	teaspoon five-spice powder
⅛	teaspoon ground cinnamon
2	teaspoons lard or sesame oil

Slice the pork along the grain into long strips, about 1 inch (2.5 cm) thick. Cut the strips crosswise against the grain so that each strip measures about 2 inches (5 cm) long.

In a small pot set over high heat, add the sliced pork tenderloin and enough water to cover. Bring to a boil, then reduce the heat to medium and briskly simmer for 5 minutes. Turn off the heat. Drain in a colander set in the sink and rinse quickly under running water to get rid of the excess scum.

In a small pot, bring 1¼ cups (300 ml) water to a rolling boil. Add the pork tenderloin, scallion, ginger, sugar, soy sauce, rice wine, salt, white pepper, five-spice powder, and cinnamon and bring everything to a boil. The liquid should just barely cover the pork. Cover, reduce the heat to low, and slowly simmer with the lid slightly ajar until the pork is soft and the liquid reduces to half, 1½ to 2 hours. As the liquid starts to reduce, rotate the pork pieces occasionally with chopsticks. Turn off the heat.

Preheat the oven to 225°F (110°C).

When the pork is cool enough to handle but still warm, remove it from the pot and shred it with your hands or a fork. Reserve the braising liquid. When all the pork has been shredded, transfer it to the bowl of a stand mixer, pour in the braising liquid, and mix with the paddle attachment on medium speed

SPECIAL EQUIPMENT:
stand mixer with the paddle attachment

until the liquid is mostly absorbed and the pork breaks apart completely and looks like pulled pork, about 2 minutes.

Transfer the mixture to a parchment paper–lined sheet pan and spread it out in a single even layer. Bake for 15 minutes, until the pork is slightly dried out. Transfer to the stand mixer and mix again with the paddle attachment on medium speed until the pieces break up even more finely, about 2 minutes. Repeat this process 4 to 5 more times, baking in 15-minute increments and then mixing with the paddle attachment for 2 minutes until the pork is completely dried out and fluffy with the texture of clumped-up floss. The final color will be reminiscent of cardboard. The total baking time will range between 1¼ and 1½ hours. After the final bake, remove the sheet pan from the oven and, while the pork floss is still hot, mix in the lard. Cool the pork floss down completely to room temperature before use. To store, transfer to an airtight jar. Pork floss can be stored at room temperature for 1 month or in the refrigerator for 3 months.

Taiwanese Soy Paste

醬油膏

Jiàng Yóu Gāo

豆油膏

Tāu Iû Kor

Soy paste is fundamental and unique to Taiwanese cuisine and adds an extra layer of depth to dishes. It's not so much a paste as it is a syrup. Thick, viscous, and reminiscent of oyster sauce without the fishy undertones, the condiment is really just thickened soy sauce plus sugar. It's available at a select number of Asian grocery stores in the West, but if you can't find it, it's easy enough to make at home. All the recipes in this book were developed using Kimlan Soy Paste, which has a hint of licorice powder. It's traditionally thickened with glutinous rice flour, though any thickening agent, like cornstarch, would work nicely.

If you're really pressed for time, don't live in an area where soy paste is easily accessible, or just don't have the will to make your own (and that's okay!), you can substitute equal parts vegetarian oyster sauce for soy paste in any recipe. Another really, really important caveat: Taiwanese soy paste isn't the same as Korean soybean paste or Chinese yellow soybean paste. Those are completely different condiments.

FOR THE SAUCE:

½ cup (120 ml) soy sauce, such as Kimlan or Kikkoman

¼ cup (50 g) coarse raw sugar, such as demerara

⅛ teaspoon licorice powder (optional)

3 tablespoons glutinous rice flour or cornstarch

In a small saucepan, whisk together the soy sauce, sugar, licorice powder (if using), and ½ cup (120 ml) water. Bring to a boil over medium-high heat, stirring continuously until the sugar dissolves.

In a small bowl, mix the glutinous rice flour and ¼ cup (60 ml) water to form a slurry. Reduce the heat to medium so that the liquid is at a brisk simmer. Pour in the slurry, immediately whisk to combine, and then cook until the sauce thickens, about 30 seconds.

Turn the heat off and wait until the sauce cools to room temperature before using. Transfer the sauce to a clean glass bottle or jar. This can be stored up to 2 weeks in the refrigerator.

Everyday Soy Dressing

Everyday Soy Dressing is my name for the delicious brown sauce found at many of street vendor stalls throughout the country. It's essentially a sweetened, diluted version of straight soy paste and is designed to be used as a dressing or a dipping sauce. Depending on the brand, soy paste on its own can be a bit too harsh to be used straight. This recipe was developed using Kimlan soy paste. If you're using a different brand, please taste and tweak the water and sugar ratio to your liking.

¼ cup (60 ml) Taiwanese Soy Paste (store-bought or homemade; page 366)

¼ cup (60 ml) water

2 teaspoons white sugar

In a small bowl, combine the soy paste, water, sugar, and stir until the sugar is fully dissolved. Add more water and sugar to taste. This can be stored for up to 2 weeks in the refrigerator.

Everyday Garlic Soy Dressing

½ cup (120 ml) Everyday Soy Dressing (this page)

2 teaspoons Garlic Puree (recipe follows) or 2 garlic cloves, minced

In a small bowl, mix together the Everyday Soy Dressing and the Garlic Puree. Taste and add more Garlic Puree if you'd like. This can be stored for up to 2 weeks in the refrigerator.

Garlic Puree

蒜泥 **Suàn Ní**
蒜茸 **Suàn Jiông**

This is a really common puree found widely at street food stalls in Tainan and used liberally as a garnish on almost anything savory. Technically, you can just use crushed garlic in any recipe that asks for garlic puree, but this method is beloved because the water softens the piquancy of the garlic.

9 garlic cloves (40 g)
3 tablespoons water

SPECIAL EQUIPMENT:
small blender or immersion blender

In a small blender, combine the garlic and water, and blend until completely smooth, about 1 minute. The puree can last about 3 to 4 days in the refrigerator.

Fried Shallots and Shallot Oil

油蔥酥 **Yóu Cōng Sū**
蔥仔酥 **Tshang Á Soo**

1¼ cups (250 g) lard, duck fat, or canola or soybean oil

8 large shallots (½ pound; 225 g), peeled and thinly sliced

In a large wok set over medium-low heat, pour in the oil, and heat it until it reaches 250°F (120°C) on an instant-read thermometer. Add the shallots and cook, stirring constantly, until the edges begin to crisp and some of them have turned a light golden brown color (there will be some purple shallots left, and that's fine because they will continue to cook when transferred to the sheet pan), 8 to 10 minutes. Turn off the heat and, with a spider strainer, immediately transfer the shallots to a paper towel–lined sheet pan and spread them out so that they're in a single layer. Let rest at room temperature until they drain completely, about 5 minutes. Store in a glass jar in the freezer for up to 1 month. Reserve the shallot oil for another use; store in the refrigerator for up to 2 weeks.

Fried Garlic and Garlic Oil

蒜酥 **Suàn Sū**
蒜頭酥 **Suàn Thâu Soo**

1¼ cups (250 g) lard, duck fat, or canola or soybean oil

30 garlic cloves (½ pound; 225 g), roughly chopped

In a large wok set over medium-low heat, pour in the oil, and heat it until it reaches 260°F (125°C) on an instant-read thermometer. Add the garlic and cook, stirring constantly, until it turns light golden brown, 7 to 8 minutes. Turn off the heat and, with a spider strainer, immediately transfer the garlic to a paper towel–lined sheet pan in a single layer. Drain completely. Store in a glass jar in the freezer for up to 1 month. Reserve the garlic oil for another use; store in the refrigerator for up to 2 weeks.

Toasted Sesame Seeds

烤芝麻 **Kǎo Zhī Ma**
烘麻仔 **Hang Muâ Á**

¼ pound (115 g) raw white sesame seeds or black sesame seeds

In a skillet over medium heat, add the sesame seeds and cook, stirring often, until fragrant, 3 to 4 minutes. The black sesame seeds won't change color, but the white sesame seeds will turn a subtle, pale shade of beige. Don't over-toast; they'll get bitter otherwise. Turn off the heat, remove from the stove, and let cool to room temperature. To store, put in the freezer for up to 2 months.

Oven-Roasted Peanuts

烤花生 **Kǎo Huā Shēng**
烘土豆 **Hang Thôo Tāu**

1 cup (130 g) raw peanuts

Preheat the oven to 325°F (160°C).

Spread the peanuts in a single layer on large sheet pan and bake until golden brown, about 30 minutes. Remove them from the oven and cool down to room temperature. If you need to skin them, rub the peanuts between your hands while they're still warm, and the skins will come right off. To store, put in the freezer for up to 2 months.

Sweet Peanut Powder

花生糖粉 **Huā Shēng Táng Fěn**
土豆糖粉 **Thôo Tāu Thñg Hún**

½ cup (80 g) roasted unsalted peanuts, skin off (page 368)	¼ cup (50 g) white sugar

SPECIAL EQUIPMENT:
food processor or immersion blender

Put the roasted peanuts in a food processor and pulse on high speed for about 30 seconds. The texture should be like fine sand. Don't overdo it; it might turn into butter. Transfer the powder into a bowl, and combine with the sugar, mixing so that the sugar is evenly distributed throughout. If you prefer, add more sugar to taste. To store, put in the freezer for up to 2 months.

Sweet Chili Sauce

甜辣醬 **Tián Là Jiàng**

This is a tangy and slightly spicy bright red sauce, reminiscent of sweet-and-sour sauce, that pairs splendidly with almost anything. This also goes really well with anything deep-fried.

¼ cup (80 g) chili sauce, such as Lee Kum Kee chili garlic sauce or Huy Fong sambal oelek	¼ cup (60 g) ketchup
	1 teaspoon rice vinegar
¼ cup (50 g) coarse raw sugar, such as demerara	2 teaspoons tapioca starch or cornstarch

In a small saucepan, combine the chili sauce, sugar, ketchup, rice vinegar, and 1 cup (240 ml) water. Bring to a boil over medium-high heat, stirring continuously until the sugar dissolves.

In a small bowl, mix the tapioca starch with 1 tablespoon water to form a slurry.

Reduce the heat to medium so that it's at a brisk simmer, and slowly pour the slurry into the saucepan, stirring so that it's thoroughly incorporated. Turn off the heat and wait until the sauce cools down to room temperature before serving. At this point, the sauce should be thick enough to gently coat the back of a spoon. If you'd like, strain the chili seeds out through a fine-mesh sieve and discard. This can be stored for up to 2 weeks in the refrigerator.

Haishan Sauce

Hǎi Shān Jiàng

Hái San Tsiùnn

Haishan sauce is the finishing touch on a lot of the island's street food dishes—most commonly dribbled on luscious oyster omelets. Haishan translates to "sea mountain sauce," and it's said to go well with everything found in the mountains and the sea, and the spaces in between. The rumor is that the sauce is a riff on Cantonese hoisin sauce, a condiment used in stir-fries and as a glaze for char siu. But over the years, it has evolved to become almost unrecognizable from its progenitor. Haishan is sweet and bright orange-red—heavy on ketchup—whereas hoisin is quite salty and dark brown. The only common denominator is that they both contain fermented soybean paste, which, in Taiwan, comes in the form of miso paste—a remnant of the Japanese colonial era. There are so many different versions of this sauce. This one is particular to southern Taiwan, where the miso is mixed with ketchup and sugar and then thickened with glutinous rice flour. If you don't have easy access to glutinous rice flour, feel free to substitute a thickener of your choice.

¼ cup (60 g) ketchup

1 tablespoon coarse raw sugar, such as demerara

2 teaspoons white miso

1 teaspoon chili sauce, such as Lee Kum Kee chili garlic sauce or Huy Fong sambal oelek

1 tablespoon glutinous rice flour or cornstarch

In a small saucepan, mix together the ketchup, sugar, miso, chili sauce, and 1 cup (240 ml) water. Heat the mixture over low heat, stirring continuously until the miso breaks down and the sugar dissolves. Bring to a boil over medium-high heat, then reduce the heat to medium so that it's at a brisk simmer.

In a small bowl, whisk the glutinous rice flour with 2 tablespoons water to form a slurry. Pour the slurry slowly into the saucepan, stirring it until it thickens, about 30 seconds.

Turn off the heat and wait until the sauce cools down to room temperature before serving. At this point, the sauce should be thick enough to gently coat the back of a spoon. This can be stored for up to 2 weeks in the refrigerator.

Just a few generations ago, this earthy, satay-inspired condiment was a heavily guarded secret made behind closed doors, but today it's sold in grocery stores and is easily accessible even outside Taiwan. Shacha can be purchased at most Asian grocery stores: look for the iconic Bullhead Barbecue Brand.

Shacha Sauce

沙茶醬
Shā Chá Jiàng

沙茶醬
Sa Te Tsiùnn

¼ cup (50 g) small dried shrimp, minced

½ cup (50 g) unsalted roasted peanuts (page 368), chopped

8 garlic cloves (30 g), minced

2 tablespoons raw white sesame seeds

½ teaspoon crushed red pepper flakes

½ teaspoon ground white pepper

¼ teaspoon five-spice powder

¼ teaspoon ginger powder

¼ teaspoon curry powder

¼ teaspoon licorice powder (optional)

1½ cups (355 ml) canola or soybean oil

1 ounce (30 g) dried flounder, sometimes known as dried stockfish, cut into 1-inch (2.5-cm) squares (see Note)

¼ cup plus 2 tablespoons (30 g) fried shallots (store-bought or homemade; page 368)

2 tablespoons white sugar

1 tablespoon soy sauce

2 teaspoons fine sea salt

1 teaspoon shredded coconut, unsweetened (optional)

In a large, heatproof, nonreactive bowl, combine the dried shrimp, peanuts, garlic, sesame seeds, red pepper flakes, white pepper, five-spice powder, ginger powder, curry powder, and licorice powder (if using). Set aside.

Heat a wok over low heat and pour in the oil. When the oil is shimmering and hot, add the dried flounder. Fry the dried flounder pieces until they turn golden brown and begin to crisp up like bacon, 2 to 3 minutes. Be careful not to burn them; they will turn bitter. With a spider strainer, remove the fried flounder from the wok and transfer to a paper towel–lined plate, reserving the oil in the wok.

Increase the heat to high and reheat the oil in the wok until it reads 375°F (190°C) on an instant-read thermometer. Turn off the heat and immediately pour the hot oil into the bowl with all the aromatics. The oil will start to bubble furiously. When it subsides, stir it with a long spoon.

When the spiced oil is cool enough to handle, pour it into a blender and add the fried dried flounder, fried shallots, sugar, soy sauce, salt, and shredded coconut (if using). Blend on high speed until smooth, about 30 seconds.

NOTES:

Dried flounder (biǎn yú 扁魚) is also sometimes labeled as brill fish, dà dì yú 大地魚, or ròu yú 肉魚. Chinese medicine stores might also have it in stock, sometimes in powdered form. If you can only get your hands on the powder, substitute it 1:1 by weight.

Shacha sauce can be stored at room temperature for up to 3 months.

Acknowledgments

This book is dedicated to my husband. Thank you for being my daily source of love, comfort, and bellyaching laughter. With you, life is a spectacular adventure full of delights and great food. To my parents and their reluctance to assimilate fully into American society, your die-hard insistence on eating Taiwanese food every single day of my childhood and lugging suitcases full of ingredients back from Taiwan (once even a whole frozen fish packed in Styrofoam) gave me an uncanny insight into my culinary heritage at a very young age.

This book would not exist without Ivy Chen, whose instructions form the heart and soul of the text. You possess an incredible wealth of knowledge; thank you for your patience and mentorship. To the incredible Wu Xin-Yun, who slid into my DMs when she heard about the cookbook deal, your incredible eye for detail and dedicated fulfillment of my research prompts have been a blessing. To food styling and photography maestros Yen Wei and Ryan Chen, whose work transformed this book into a stunning visual feast, your joint commitment to historical and cultural accuracy was not only inspiring but educational. And a very special thank you to the Taiwan Bowl and Dish Museum, the Museum of Old Taiwan Tiles, and Chin Chin Pottery for lending us pieces from your invaluable collections for our photo shoot.

Thank you to my editor, Justin Schwartz, who oversaw this project from beginning to end; I am eternally grateful for this opportunity. To my agent, Nicole Tourtelot, who has steadfastly believed in me throughout the years. To Jen Wang, for the gorgeous book design. To the team at Simon Element, for making this a book a dream come true.

I'm grateful to Cam Chao, for overseeing all the Taiwanese language translations; James Lin, for your meticulous notes on Taiwan's history; Ozzy Hsieh at Yu Ding Xing, for all your help on the nuances of Taiwanese soy sauce; Aeles Lrawbalrate, for opening up your home to me and teaching me so much about indigenous Taiwan; Huang Teng-Wei and Chou Pei-Yi, for continuously inspiring me in all things rice; Chieh-Ting Yeh, for your feedback on select essays; Joelle Chevrier, for giving me much-needed context about rice varieties; Brian at Brian Cuisine, for your advice on wheat flour; Acer Wang, for your enthusiasm; Hank Hsieh, for taking us around Hsinchu; Amy Yu, for your friendship; David Tsay, for constantly teaching me about tea.

To every single person featured in this book, thank you so much for entrusting me with your stories and recipes; I hope I did them justice. I owe drinks to the small village of people around the world who helped me test the recipes, including Scott Hocker, Laura Manzano, Leanna Rongavilla, Hunter White, Joy Huang, Katharin Dai, Marie Vilà, Rachel Karasik, Sean Peters, Denny Cheng, Layla Schlack, Christine Gallary, Yuting Yeh, Chloe Rose-Crabtree, Gretchen L. B. Brown, Ting Lin, Jane Pan, Grace Lee, Nora Landis-Shack, Caroline Lo, Caroline Chang, Matt Gross, Christine Su, Eric Lam, Rachel Balota, Joshua Gottemoller, Wan-Yuan Kuo, Mina Park, Hannah Kirshner, Emma Scarpino, Kate Lewis, Steph Hsu, Irene Hua, Sophia J. Chang, Christina Lee, Joshua Sadinsky, Bryan Chen, Rachel Ng, Cindy Young, Sarah Hodge, Enos Feng, Jill Chen, Joey Wendel, Morgan Finn, Erin HouYing Chen, Stephanie Hsu, Mink Lin, Serena Wang, Tiffany Ran, Elli Shanen, Anikah Shaokat, Hattie LeFavour, Vicky Liaw Hsu, Evan Hamilton, Christina Yu, Gary Lo, Alexander Chen, Phillip Chu, Gina Song, Andrew Shiue, Phaedra Fang, Emily Wu Pearson, Jean Lim Flores, and Robyn Lee. If I've forgotten your name here, I owe you two drinks. And last but not least, to the people of Taiwan, wherever you may be in the world. Despite the odds, we are an incredibly resilient people. I hope this book made you proud to be Taiwanese. 台灣加油.

Index

SIMON
ELEMENT

An Imprint of Simon & Schuster, Inc.
1230 Avenue of the Americas
New York, NY 10020

First Simon Element hardcover edition
September 2023

SIMON ELEMENT is a trademark
of Simon & Schuster, Inc.

For information about special discounts for
bulk purchases, please contact Simon &
Schuster Special Sales at 1-866-506-1949
or business@simonandschuster.com.

The Simon & Schuster Speakers Bureau can bring
authors to your live event. For more information
or to book an event, contact the Simon &
Schuster Speakers Bureau at 1-866-248-3049 or
visit our website at www.simonspeakers.com.

Interior design by Jen Wang 王明圓

Manufactured in Malaysia

10 9 8 7 6 5 4

Library of Congress Cataloging-in-Publication
Data has been applied for.

ISBN 978-1-9821-9897-8
ISBN 978-1-9821-9898-5 (ebook)

Styling and Photography by Yen Wei 嚴葳
and Ryan Chen 陳志華

Research by Wu Xin-Yun 吳昕芸

CLARISSA WEI is a freelance journalist based in Taipei. Born in Los Angeles but raised on the food of Taiwan, she has been writing about the cuisines and cultures of Taiwan and China for over a decade. Her writing has been published in the *New York Times*, the *New Yorker*, the *Los Angeles Times*, *Serious Eats*, and *Bon Appétit*. She has produced videos on cross-strait tensions for *VICE News Tonight*, *60 Minutes*, and *SBS Dateline*. Clarissa was previously a senior reporter at Goldthread, a video-centric imprint of the *South China Morning Post* in Hong Kong, where she made more than one hundred videos on the foods and cultures of China, Hong Kong, and Taiwan over the span of two years. In her spare time, she tends to a subtropical food forest on the outskirts of Taipei.